Rethinking the French Revolution

Rethinking the French Revolution

Marxism and the Revisionist Challenge

◆

GEORGE C. COMNINEL

VERSO

London · New York

First published by Verso 1987
Second impression 1990
© 1987 George Comninel
All rights reserved

Verso
UK: 6 Meard Street, London W1V 3HR
USA: 29 West 35th Street, New York, NY 10001 2291

Verso is the imprint of New Left Books

British Library Cataloguing in Publication Data

Comninel, George C.
  Rethinking the French revolution:
  Marxism and the revisionist challenge.
  1. France—History—Revolution,
  1789–1794   2. France—Politics and
  government—Revolution, 1789–1799
  I. Title
  944. 04   DC161

ISBN 0-86091-890-4 Pbk
ISBN 0-86091-179-9

US Library of Congress Cataloging in Publication Data

Comninel, George C.
  Rethinking the French Revolution: Marxism and the revisionist
challenge/George C. Comninel; with an introduction by George
Rudé.
    p.   cm.
  Bibliography: p.
  Includes index.
  ISBN 0-86091-179-9: $34.95 (U.S.).   ISBN 0-86091-890-4 (pbk.):
  1. France—History—Revolution, 1789–1799—Historiography.
2. Marxian historiography.   I. Title.
DC147.8.C74 1987
944.04—dc19

Typeset in Times by P.R.G. Graphics Ltd
Printed and bound in Great Britain by
Biddles Ltd, Guildford and King's Lynn

Contents

Acknowledgements

This book is a revised and rewritten version of a doctoral dissertation presented to the Graduate Programme in Social and Political Thought at York University. My studies and the writing of much of this text were made possible in part by a fellowship from the Social Sciences and Humanities Research Council of Canada.

There are several people whose contributions to this work I would like to acknowledge. William Irvine and Nicholas Rogers advised and commented on the text of my dissertation, and each helped to steer me towards some important questions, and away from a few pitfalls. Neal Wood also commented on that early text, while Robert Brenner read and commented upon the revised manuscript.

For introducing me to the range of historiography on the ancien régime, I am greatly indebted to J. F. Bosher. He does not, of course, bear any responsibility whatever for the use I have made of the rich history which I discovered through his generous assistance.

My interest in the class relations of the French Revolution was first stimulated by the work of George Rudé, who retrieved the lives of common people from forgotten documents to make meaningful their political acts. I was fortunate to have been able to study briefly with Professor Rudé, and even more fortunate since then to have benefited from his kindness, interest, and good advice. I want to thank him for his comments and suggestions, and look forward to taking up those for which there was no room here in a future work.

I am especially grateful for Ellen Meiksins Wood's generous and invaluable assistance over the many years since she first agreed to supervise my dissertation. Her original and critical approach to the questions of class and state in pre-capitalist society and the transition to capitalism was an important influence in the development of my ideas. She has unstintingly contributed her questions, comments, and criticism, and this work has been greatly improved as a result. I have learned a great deal both from her work and from working with her.

Finally, for her support, good humor, and understanding, I dedicate this book to my partner and wife, Ann Ball.

Foreword

George Comninel's book is a hard-hitting and contentious work that is bound to raise some flak from historians of the Revolution, both among those whom he calls 'revisionists' and those 'orthodox' Marxists and others whose judgements they have been proposing to 'revise'. But it is also a very thoughtful, original and well-researched book from a young historian whose arguments, though he is a newcomer to the field, deserve to be carefully examined and widely read.

The main thrust of Dr Comninel's contention is that, while the French Revolution has been widely debated, that debate has often been based on the erroneous premise that it was a 'bourgeois' revolution, in which the bourgeoisie, in challenging the old feudal-aristocratic régime, sought to replace it by a liberal-bourgeois political and social order favorable to the development of a capitalist mode of production. The major fallacy in this perspective, as he sees it, lies in the mistaken view that the French eighteenth-century bourgeoisie and aristrocracy belonged to two fundamentally hostile classes whereas (in his view) they were bound by a common interest to exploit the material resources of the state while leaving the old social order virtually intact. So the major issue over which the French Revolution was fought (and the author in no way denies its importance) was not, as Lefebvre and Soboul and other 'social interpreters' have maintained, to uproot the old 'feudal' order but rather to give the bourgeoisie, the despised junior partners of aristocracy, a larger – and ultimately preponderant – share in the *political* control of the state, involving the eventual demise of both aristocratic privilege and the absolute power of the King. And it is for being the first to expose this fallacy of the 'social interpreters', or school of 'orthodox' Marxist historians, that Alfred Cobban has earned the author's praise; yet he goes on to argue that neither he nor the French and American 'revisionists' that followed him have offered an acceptable alternative explanation of what the French Revolution was really about.

So the main purpose of Dr Comninel's book is to explore this whole problem anew, both as to its origins and to its possible eventual solution. How, then, to begin with, did this mistaken perspective of a 'bourgeois' revolution arise? It started, the author believes, with none other than Marx himself, or, more exactly, with Marx's failure to extend his rigorous critique of bourgeois-liberal political economy to the study of the history of pre-capitalist society. So Marx, although he had already (from 1843 onwards) begun to evolve his new theory of historical materialism, took over almost unchanged from the French liberal historians of the 1820s and their 'philosophical' pre-decessors their ideas of a 'bourgeois' revolution and its particular application to the revolution of 1789. The liberals of the 1820s, as well as the eighteenth-century *philosophes* and the *patriote* leaders of the Revolution itself, had sound social and political reasons for seeing the conflicts preceding and accompanying the Revolution as they did: in bourgeois-materialist terms as an ineluctable struggle of right against wrong, of future against past, of the nation against the privileged; and, more specifically, as a revolution of a forward-looking bourgeoisie and its allies against an entrenched aristocracy buttressed, when it came to the point, by its protector, the absolute monarch. In the author's own words:

> The essential classes in this continuum were the aristocracy and the bourgeoisie: the idle, decadent descendants of the feudal order of Germanic conquerors, and the productive, innovative, and virtuous.

A weakness of course, in this theory was the liberals' virtual refusal – except among their more radical element – to appreciate the positive role played by the popular masses without whose intervention (as the author insists) the bourgeois and liberal-aristocratic revolutionaries could not have realized their goals. It was a weakness, he adds, that was later shared by the 'revisionist' critics of the 'social interpreters' (who, at least in this respect, had redeeming virtues), like Furet and Richet in France, with their claim that once its liberal phase had been completed (by 1792) the Revolution fell into *dérapage* (came off its tracks).

How, then, could the founder of historical materialism, with its revelation of the hidden laws of class struggle and the 'alienation' and exploitation of labor under capitalism, fail to apply the same principles to a society of a mere half-century before – all the more so as his adopted model of a 'bourgeois' revolution had emanated from the same liberal-philosophical source whose errors he had already been exposing for some years past? According to Comninel, the reasons are twofold. On the one hand, once *The German Ideology* and *The Manifesto* had been written (both with Engels) in 1846–8, Marx had become increasingly preoccupied with the problems that for him overshadowed all others, those relating to capitalist society and capitalist class relations, to the consequent neglect of such matters of secondary concern as the exact nature of the society out of which the French Revolution erupted in 1789. But there was also another, possibly more compelling, reason: the attraction that the notion of a 'bourgeois' revolution, set in the late eighteenth and early nineteenth centuries, had for Marx in that it appeared to offer a justifiable historical precedent for the *proletarian* revolution, which he believed to be maturing and to whose development he was by now devoting ever more of his time and attention.

Finally, the author asks, if the French Revolution has been viewed in a false light – whether by 'orthodox' or structural Marxists or by 'revisionists' and others – how can the blinkers be removed and the debate be resumed with a greater concern for historical truth? Only, he insists, by returning to the rigorous principles of historical materialism that Marx evolved from his long-standing critique of bourgeois-liberal political economy and that, after twenty-five years, found its mature expression in the publication of *Capital*. Such a reorientation he hopes to accomplish in a later volume as a successor to this one; but, meanwhile, in his conclusions, he sketches its guiding principles as follows:

1. First, to make a close study of class relations in eighteenth-century France. From this should emerge: a) that, in sharp contrast with contemporary Britain, capitalist class relations did not yet exist in France either in the towns or countryside; b) that the bourgeoisie, far from being a capitalist class basically opposed to aristocracy, shared with it 'the essential social relations of property ownership [particularly in land] and state

office'; and c) that, in consequence, these two should be seen as partners in exploitation rather than as being at each others' throats.

2. Yet the partnership was an unequal one and it was over the *political* control of the state and the spoils of high office – as in the army and administration – that a conflict arose that led to the Revolution. Its outbreak was precipitated by the 'aristocratic revolt' of 1787 by which the nobility challenged the authority of the monarchy itself, making a firm bid for a greater share without any intention of sharing its fruits with the bourgeoisie. And the conflict sharpened as the Revolution continued, both because of the growth of an anti-'aristocratic' ideology and the bourgeoisie's success in uniting the nation, including the rural and urban masses, to achieve its goals.

3. A major result of the Revolution was both to unify the nation and to centralize the state far more than had ever been done before, but it was not to transform the essential social relations of production or to create a new capitalist society. This would only happen in the half-century that followed.

Yet in an earlier chapter, the author adds an observation (borrowed from the Dobb–Sweezy debate on the transition to capitalism) that may perhaps give some comfort to the proponents of a 'social interpretation'. It is that it might be reasonable to recognize the existence of an interim or *transitional* period between feudalism and capitalism and one, therefore, that would presumably not be marked by the same basic social conflicts out of which a 'social' revolution might be expected to arise. In this respect, it may perhaps be appropriate to cite the example of the small Parisian consumers or sans-culottes who, in the century before the French Revolution, fought their main battles with wholesalers and merchants – being more concerned with bread than with wages – at the point of *consumption* rather than at the point of *production*, with all the convulsions that this led to both on the eve and in the course of the Revolution.

While I cannot in all honesty saddle the author with a reflection that is clearly mine rather than his, it may perhaps serve to illustrate his point (if I have understood him correctly) and to underline at least one of the problems that he may encounter on embarking on his coming volume. In any case, it seems likely that his readers, having carefully studied his case and the cogent arguments he has put forward to support it – not to mention his outline of what he hopes to offer them next – will have their appetites whetted by the prospect of a second volume to crown the considerable achievement of the first.

George Rudé
Montreal

Introduction

This book was first inspired by a desire to understand *precisely* how a revolution emerges from class society. Like so many others, my interest in the French Revolution had been originally directed towards understanding the social radicalism of the popular movement, for which the social interpretation of the Revolution as a bourgeois revolution seemed to provide a lucid and logically necessary backdrop. It was striking, however, that while the history of the popular movement had been set out in great social and political detail, there was nowhere to be found a comparably detailed account of the bourgeoisie, their interests as a rising capitalist class, and the political dynamics of their revolutionary career. Indeed, when the snippets of evidence offered in demonstration of the emergence of a capitalism were actually pinned down, one was left with the unmistakable impression that despite the strength of the *theory* of bourgeois revolution, its *history* was marked by looseness and vague allusions. Most troubling was the fact that the strongest evidence with regard to the social and political interests of the bourgeoisie seemed to be that offered by Alfred Cobban in his polemically charged attack upon the Marxist position. Approaching, then, the Revolution from a Marxist theoretical perspective that was virtually predicated upon the existence of bourgeois revolution, it came at first as something of a shock to discover just how much of a case against it had been made by revisionist historians in Cobban's wake.

For, over the last two decades, a truly radical transformation

1

has taken place in the opinions prevailing among historians as to the causes and meaning of the French Revolution. It is now generally recognized that with Cobban's publication of *The Social Interpretation of the French Revolution* a new era in the historiography of the Revolution has opened.[1] Through the mid 1960s, the long-established 'orthodox' conception recognized in the Revolution an epochal *social* phenomenon – the political expression of fundamental changes in economic conditions and the balance of classes. Historians generally, and not only Marxists, held that the Revolution marked the ascendancy of the bourgeoisie as a class, the defeat of a more or less feudal aristocracy, and, hence, the triumph of capitalism.

Before Cobban, as will be seen, there had been other challenges to the interpretation of bourgeois class revolution. On the one hand, an alternative reactionary interpretation viewed the Revolution as a calamity for which 'the Mob' or 'the lower orders' were responsible; and on the other hand, there had been a tendency for conservatives to quietly downplay the role of class interests, without challenging the standard social interpretation itself. Cobban, however, accepted all the standard scholarship associated with the social interpretation and yet forcefully argued that the social interpretation was inconsistent with it. In particular, he argued, the evidence demonstrated that the French aristocracy was not feudal, the bourgeoisie was not capitalist, and the Revolution itself did not consolidate the triumph of a capitalist society.

Indeed, the new 'revisionist' historiography is to an important extent – but *only* in part – precisely the product of the many decades of increasingly sophisticated and thorough historical research inspired by the social interpretation. Our knowledge of the ancien régime has been impressively expanded by both extensive and highly detailed studies of its social history – further informed by the development of the sub-disciplines of economic, demographic, and regional history. Pre-eminent among the standard bearers of this research was Georges Lefebvre, who had a great deal to do with the nearly universal acceptance of the social interpretation. The breadth and nuances of Lefebvre's own exposition of this interpretation – as most clearly expressed in *The Coming of the French Revolution*[2] – were further enhanced by both admiration of his ground-breaking monographic studies, and respect for his Chair in the History of the Revolution at the Sorbonne. Yet, within a few years of Cobban's book, in both France and the English-speaking world, the revisionist approach to the Revolution had simply routed the social interpretation, and gained ascendancy.

This revisionist history, which has by now acquired the status of a 'new international consensus',[3] follows Cobban in arguing that the entire body of social historiography of the ancien régime stands in refutation of the idea of bourgeois class revolution. The implications of the revisionist challenge therefore reach far beyond the historiographical issues of the French Revolution itself, to embrace fundamental issues of method in historical analysis. Cobban himself pointedly maintained that it was the considerations of 'abstract social theory' and historical sociology – that is to say, Marxist theory – that had led historians to misconstrue the facts and impose a preconceived model of the social origins of modern capitalist society upon the history of France. The whole subsequent development of the revisionist historical perspective has continued this attack on Marxism, both explicitly and implicitly. Indeed, agreement has been reached among the revisionists not so much on any new interpretation of the Revolution, as on the way that facts have been distorted by theory among the proponents of the social interpretation. While attacks on Marxism are nothing new, the revisionist historians have enjoyed remarkable success in reversing this outstanding instance of Marxist credibility, because their challenge has in fact been backed by substantial and very compelling historical evidence.

Virtually all non-Marxist historians have now been won away from the social interpretation, essentially because – ideological issues aside – its supposed historical foundations have simply been found wanting when subjected to scrutiny. Powerfully challenged on the 'facts' which had for long been taken for granted, Marxists have increasingly been reduced to defending the idea of bourgeois revolution through purely theoretical arguments, based on abstract conceptions of the transition from feudalism to capitalism. Reformulations of the Marxist interpretation have been put forward from both structuralist and 'orthodox' perspectives, but neither has been successful in resolving either the real historical inconsistencies or the underlying theoretical problems of the original account of bourgeois revolution.

It must now be accepted that the long-standing claims to historical validity of the Marxist interpretation of the French Revolution have been exploded. Granting this, but also upholding a commitment to understanding the role of class relations in historical development, the primary purposes of this work will

4

be: to argue that, despite his incisive criticism of the ideology of political economy, it was Marx's own *uncritical* appropriation of bourgeois-liberal[4] materialist history that introduced distortions into Marxist history; to demonstrate, however, that the method of historical social analysis which Marx actually created is *not* implicated in these distortions; and, finally, to consider both the nature and practice of this method itself – historical materialism – as the necessary foundation for a new interpretation of the French Revolution as an event in the historical development of class society. In order to justify this contentious line of argument, the responses which already have been made to the revisionist challenge by other Marxists will be examined to reveal the sources and extent of their weaknesses. Perhaps the central point of this work will be that the theory of bourgeois revolution did not originate with Marx, and in fact is not even consistent with the original social thought which Marx did develop.

While this book emerges from a recognition of the need to develop a new interpretation of the French Revolution, based on a fresh analysis of the ancien régime as a class society, that task must itself await a future work. The unfortunate extent to which the theory of bourgeois revolution, and the whole conception of 'historical' modes of production associated with it, have been understood to be *the* key to Marx's historical social theory has made an initial theoretical ground-clearing necessary. By way of a conclusion, however, a 'preface' to a historical materialist account of the origins and dynamic of the Revolution will be offered, indicating in broad strokes the sort of analysis which can be expected on the basis of current evidence.

Notes

1. Alfred Cobban, *The Social Interpretation of the French Revolution*, London 1968.
2. Georges Lefebvre, *The Coming of the French Revolution*, New York n.d.
3. William Doyle, *Origins of the French Revolution*, Oxford 1980, p.24.
4. Throughout this work, the term 'liberal' is used to convey the meaning of a commitment to representative government and civil liberties, and/or a commitment to freedom of trade and enterprise. It is clear that virtually everyone in British public life after about 1720 falls into this category, including many Tories who would not usually be classified as 'liberals'. One of the points of this work, however, is precisely that no such liberal consensus existed in *France* until the twentieth century. The term 'bourgeois-liberal', which is usually used by Marxists to convey this meaning, will generally be avoided because it begs the question of what is meant by 'bourgeois'.

1

The French Revolution as Bourgeois Revolution: Orthodoxy and Challenge

The Social Interpretation and Bourgeois Revolution

In the mid 1960s, after a decade in the chair of French History at the University of London, Alfred Cobban returned to the provocative theme of his inaugural lecture, *The Myth of the French Revolution*.[1] With his slender but highly charged volume, *The Social Interpretation of the French Revolution*, Cobban attacked head-on a broad and long-established consensus over the general character and meaning of the French Revolution.[2] This 'social' interpretation was the established academic opinion, refined over time by the most notable historians of the Revolution, with an appropriate range of scholarly variation on its basic theme. What Cobban most took issue with – and what was central to this interpretation – was viewing the Revolution as a *social* revolution, one that embodied fundamental and necessary processes of historical development. Cobban did not object to examining the origins or events of the Revolution in terms of social or economic interests. On the contrary, Norman Hampson criticized Cobban for having produced no more than a 'non-Marxist economic interpretation of the revolution'.[3] What Cobban rejected, as he saw it, was history written to reflect 'the deterministic operation of an historical law', history which had been combined with 'general sociological theories'.[4] In his eyes this was both the defining characteristic and the cardinal sin of Marxist history, and it was as Marxist history that Cobban took on the social interpretation. Indeed, as has since come to be true of much of the revisionist 'new consensus', Cobban's criticism was explicitly intended to be at least as much an attack on Marxist historical

5

sociology, as such, as an effort to shed new light on the Revolution.

Cobban recognized Georges Lefebvre's work to be the most authoritative expression of the social interpretation, and the central idea to which he objected was clearly stated by Lefebvre:

> The revolution is only the crown of a long economic and social evolution which has made the bourgeoisie the mistress of the world.[5]

All the elements central to interpreting the Revolution as a bourgeois social revolution are incorporated in this statement: that the Revolution was only the 'crown' of a more fundamental historical process; that behind this historical development lay social, and particularly economic, progress; and that the agent and chief beneficiary of this evolution was the bourgeois class that rose to social ascendancy in liberal capitalism.

Lefebvre was a consummate practitioner of the historian's craft, justly noted for the depth of his research and for his grasp of the historically concrete, and he applied this attention to detail even to so sweeping an interpretive perspective as this. Not only did Lefebvre recognize that 'many motives combined to bring the French people to their supreme dilemma', but he specifically developed the idea that the Revolution was at once *four* different revolutions – those of the aristocracy, the bourgeoisie, the sans-culottes, and the peasantry.[6]

Yet, beyond the proximate causes of the many separate elements which went into the Revolution in its distinctive complexity, Lefebvre did not hesitate to identify a 'deeper cause of the French Revolution', one which revealed these four revolutions to be expressions of an integral whole, a necessary bourgeois social revolution:

> The ultimate cause of the French Revolution of 1789 goes deep into the history of France and of the western world. At the end of the eighteenth century the social structure of France was aristocratic. It showed traces of having originated at a time when land was almost the only form of wealth, and when the possessors of land were the masters of those who needed it to work and to live. . . .
>
> Meanwhile the growth of commerce and industry had created, step by step, a new form of wealth, mobile or commercial wealth, and a new class, called in France the bourgeoisie. . . . This class had grown much stronger with the maritime discoveries of the fifteenth and sixteenth centuries. . . . In the eighteenth century commerce, industry and finance occupied an increasingly important place in the national economy. . . . The role of the nobility had correspondingly

declined; and the clergy . . . found its authority growing weaker. These groups preserved the highest rank in the legal structure of the country, but in reality economic power, personal abilities and confidence in the future had passed largely to the bourgeoisie. Such a discrepancy never lasts forever. The Revolution of 1789 restored the harmony between fact and law. This transformation spread in the nineteenth century throughout the west and then to the whole globe, and in this sense the ideas of 1789 toured the world.[7]

This was the established interpretation of the Revolution, offered from the Chair in History of the French Revolution at the Sorbonne, and it clearly embraced the concept of bourgeois revolution as its general theory of cause.

The implications of the concept of bourgeois revolution by far transcend the issue of interpreting the French Revolution. In the first place, of course, it is a *general* historical concept: prior to the revisionist challenge, even non-Marxists were often willing to admit some such measure of commonality between the French Revolution and the English Civil War, even among a whole range of eighteenth-century 'Atlantic' revolutions. Marxists have defined such revolutions far more rigorously as instances of bourgeois class revolution, and, taking this to be a normal expression of necessary social development, have looked for it in all modern national histories. In this sense, then, 'bourgeois revolution' implies an entire theory of historical process, a conspectus of world-historical development. At this level of explicit theorizing, 'bourgeois revolution' is far more than an interpretation of the causes and character of a given political revolution; it is a concept which places that political conflict in the context of a fundamental transformation of the entire structure of material, institutional and cultural reproduction in society.

This is the sense in which Marxist theory has embraced the idea of bourgeois revolution. It has been taken to express a necessary stage of the development of class society in world history. (Whether or not a *discrete* bourgeois revolution and a corresponding stage of bourgeois democracy is necessary in historical development became a prime issue of polemical dispute between Stalinists and Trotskyists; it is important to be cognizant of such implications without being paralyzed by them – particularly since the main point of this work is to question the whole framework of that debate.[8]) Marxism, as will be seen, has been particularly concerned with stages of history; and bourgeois revolution – the political expression of the transformation of feudal society into capitalist society by the bourgeoisie – is a major theoretical element of this historical perspective. Indeed, in terms of both historical analysis and political theorizing, there have been few if any ideas more central to Marxism than bourgeois revolution.

The most celebrated characterization of bourgeois revolution as such appears in the *Communist Manifesto*:

- Each step in the development of the bourgeoisie was accompanied by a corresponding political advance of that class . . . the bourgeoisie has at last, since the establishment of Modern Industry and of the world market, conquered for itself, in the modern representative State, exclusive political sway. . . .

- The bourgeoisie, wherever it has got the upper hand, has put an end to all feudal, patriarchal, idyllic relations. . . .

- The bourgeoisie keeps more and more doing away with the scattered state of the population, of the means of production, and of property. . . . The necessary consequence of this was political centralisation. Independent, or but loosely connected provinces with separate interests, laws, governments and systems of taxation, became lumped together into one nation, with one government, one code of laws, one national class interest, one frontier and one customs tariff. . . .

- We see then: the means of production and of exchange, on whose foundation the bourgeoisie built itself up, were generated in feudal society. At a certain stage in the development of these means of production and exchange . . . the feudal relations of property became no longer compatible with the already developed productive forces; they became so many fetters. They had to be burst asunder; they were burst asunder. [9]

An important discussion of this conception in a more analytical vein can be found in Marx's 'Moralizing Criticism and Critical Morality', a response to the ideas of Karl Heinzen, and it is implicit or taken for granted in much of the rest of Marx's work. [10]

The Prevalence of the Social Interpretation

The concept of bourgeois revolution has always held a central place in Marxist theory and history, [11] with the result that the term itself has tended to have only limited academic currency outside Marxist circles, particularly in the English-speaking countries. Nevertheless, some version of bourgeois revolution can be found at the heart of most of the historical interpretations of the French Revolution put forward since the founding of the

Third Republic. Throughout this century, a wide variety of historians, and not only those closely associated with the 'official' orthodox account, have treated the origins and social consequences of the Revolution in terms which have reflected the general perspective of bourgeois revolution.[12]

In France, until after the end of the Fourth Republic, there was more than similarity between the liberal and Marxist interpretations of the Revolution – they were clearly identical. The social interpretation was shared unhesitatingly by left-liberals everywhere, for in its 'official' version it was as much Republican as Marxist. Between the Paris Commune and World War II, Western liberal democracy simply could not be taken for granted. The virtues or vices of political and economic liberalism; the celebration or disparagement of enlightenment and modern society; the affirmation or denial of historical progress: all these continued to be vital issues of contention, and not least for historians.

Wherever popular democracy was a real issue, and particularly in the political context of the Third Republic where serious right-wing opposition to liberal republicanism had long been a factor, it was unavoidable that the historiography of the Revolution should become confused with contemporary politics.[13] Indeed, everywhere, whether as an expression of the immediate political context, or as an echo of distant conflicts and underlying ideology, the Revolution tended to be simplified from the complex struggle of aristocracy, bourgeoisie, sans-culottes, and peasants, to fit either of a pair of archetypal conflicts: 'the People vs. Aristocracy', or 'Society vs. the Mob'. Under such circumstances, liberals were politically constrained to identify with the Revolution as a whole, to defend it against anti-popular reactionaries, on the grounds of its announced ideals, however much they may have regretted the Terror. Liberals, radicals and Marxists were uneasily allied in defending the liberal-democratic Republic, and this meant defense of the principles of the Revolution as well – however each group chose to construe them. This general political alignment was not limited to France; it was recognized everywhere that the Revolution had brought down the ancien régime and its absolutism in order to replace political aristocracy with liberal democracy.

Interpretation of the Revolution therefore closely conformed to the lines of conflict drawn by its own ideology: the achievement of political democracy, legal equality, and civil liberty through overthrow of the old order of aristocracy. For liberals everywhere, the Revolution stood as one expression, a central expression, of the general social and political progress associated with the Enlightenment. The liberal goals of the Revolution being both reasonable and progressive, it was not hard for liberals to deduce that the 'excesses' of the Terror were somehow necessary, if regrettable; or that they had been called down upon the aristocracy by its own intransigence in the face of the people's legitimate aspirations. At worst, for conservative liberalism the Terror was an unavoidable symptom of the 'disease' of revolution, a 'disease' brought on by the inability of old institutions and 'modes of thought' to cope with the stresses inherent in the progress of 'modernizing' society.

This latter interpretation of the Revolution, perhaps the most conservative that still embraced liberalism, was well expressed in the avowedly anti-Marxist and non- 'Republican' historical work of Crane Brinton.[14] Brinton has not loomed large in the historiography of the French Revolution. He is remembered, however, for his ideas on revolution in general, and particularly for his remarkably conservative conception of revolution as a 'fever', which a growing society might have to endure in order to restore a 'normal' and 'healthy' state of social equilibrium.[15] This allowed him to describe one of the primary 'symptoms' of revolution as 'a feeling on the part of some of the chief enterprising groups that their opportunities for getting on in this world are unduly limited by political arrangements', while asserting that this 'is rather less than what Marxists seem to mean when they talk about the revolutions of the seventeenth, eighteenth, and nineteenth centuries as deliberately the work of a class-conscious bourgeoisie'.[16]

Brinton carefully separated the politics of liberalism from both class interests and the disorder of social revolution, for unlike the French republicans and left-liberal historians, he had no enthusiasm for conceptions of a heroic people driven to arms by tyranny. Indeed, Brinton anticipated the revisionist historians by forty years in his insistence that the 'real' Revolution was fully realized *before* 'the lurid affair of the Bastille', simply by the creation of the National Assembly.[17] Yet, even this profoundly conservative historian accepted the essential premises of the official social interpretation: that the Revolution of 1789 was the necessary work of the bourgeoisie in bringing about modern, liberal-capitalist society,

working for a bourgeois domination, for that triumph of natural rights over prescription which meant the triumph of the businessman over the gentleman.[18]

Even in America, then, some variation of the social interpretation of the Revolution as a bourgeois revolution was the norm among historians. Among those who saw the Revolution as a *philosophical* expression of the emergence of democracy from the 'Age of Reason', there was still a ready identification of egalitarianism, civil nationalism, anti-clericalism, and organizational rationalism with the self-made men of commerce, industry, and the professions. The growth of trade; the industrial revolution; the ascendancy of science and rationality; the emergence of religious tolerance and secular society: all have been taken as being of a piece with the establishment of democracy and civil equality, and all together have been seen as the substance of *progress*.[19] Initiative, talent, and knowledge have been the cardinal virtues of progress – and of liberalism – and these were most demonstrably possessed by those who made their way in the world without special privilege or favor. Thus, even R. R. Palmer, whose interpretation of the Revolution is almost purely political – couched in terms of the necessary and proper advance of democratic principles in the whole of the Atlantic world, which economic conditions simply encouraged – can be seen to share in the general perspective of bourgeois revolution, while virtually denying its social character.[20]

These conservative, and primarily American, perspectives on the Revolution occupied the margins of established historiography. In the main, historians were far less reluctant to admit to a 'social' dimension of history, clearly associating both progress and the Revolution with 'the rise of the middle classes' and the growth of capitalism and industry. J. M. Thompson expressed well the more typically British liberal perspective on the Revolution:

It has become fashionable to condemn 'a bourgeois revolution'. There is a sense, and one creditable to the intelligence and energy of the middle class, in which every revolution is a bourgeois revolution. The French nation at the end of the eighteenth century was not exceptional in having to rely on its professional and propertied minority for liberalism and leadership. It was unusually fortunate in that this minority was too weak to establish its rule without the help of the majority, and too patriotic to exploit its private interests until it had carried through a programme of national reform.[21]

Despite, therefore, the obvious reluctance of some, who took pains to qualify their agreement with the Marxists, liberal historical opinion was on the whole consistent with the theory of bourgeois revolution. Cobban acerbically took note of this 'Whig' perspective in observing that 'as every schoolboy knows, the perfect cliché for any period in history since the expulsion from the Garden of Eden is the rise of the middle classes'.[22] The role of this perspective in the development of not only liberal but also Marxist thought will be explored at some length later in this work, but nowhere was its impact more clear than in interpreting the French Revolution.

The Social Interpretation as 'Official' History

There is a vast and well-known historiography of the French Revolution. Historians have long recognized the connections between this body of history and a range of republican, radical, socialist, and counter-revolutionary political positions.[23] To summarize: during the Second Empire and the early years of the Third Republic, Michelet's history, renowned for its 'mystical' evocation of *the people* as the generative principle of the Revolution, held sway. 'The people' included the whole of the Third Estate; the downfall of their Republic was disunity – the mutual recriminations of Girondins and Montagnards in the Convention – a disunity for which there was no real basis but misunderstanding.[24] Michelet's history reflected the frustration of popular and bourgeois liberal-republican aspirations, and it was not to be superseded before the Third Republic was well established.[25] It is unsurprising that Marx's description of bourgeois revolution as an essentially selfish expression of class interest, the founding act of brutal and exploitive capitalist society, found no place among the non-communist thinkers of the time.

During the early days of the Third Republic, right-wing opposition to the Revolution's liberal-radical legacy found its pre-eminent historiographical expression in the work of Hippolyte Taine.[26] Taine held that it had been heedless adherence to the abstract ideology of democracy that had been responsible for rejection of the royal proposals of June 1789 by the National Assembly, fatally opening the floodgates to mob anarchy and Terror. With fears of popular uprising still fresh from the Paris Commune – only heightened by the bloodiness with which it was suppressed – Taine's history had unmistakable political significance. Until the Republic had weathered the crises of its first decades, this interpretation hung over it like a pall. Then, as republicanism asserted itself, while still facing considerable opposition, a response to Taine appeared in the form of a new interpretation of the Revolution.

Alphonse Aulard, first historian to hold a chair in the Revolution at the Sorbonne, established the tradition of official Republican interpretation of the Revolution by putting forward a version of the theory of bourgeois revolution that was imbued with a radical-socialist political perspective. Aulard embraced a radical republicanism that was 'social' without being socialist; fundamentally liberal, his perspective was far removed from Marxism.[27] His 'socialism' called only for a more just distribution of wealth and greater equality of opportunity, and it really constituted an expression of that left republicanism which had emerged between the increasingly 'centrist' politics of the leading conservative liberals and the growing socialist movement.

Despite their profound differences, these groups were all together on the side of the Republic, and hence the Revolution.[28] Faced with counter-revolutionary claims that any attempt to implement the principles of the Revolution in real government policy would inevitably lead to mob rule, this Republican alliance could not afford – and did not now need – to hold to those apologetic interpretations that had previously separated the politics of 1789 from Jacobin Republicanism, and the Terror. The establishment of the Republic and introduction of universal suffrage now had to be portrayed as integral and necessary advances upon the initial gains of 1789 – and not as loss of social control to the mob. Republicans such as Aulard could disdain Robespierre as an individual, but the Terror itself had to be upheld as essential to the defense of the Revolution and achievement of its goals.

In order to portray the Revolution in this light, an opening was made towards the socialist analysis of bourgeois revolution which followed Marx. In Aulard's history – the 'official' history – the year 1789 became the limited product of a no doubt progressive, but also self-serving, even 'privileged', bourgeoisie.[29] This bourgeoisie promulgated the principles of the Revolution in the Declaration of Rights; but in their own interests they blocked the actual implementation of these principles – especially by dividing the nation into the categories of 'active' and 'passive' citizens for purposes of the franchise. It was thus *necessary* for the Revolution to be continued. Subsequently, it was not the bourgeoisie but the *French* who formed themselves into a Democracy and a Republic.[30] For Aulard, it was the men of 1789 who could better be called renegades than those of 1793; but he held that, in truth, *all* were 'worthy Frenchmen who acted for the best'.[31]

From the socialist perspective, this was history that borrowed only timidly from Marx, and it was soon followed by the avowedly *socialist* history of Jean Jaurès.[32] This study, which Aulard praised, systematically subjected the history of the Revolution to the terms of Marxist analysis, as understood by Jaurès. (In recent years, Marxists have generally judged the work not to have been distorted by its simultaneous appreciation of the work of Michelet.[33]) This influential but 'unofficial' history, squarely situated in the *Manifesto*'s economic determinism and its description of bourgeois revolution, was superseded without being refuted when Albert Mathiez succeeded to Aulard's chair.

Mathiez pulled official Republican historiography farther to the left by taking up the cause of Robespierre against Aulard, and particularly by examining the *social* content of political conflicts in the course of the whole Revolution.[34] The stages of the Revolution which Mathiez distinguished went significantly beyond Aulard's merely political periodization in their social substance: before the specifically bourgeois revolution of 1789–91, the revolt of the nobility was based upon *their* social conditions; in governing the Republic created by popular insurrection, the Girondins 'confined themselves to a narrow class policy benefiting the middle classes only'; in turn, not only was June 2nd, 1793 'more than a political revolution', but in response to the social crisis and demands of the sans-culottes, the Revolutionary Government went beyond the limited perspective of the Hébertistes to attempt to make the Terror into a genuine *social program*.[35]

Against the continuing threat of counter-revolutionary ideology, historiographical identification of the real meaning, achievements, and potential of the Revolution shifted progressively from the merely liberal perspective of 1789 to the more radical promise of the Republic, and then to the Revolutionary Government itself. Awareness of contemporary social conflicts, and the growing influence of the socialist movement generated by capitalist society under the Third Republic, fostered in turn a sympathetic analysis of the social conflicts of the Revolution. This involved an emphasis upon the *class* character and purposes of bourgeois revolution, and increased use of the concept of class struggle. With the claims of monarchism, as such, supplanted by a right-wing political determination to keep popular forces in line through strong government, the Revolution was no longer conceived merely in terms of a *political* struggle for republican democracy, but acquired the sense of *social revolution*. Interpretation of the Revolution from anywhere left of center increasingly corresponded, at least in general terms, with the Marxist interpretation. This was perhaps facilitated by a preoccupation with polemicism rather than theory within formal Marxism at the time: generally unconcerned with scholarly exposition, Marxists for the most part simply used history in the service of contemporary political purposes. Increasingly, therefore, the official historiography of the Revolution not only reflected, but *was taken to be* – even by Marxists – the essence of socialist history.

Among the distinguishing characteristics of this 'socialist history', three criteria may be taken as essential. The first – analysis in terms of class struggle, however construed – had already been implicit in Aulard, was further spelled out by Jaurès, and was substantially extended by Mathiez. The second – analysis of conflict in terms of actual socio-economic interests – was put forward by Jaurès through his economic determinism, but was made both more general and less mechanical by Mathiez. Under this general rubric of 'social' analysis, study of the specifically *economic* aspects of the causes and course of the Revolution proceeded from Jaurès through Mathiez, to find notable expression in the work of C. E. Labrousse.[36] Both class struggle and socio-economic analysis, however, still awaited the addition of a third element: *history from below*.

This found expression in the work of Georges Lefebvre, who added the social movement of the peasantry to that of the urban people, as the necessary complements to a bourgeois class revolution against aristocratic social paralysis. Succeeding Mathiez, Lefebvre helped to establish new standards for detailed historical research, while synthesizing the several strands of republican-socialist history with the social perspective of the participants in revolution.[37] In developing upon Mathiez's social analysis by suggesting the existence of four individual revolutionary social movements – of the nobility, bourgeoisie, peasantry, and sans-culottes – he emphasized that while each had its distinctive social origins and course, they reflected together the crisis of the ancien régime, and together formed a *single* social revolution.[38] This, then, became the classic conception of the social interpretation, pre-eminent both as established scholarship and as 'socialist history'.

Lefebvre's work was the definitive formulation of the social interpretation precisely because he was able to bring together so much information, based on such thorough research, and give nuance to so many aspects of the Revolution by carefully situating them in context. He won praise for the many parts of his analysis, and respect for the argument as a whole – even from those who conspicuously rejected Marx's analysis, as such. (Such as R. R. Palmer, who translated *The Coming of the French Revolution*: in his preface, he happily pointed to Lefebvre's observation that the bourgeoisie owned as much land as the nobility, a fact that was 'singularly awkward to a purely materialist theory of class conflict' – anticipating Cobban's point without bringing it to bear on Lefebvre.) The great majority of liberal historians were prepared to accept the three central aspects of socialist history, *provided* they were not explicitly presented in Marxist terms. This ambiguity, perfectly captured by Lefebvre, was the key to the continued success of the social interpretation.

Albert Soboul, Lefebvre's successor, *did*, however, squarely situate the social interpretation in the terms of the Marxist analysis to which it alluded, while at the same time extending 'history from below' to the sans-culottes and their complex relations with the Revolutionary Government.[39] Yet from a strictly Marxist perspective, all that really was required was a history which, as a whole, supported the historical sketch in the *Manifesto*. Eric Hobsbawm's *The Age of Revolution*, exceedingly rare in being a history of both the political and economic revolutions of the bourgeoisie as sketched by Marx, simply offers Lefebvre's detailed history as a full account of the immediate causes of the Revolution, contingent expressions of the underlying class conflict with which Marx was concerned.[40] The central points from the Marxist point of view remained that the bourgeoisie had been the agent of growth in commerce and industry; that the aristocratic and absolutist structure of the ancient régime had been, in various senses, a feudal hindrance to this growth; and that the bourgeoisie had led the Revolution to overthrow this system, clearing the ground for the bourgeois capitalist society whose mature form was apparent in the nineteenth century. These points were taken to corroborate the idea that the Revolution had been a bourgeois class revolution, in turn corroborating the Marxist analysis of class.

Lefebvre embraced each of those three points, and, despite Palmer's perception that his work stood as a challenge to the

Marxists, he embraced the idea of bourgeois revolution as a whole. He did so, however, by demonstrating that the conclusions reached through his own careful synthesis tended to support the Marxist interpretation, rather than by declaring at the outset that history is the study of class struggle. His analysis was, if anything, *more* dangerous to opponents of Marxism than Soboul's for this reason. It was Lefebvre who required serious attention. It is not surprising, therefore, that the revisionist challenge to the social interpretation began as an attack on the 'myth' of the Revolution's intrinsic *unity* as Lefebvre had presented it, and developed as a criticism of Lefebvre for being seduced by the Marxist 'general theory'.[41]

This or that author might offer reservations on one point or another of the republican-socialist interpretation; or accept much of its detail while rejecting a 'purely materialist' conception of causes; or perhaps fuss over the fact that Estates were not defined in the economic terms appropriate to *classes*. In the English-speaking world generally, a more conservative version of the interpretation did in fact prevail. Nevertheless, no critic was able to pose an alternative interpretation of comparable scope, comprehensiveness, and harmony.

One of the particularly compelling aspects of the social interpretation, even for many of the decided non-Marxists, was that it did not rest on suspiciously *moral* judgements – as the counter-revolutionary interpretations did for the most part – but instead claimed that there was a historical inevitability to social and economic progress, which entailed the changes brought about by the Revolution. This analysis claimed to rest on historical social science, and to provide the convincing detail of a society brought to the inevitable outbreak of revolution; it called on the facts of price movement, food supply, economic growth, and fiscal crisis, together with the effect of enlightenment and rationality in creating resistance to absolutism and opening the state to reform. Lefebvre and Soboul gave even further depth to this analysis by revealing the specific social manifestations and intellectual development of the common people of town and country, as they gave their impetus to the Revolution. The social interpretation was conceptually based on the theory of bourgeois revolution, but it drew upon and invited ever more detailed historical research – not only to support it, but to give it nuance. The enormous number of monographic investigations into the social circumstances of the Revolution which were undertaken as late as the mid 1960s were generally perceived to have been carried out under the umbrella of the social interpretation.

The Revisionist Challenge

For all the inspiration and accommodating flexibility which the social interpretation for so long afforded historians of the Revolution, it is no less true that, as Cobban first contended, their researches have instead provided substantial evidence *against* the view that a capitalist bourgeoisie overthrew a feudal aristocracy in order to break the fetters of the old regime. Cobban underlined the disjuncture between the historical evidence, as it emerged, and the cardinal points of the social interpretation: that feudalism had remained a central component of the productive relations of the ancien régime; that the revolutionary bourgeoisie had been an emerging capitalist class, necessarily opposed to the feudal restrictions of aristocratic society; and that the Revolution marked the launching of significant capitalist growth in a new society. In the opinion of the great majority of historians of the ancien régime and the Revolution – including, as will be seen, many Marxists – there is now little doubt that the whole body of serious historical research stands in refutation of the idea that a capitalist bourgeois class was driven to overthrow a feudal aristocratic ruling class to which it was intrinsically opposed.

As will be argued throughout this work, no adequate synthesis of the historical evidence yet exists: the Marxists have been wrong, while the revisionists are incapable of providing a coherent alternative that *explains* the Revolution. The very point of this work is to develop a method of historical social analysis with which to interpret the Revolution on the basis of the evidence. It is not possible to present the evidence which argues against the social interpretation in any systematic or thorough fashion at the same time. William Doyle has summarized the revisionist case very ably, and the Bibliography cites most of the significant work which has been brought to bear on the subject. In the arguments that follow, and in the conclusion which stands as a 'preface' to a new interpretation, the most essential points therefore will be introduced without the substantive discussion they merit.

While Cobban unquestionably played a central role in revising the established social interpretation, his work laid the foundation for the current 'revisionist' mainstream *without* actually belonging to it. Cobban's argument was that the social interpretation went astray from the start, by *beginning* with the notion of bourgeois capitalist class revolution – the idea of *social* revolution. This he saw as a 'semi-religious' tenet of Marxism, a product of 'abstract historical sociology', which was burdened by an 'anachronistic' use of the concept of *class* – which Cobban understood to be an economic category, peculiar to capitalism. He argued that though the Revolution was made by the bourgeoisie, the bourgeois revolutionaries were not capitalists; that they shared with the nobility a proclivity for agrarian property, and as *rentiers* shared in the full range of landed income – including that relatively small portion derived from feudal dues; and finally, that the Revolution did not give rise to capitalist production, but if anything hampered it, preserving the essential social characteristics of the ancien régime.

Unlike the later revisionists, however, Cobban maintained his own version of an essentially 'bourgeois' revolution, led by a non-capitalist bourgeoisie for non-capitalist social objectives against an aristocracy which was in fact *capitalist*.[42] This idiosyncratic interpretation has never found much favor. Instead, his primary contributions were to demonstrate the gulf between the orthodox conception of bourgeois revolution and the historical evidence, and to argue that this discrepancy was a refutation of Marxism itself. The subsequent wave of revisionist historians have concurred on both of these points.

Among the English-speaking historians who first contributed to the revisionist challenge, George V. Taylor and Elizabeth Eisenstein had greater influence than Cobban on the direction of revisionist thought. Taylor argued that the bourgeoisie could not be differentiated from the nobility in their forms of wealth and income, while Eisenstein recollected that liberal members of the nobility had played a critical role in forging the political movement of the Third Estate in 1788–9.[43] Taken in combination with the considerable body of historical research that had exploded the idea that the nobility had been simply a hereditary, feudal aristocracy, this new direction quickly led to the emergence of the central conception of the new revisionist consensus.

The essential proposition is that, since both the nobility and the bourgeoisie had marked *internal* differentiation, and no impermeable social boundary existed between them, and the two statuses had a great deal in common in terms of their forms of wealth, professions, and general ideology, it therefore would be more accurate to recognize a *single* 'elite' in the ancien régime – or, more precisely, a dominant social stratum comprising several different, but sometimes overlapping 'elites'.[44] On the basis of this analysis, the 'aristocratic offensive' of 1787–8 and the subsequent agitation of the Third Estate in 1788–9 can be conflated into a single movement of reform, reflecting the emerging institutional requirements of the entire elite stratum and their emerging ideological consensus. In place of class struggle, therefore, there is a movement of national renovation – which in opening society to the new reality also opened it to the potential for tumult, yet which ultimately secured expression in the Napoleonic society of the *notables*. While the English-speaking historians were originally prominent in developing this revisionist perspective, it quickly became a fixture of the *Annales* school of historians in France, leaving Marxist historians thoroughly isolated in their attempts to retain the once orthodox social interpretation.

The Conservative Liberalism of the Revisionist Challenge

The shift to the revisionist interpretation of the Revolution has been a shift to a markedly more conservative liberalism. The central task of the Revolution is now interpreted as simply the overthrow of despotism, a task which united the entire 'elite', and was perhaps even led by the *nobility*:

> But the struggle between 'Aristocrates' and 'Nationaux' in no way weakened the common will to overthrow 'despotism'. And the program of the 'Aristocrates', however conservative it may have been on the terrain of privilege, was not less liberal than that of the 'Nationaux' . . . Privilege had not only been, as Jean Meuvret put it, the refuge of liberty, it had been its true ancestor, legitimate parent, authentic source. Throughout the passage from 'gothic barbarism' to the Enlightenment of reason, it was the nobility which fathered that revolutionary system of values: liberalism.[45]

The growth of liberalism still appears to be as inexorable, and as much tied to economic and social progress, as in the social interpretation, but in this version the liberal protagonists are the enlightened nobility and the upper reaches of the bourgeoisie. (Precisely how classically liberal this conception is will be discussed in a subsequent chapter.) For the revisionists, the Revolution was a natural and necessary development, a just effort to reform society; but at the same time, from this perspective, the manner in which the Revolution went 'skidding off course' into the period of the Revolutionary Government, *sans-culottisme*, and the Terror, must seen as *unnecessary*.[46] As had previously been the case with liberal apologists prior to the Third Republic, the Revolution is no longer to be treated as a 'bloc' in this interpretation. From the revisionist perspective, the Revolution is properly bracketed by the Assembly of Notables and the society of *notables*, and the revolutionary years of 1791–4 stand out as a more or less lamentable aberration along the way.

The revisionist consensus, in fact, is in many ways a contemporary reworking of the perspective of Tocqueville, or Brinton. Tocqueville, in the wake of 1848, was the first to identify with the liberal goals of the Revolution but to characterize the Revolution itself as tragic – perhaps inevitable, but not *necessary*. It was Tocqueville's view that the monarchy under Louis XVI had been far from reactionary. The very progress made by the ancien régime in reducing the misery, irrationality, and despotism of the past was seen by Tocqueville to have simultaneously destabilized society. It facilitated the heroic work of social reorganization in 1789, but also, through the dissolution of established structures of public control and the inexperience in leadership of the 'cultured elite', set the stage for the 'mastery' of the masses in their 'lust for revenge'.[47]

Brinton had a less tragic conception, for he frankly maintained that the Revolution had not even been inevitable. Instead, he argued that the Revolution had *already been won* before the taking of the Bastille, and that the court had had no intention of making a counter-coup against the National Assembly, but could have learned to live with the liberal constitutional order the bourgeois delegates were determined to have.[48] Brinton has not often been followed in this judgement. The revisionist account is further complicated by its recognition of *two* liberal currents of opposition to despotism ('Aristocrates' and 'Nationaux'). Despite their inclination to see the Revolutionary Government as a *dérapage*, then, the revisionists see the revolution of *1789* as in some sense both inevitable and necessary. Which is to say, it was *about* something, even if it occurred within an integrated elite.

Unfortunately, precisely *what* this liberal revolution was about – what the source of this intense struggle was if *not* a conflict between bourgeois and aristocrats – is something that the revisionist account has not been able to explain. Colin Lucas, indeed, has taken Doyle's effort at synthesis to task on just these grounds: *why*, if there was no fundamental social conflict at issue, was there 'the sustained intensity of the revolutionary will to impose a new social organization' exhibited by the Constituent?[49] Yet from the revisionist perspective, what the Revolution *was* about is less important than what it was *not* about; and there has been complete agreement with the previous conservative-liberal positions that, by whatever date the accomplishments of 1789 can be deemed to have been fulfilled, it was then both unnecessary and regrettable for the Revolution to have gone further.

By judging the course of the Revolution after 1791 to have been unnecessary, and hence a violent and even anarchic 'skidding off course', the revisionists generally endorse the long-standing conservative position on the popular movement – particularly with regard to the period of the Terror. The popular movement has played a major role in the historiography of the social interpretation ever since Lefebvre identified the sans-culotte revolution as one of the integral revolutionary movements making up the whole of the bourgeois revolution. Quite aside from the sympathy and enthusiasm which left-liberals and Marxists have felt for the *menu peuple*, the popular movement has provided the social interpretation with the necessary explanation of how the bourgeoisie were able to prevail against the aristocracy. It also has accounted for the internal political history of the Revolution, the course of which has been attributed to the complex – even dialectical – dynamic interaction of the separate but parallel bourgeois and sans-culotte revolutionary movements. By denying that there was a necessary and coherent bourgeois revolution in continuous development between the National Assembly and the Directory, the revisionist interpretation has simultaneously deprived the popular movement of its 'legitimate' role as driving force and ally.

On the one hand, in writing revisionist histories which have been less enthusiastically *for* the Revolution, there has been a tendency to lay blame for the violence of an 'unnecessary' revolutionary *dérapage* upon the people and a 'handful' of ambitious politicians. On the other hand, in arguing that the heights of revolutionary zeal were not in fact essential and worthy, the revisionists have also played down the general level of popular political consciousness and commitment, emphasizing instead the role played by a relatively few popular agitators, both bourgeois and sans-culotte. These tendencies are apparent in the

more conservatively liberal histories offered by Cobban and
Furet and Richet, which in their accounts of popular revolutionary action have emphasized the persistence of *traditional*
popular responses, the jealous manipulations of petty fire-
brands, and the significance of degradation, misery, and even
alcoholic hysteria as revolutionary motivations.[50]

The revisionists do not reproduce the anti-democratic fulmi-
nations of counter-revolutionary ideologues, but they offer a
decidedly less generous perspective on the revolutionary process
than had come to be the norm. While Doyle provides a more
favorable picture of the Parisian people, his focus is on 1789, and
does not require him to come to terms with the *dérapage*.
Cobban, Furet and Richet, and Louis Bergeron, however, are
among those who have insisted on distinguishing between a
minority of sans-culotte activists and the *menu peuple* in general
– who at times burst, and were at times cajoled, onto the political
stage.[51] This analysis makes the militants into just another
example – if a rather crude and inferior one – of the several
'sub-elites' which, according to Furet, entered into political contention after the 'opening' of French society by the Revolution.[52]
This 'autonomous political and ideological dynamic' of struggle
among 'elites' is the means by which Furet accounts for the
dérapage of the Revolution.

In all this, despite the differences between conservative
liberalism and genuine counter-revolution, there is an unmistakable tendency for 'the people', shorn of their solemn obligation
to uphold and carry forward the Revolution through the Terror,
to be reduced once again to little more than 'the mob' (which has,
after all, always been alleged to be no more than a fraction of the
largely passive 'good folk'). No doubt the impression of sternly
self-denying, revolutionary sans-culottes could in fact be tempered by an appreciation of the role of wine shops in Parisian
political life. But in the context of the revisionist challenge, the
faint echoes of Taine which can be discerned in descriptions of
drunken bloodlust have unmistakable political implications. If
the nobility had largely been enlightened, and the real goals of
the Revolution were achieved with the Constitution of 1791,
then the social violence of the Terror can be cast aside as darkly
mindless terrorism, a product of ambition, jealousy, and
anarchy.

Although this conservative reconstruction of the relationship
between the popular movement and the Revolution as a whole is
quite remarkable, it is in fact only a logical consequence of

replacing the revolutionary bourgeoisie with a liberal reforming 'elite'. In the first bold attack of the *Annales* historians directly upon the Marxist conception of the Revolution (cited above), Denis Richet elaborated on the broad, liberal character of the elite's struggle. This general revisionist conception denies the bourgeoisie any precedence in the leadership of the Revolution, while also denying the existence of any fundamental social conflict between 'Aristocrates' and 'Nationaux'. Yet, in accepting the classic liberal account of the Revolution's origins, the revisionists have also reaffirmed the liberal conception of 'progress'. They still recognize a 'natural' and historically necessary correlation between the growth of commerce and industry, the development of social and economic rationalism, and the emergence of political liberalism – without, however, in any way relating this progress to class struggle. Richet argued that there was indeed a long, slow capitalist social 'revolution' between the sixteenth and nineteenth centuries, whose decisive stage arrived only in the second half of the nineteenth.[53] This whole, long process he would allow the title of 'bourgeois revolution'.

What remains is 'progress' without class revolution, stripped of all connotations of class struggle, deleting all references to the vigor and vigilance of the people in winning and preserving democracy. On these grounds:

> to enclose the French Revolution of 1789 in the Marxist theory of revolution – one of the weakest and least coherent aspects of Marx's gigantic oeuvre – seems to us doubly impossible.[54]

Not all revisionist historians have polemicized against the Marxists in quite the way that Furet has; but the conception of history as a product of social development is now almost entirely focused on *demographic* development, to the exclusion of considerations of class. The association of republican history with socialist history has been ruptured – probably forever – in favor of the perspectives of Tocqueville, Brinton, and Cobban.

This embrace of *conservative* liberalism – one which clearly gives political precedence and legitimacy to a 'cultured elite', while denigrating the theory and practice of popular democracy – must be taken in the context of the changed political climate in France since World War II. Serious anti-liberal political forces were soundly defeated at the Liberation, and the diminishing threat of the anti-liberal Right virtually disappeared after the

Gaullist foundation of the Fifth Republic. Without such a threat, there were no longer grounds for a tacit alliance or 'Popular Front' of understanding between conservative – or centrist – liberals and Marxists.

At one time, conservative liberals were seriously constrained by the anti-liberal political forces on their right. Left-liberals were at the same time conscious of a betrayal of the 'social' promise of Republicanism by governing conservatives, while the *socialist* left went so far as to call into question the very nature of the Republic, as a bourgeois class state. Given the necessity of making common cause against the right, both at home and abroad, these differences tended to foster a leftward drift in the 'official' interpretation of the Revolution. The political center was largely obliged to keep still – or risk open identification with the right – while the social interpretation grew steadily more emphatic in its class analysis. In the end, the conservatives were confronted with an outspoken Marxist in the Sorbonne.

Yet with real changes in the political realities, the tide of ideas began to turn. The development of profoundly conservative liberal sociological theories in the United States, to counter the more critical traditions of social theory, began to influence French social history in ways which were not at first obvious. Emmanuel Le Roy Ladurie, for one, went in search of Marx, but found Malthus. When, at the same time, the official historiography of the Revolution was becoming ever more explicitly grounded in Marxist theory, and both Montagnard politics and the revolutionary popular movement were being sympathetically evoked by Rudé and Soboul, the appearance of a conservative, revisionist interpretation of the Revolution should not be surprising.

Notes

1. Alfred Cobban, *The Myth of the French Revolution*, London 1955, reprinted in A. Cobban, *Aspects of the French Revolution*, London 1968, pp. 90–112.

2. Cobban, *The Social Interpretation of the French Revolution*, London 1968.

3. *Irish Historical Studies*, xiv (1964–5), 192, cited in Doyle, *Origins*, p. 15.

4. Cobban, *Social Interpretation*, pp. 8–14.

5. Georges Lefebvre, *Etudes sur la Révolution française*, Paris 1954, p. 246, cited by Cobban, *Social Interpretation*, p. 8.

6. Georges Lefebvre, *The Coming of the French Revolution*, New York n.d. p. 179, p. 5.

7. Lefebvre, *Coming*, pp. 3–4.

8. Marx's own thoughts on this topic are explored with care and intelligence by Hal Draper in *Karl Marx's Theory of Revolution*, 2 vols, New York 1977, 1979.

9. Karl Marx and Frederick Engels, *Manifesto of the Communist Party*, in Marx–Engels, *Collected Works* vol. VI) 50 vols, New York 1976, pp. 486–9.

10. Marx, 'Moralising Criticism and Critical Morality', *Collected Works* vol. VI, pp. 312–40.

11. For an indication of its role, see J. Montreau [J. Bruhat], 'La Révolution française et la pensée de Marx', *La Pensée*, 3 (Dec. 1939), 24–38.

12. For the historiography of the social interpretation: George Rudé, *Interpretations of the French Revolution*, Historical Association Pamphlet 47 (General Series), London 1972; Raphael Samuel, 'British Marxist Historians, 1880–1980; Part One', *New Left Review*, 120 (1980), 21–96; Paul Farmer, *France Reviews Its Revolutionary Origins*, New York 1963; Albert Soboul, 'L'Historiographie classique de la Révolution française', *La Pensée*, 177 (1974), 40–58. Stanley Mellon offers a masterly study of the historiography of the Restoration period in *The Political Uses of History*, Stanford 1958.

13. Farmer's book deals directly with this theme.

14. Crane Brinton, *The Anatomy of Revolution*, revised edn, New York 1965; *A Decade of Revolution*, New York 1963.

15. Brinton, *Anatomy*, pp. 16–18.

16. Ibid., pp. 34–5.

17. Brinton, *Decade of Revolution*, pp.5, 26.

18. Ibid., p. 26.

19. A critical approach to this treatment of 'progress' in history is offered by Herbert Butterfield in *The Whig Interpretation of History*, London 1931.

20. R. R. Palmer, *The Age of Democratic Revolution*, 2 vols, Princeton, NJ 1959, 1964.

21. J. M. Thompson, *The French Revolution*, Oxford 1943, cited in Frank A. Kafker and James M. Laux, eds, *The French Revolution: Conflicting Interpretations*, 2nd edn, New York 1976, p. 84.

22. Cobban, *Social Interpretation*, p. 25.

23. Besides the discussions of these connections in the works by Cobban, Brinton, Rudé, Farmer, and Mellon cited above, see A. Gerrard, *La Révolution française: mythes et interprétations*, Paris 1970.

24. Jules Michelet, *Histoire de la Révolution française*, 2 vols, Angers 1952.

25. Farmer, *Revolutionary Origins*, p. 38.

26. For a discussion of Taine, see Farmer, *Revolutionary Origins*, pp. 28–37; Rudé, *Interpretations*, pp.9–11; Gerard, *Mythes et interprétations*, pp.60–64.

27. Alphonse Aulard, *The French Revolution: A Political History*, 4 vols, New York 1910.

28. For an illuminating discussion of the special role which the Revolution and the Republic continued to play in left-wing ideology, see Ronald Tiersky, *French Communism, 1920–1972*, New York 1974.

29. Aulard, *French Revolution*, p. 9; p.157; pp. 171–2.

30. Ibid., p. 9.

31. Ibid., p. 157.

32. Jean Jaurès (ed. Albert Soboul), *Histoire socialiste de la Révolution française*, 2 vols, Paris 1969.

33. Ibid., vol. 1, pp. 29–33.

34. Albert Mathiez, *The French Revolution*, New York 1928; Rudé, *Interpretations*, pp. 19–20.

35. Mathiez, *French Revolution*, pp. 4–9, 327, 448–52.

36. C. E. Labrousse, *La crise de l'économie française à la fin de l'Ancien Régime et au début de la Révolution*, Paris 1944; *Esquisse du mouvement des prix et des revenues en France au xviiie siècle*, Paris 1933.

37. Georges Lefebvre, *The Great Fear of 1789: Rural Panic in Revolutionary France*, New York 1973; *Les Paysans du Nord pendant la Révolution française*, 2nd edn, Paris 1972.

38. Lefebvre, *Coming*, pp. 3–5.

39. Albert Soboul, *The French Revolution, 1787–1799*, 2 vols, London 1974; *Les sans-culottes parisiens en l'an II: mouvement populaire et gouvernement révolutionnaire, 2 juin–9 thermidor an II*, Paris 1958.

40. Eric Hobsbawm. *The Age of Revolution*, New York 1962.

41. Cobban, 'Myth of the French Revolution'; *Social Interpretation*.

42. Cobban, *Social Interpretation*, pp. 54–67, 162–73.

43. George V, Taylor, 'Types of Capitalism in Eighteenth Century France', *English Historical Review*, lxxix (1964), 478–97; 'Noncapitalist Wealth and the Origins of the French Revolution', *American Historical Review*, lxxii (1967), 469–96; Elizabeth Eisenstein, 'Who Intervened in 1788?', *American Historical Review*, lxxi (1965), 77–103.

44. As summarized by William Doyle, *Origins of the French Revolution*, Oxford 1980. The development of this proposition can be followed in: Taylor, 'Types of Capitalism', 'Noncapitalist Wealth'; Denis Richet, 'Autours des origines idéologiques lointaines de la Révolution française: Elites et despotisme', *Annales: Economies, Sociétés, Civilisations*, xxiv (1969), 1–23; François Furet, *Penser la Révolution*, Paris 1978 (recently translated as *Interpreting the French Revolution*, Cambridge 1981); Colin Lucas, 'Nobles, Bourgeois and the Origins of the French Revolution', *Past and Present*, 60 (1973), 84–126; 'Notable against Notable', *Times Literary Supplement*, May 8, 1981; Guy Chaussinand-Nogaret, 'Aux origines de la Révolution: noblesse et bourgeoisie', *Annales: ESC*, xxx (1975), 265–78.

45. Richet, 'Origines idéologiques', p. 22. (my translation)

46. The theory of the *dérapage* of the Revolution was first suggested, and then emphasized, by Furet and Richet in *La Révolution française*, 2nd edn, Paris 1973.

47. Alexis de Tocqueville, *The Old Regime and the French Revolution*, New York 1955, pp. 206–10.

48. Brinton, *Decade of Revolution*, pp. 26–7, 33–5.

49. Lucas, 'Notable against Notable'.

50. Cobban, *Social Interpretation*, pp. 126–8; *A History of Modern France*, vol. 1, Harmondsworth 1963, pp. 137–8, 226–8; Furet and Richet, *La Révolution française*, pp. 204–7, 211–13.

51. Cobban, *Social Interpretation*; Furet and Richet, *La Révolution française*; Louis Bergeron, in Furet, Mazauric and Bergeron, 'The Sans Culottes and the French Revolution', in Jeffry Kaplow, *New Perspectives on the French Revolution*, New York 1965, pp. 226–53.

52. Furet, 'Le catéchisme révolutionnaire', in *Penser la Révolution*, pp. 145–52, 170–71.

53. Richet, 'Origines idéologiques', p. 22.

54. Ibid., pp. 22–3. (my translation)

2

The Marxist Response

From the start, the revisionist interpretation of the French Revolution has been framed as much in terms of an attack upon Marxism itself as in terms of a new historiography. Cobban's challenge was indeed primarily an argument against incorporating Marxist theory into historical analysis, going so far as to attribute the historiography of the popular movement to the dictates of Marxism-Leninism.[1] Furet, similarly, indulged in a favorite liberal mode of criticism by discussing at length the Marxist interpretation of the Revolution in the terms of 'catechism'.[2] Aside from these glosses, however, it is widely felt that the revisionist debunking of bourgeois-capitalist social revolution stands as a sufficient repudiation of Marxist historical claims. From the point of view of a class analysis of historical development, then, the obvious questions must be: is there any validity to the revisionist challenge, and, if there is, does this truly repudiate Marx's contribution to class analysis?

Bourgeois Revolution in Marx's Thought

That the validity of Marxist analysis as a whole should appear to have been called into question is in some measure a reflection of the central position that the theory of bourgeois revolution has held in Marxism. The whole of Marx's early thought was oriented towards the questions raised by – and the world created by – the French Revolution.[3] The conclusion that the French Revolution was indeed epochal and progressive, but only as the

28

achievement of the most advanced, and final stage of class society; which in turn was to be overthrown by a revolution of the proletariat, the 'universal class' of humanity, realizing true human emancipation: this was the distinctive and central conclusion of Marx's early maturity, which set him to the task of studying the bourgeois capitalist society that would produce the proletarian revolution.

That Marx's definitive statement of the concept of bourgeois revolution comes in the *Manifesto* – when he was rendering credit due to the bourgeoisie for their accomplishments, while proclaiming the time for their passing – is precisely indicative of the role the Revolution played in Marx's thought. The French Revolution appeared to be the most important expression of the epochal rise of the bourgeoisie, which, bringing in train modern industry and communications as well as the social relations of bourgeois society, had put the task of socialist revolution on the agenda. The direct fruits of bourgeois class revolution were political liberalism (which was an important asset for the proletariat as well), the sweeping away of feudal impediments to the growth of capitalist productive forces, and effective bourgeois class rule. These were the integral components of bourgeois society, aside from capitalism itself. Together with capitalism's constant revolutionizing of productive forces, they would figure in the ongoing development of class struggle and the growth of contradictions between society's creative potential and the constraints imposed by capitalist class relations of production.

One of the central problems of political theory which Marx faced between 1843 and 1848 was posed by the fact that Germany had not, like England and France, had its ancien régime transformed by bourgeois revolution. Would the proletariat and bourgeoisie *join* in making a liberal democratic revolution, as the bourgeoisie and the people had in France? Or would the proletariat instead be faced with a bourgeoisie that opted to stand with the absolutists and aristocrats – creating a very different struggle, with social implications reaching far beyond a joint program of republican democracy?

Hal Draper has examined the development of Marx's ideas on this aspect of bourgeois revolution in considerable detail.[4] Draper points out that the *Manifesto* (written between December 1847 and January 1848) incorporated the idea that the bourgeoisie would *be compelled* to make a bourgeois democratic revolution, even if it would immediately be followed by proletarian revolution (though in previous years Marx and Engels had thought otherwise).[5] By 1850, however, Marx and Engels had come to the conclusion that the bourgeoisie would *not* be forced to lead a revolution merely because an aristocratic-absolutist old regime still held power. A revolutionary seizure of power by the bourgeoisie was neither actually *necessary* for the immediate development of capitalism, they decided, *nor likely* in the face of the social revolutionary demands of proletarians, petty bourgeois, and peasants.[6] This area of Marxist revolutionary theory, particularly as it is applied outside the context of Western Europe (for instance, Russia) still raises one of the most contentious issues of early-twentieth-century Marxism: the character of revolution in societies where 'feudal' absolutism reigns, and whether or not a 'permanent revolution' can lead to socialism without an intervening stage of stable bourgeois ascendancy. It will suffice here to note the continued centrality of bourgeois revolution and its political implications, and to observe that discussion of the issue is still marked by positions staked out during the struggle between Stalin and Trotsky.[7]

Aside from this issue, however, it is important to note that while Marx continued to analyze the political situation in terms of the configuration of class struggle suggested by the concept of bourgeois revolution – the bourgeoisie struggling with the aristocracy for power and the establishment of liberal society, pushed from behind by the proletariat – after 1848 he tended to see *bourgeois-led revolution* as a thing of the past. In this regard the bourgeois of the nineteenth century were substantially different from those of the French and English Revolutions, although their overall class position was essentially the same. The bourgeoisie of the nineteenth century was not heroic, and would not risk its property and the maintenance of social order to overthrow a more or less accommodating absolutism and its feudal trappings. These goals, however, remained as part of the social ground-clearing necessary in order to realize the socialist future. The bourgeoisie might on occasion be goaded to take action in the ongoing struggle, but the real drive for bourgeois democracy would increasingly come from the proletariat, whose objectives of course went far beyond it.

In a sense, therefore, there was nothing more to be learned from bourgeois revolution as such – and Marx never returned to study the question seriously. Yet, at the same time, it has been treated by Marxists as the central point in the history of class society, because it either gives birth to, or becomes the task of, the autonomous class struggle of the proletariat. The class analysis expressed by the theory of bourgeois revolution primarily concerns the change from a class struggle between aristocracy and bourgeoisie to the class struggle between bourgeois and proletarians. This class analysis has shaped the way Marxists have analyzed the development of capitalist society out of pre-capitalist agrarian societies, and how in turn capitalist society will develop to revolution and socialism.

The revolutionary transformation of capitalist society is the whole point of Marxism. Nothing is more indicative of its complete appropriation of the French Revolution for theoretical purposes than the use of 'bourgeois' as an exact synonym for the rigorously defined term 'capitalist', a terminology which also suggests the continuity of class relations between medieval burghers and contemporary capitalists. The importance of the Marxist interpretation of the Revolution within Marxism as a whole was further reinforced by the longstanding acceptance it enjoyed with official historiography. This confluence of Marxist and Republican interpretations marked what seemed to be the single most influential and sustained inroad of Marxist ideas upon generally accepted 'bourgeois' social and historical thought. The very reluctance of conservatives such as Brinton to recognize the Marxist account seemed a satisfying confirmation of its inherent value, and the importance of its otherwise widespread acceptance.

The concept of bourgeois revolution was referred to by Marxists with easy confidence, and it became a benchmark of class analysis, as well as a claim-stake to historical validity. These traits are nowhere more obvious than in Eric Hobsbawm's *Age of Revolution*.[8] The epochal character of the Revolution made the success of the concept of bourgeois class revolution doubly significant; for, however much the inevitability of proletarian revolution might be doubted, there would always remain this generally accepted, prior instance of class revolution.

The concept of bourgeois revolution, therefore, has been consistently treated as a central aspect of Marxist theory. Though after 1848 Marx and Engels occupied themselves with the theory of *socialist* revolution, based on developments of the nineteenth-century workers' movements, they freely and frequently referred back to the theory of bourgeois revolution. Subsequently, it has been used by Marxists as an analytical tool in approaching other issues of contemporary relevance, and it has of course figured centrally in Marxist historiography as such. For all these reasons, and given the ideological character of the revisionist attack, it is not surprising that the general Marxist response to revisionism was to stand firm.

The Initial Marxist Response

The very first salvo of the revisionist attack came in Cobban's 1955 inaugural lecture at the University of London.[9] Lefebvre's quick reply granted no ground to Cobban. He argued that, through a wrongheaded denial that payment of feudal dues meant the same thing as 'feudalism', and through an over-emphasis upon the occupations of the men in the Assembly, Cobban was attempting to conjure away the reality of a social revolution.[10] The class interpretation of the Revolution would not yield to mere semantics or conjurers' tricks, and Cobban's arguments were not to be taken seriously.

The history of the French Revolution which François Furet and Denis Richet produced in the late 1960s, however, *was* recognized to be a fundamental challenge to the Marxist concep-tion of the Revolution as a 'bloc'. The convergence of the Cobban, Taylor, Eisenstein line of criticism with the favorable reception accorded to this revisionist history prompted a more substantial Marxist response, in a collection of critical essays by Claude Mazauric.[11] Mazauric exhibited a more thorough under-standing of the revisionist challenge than had Lefebvre (having a great deal more of it to contend with), and he both took note of the *polemical* purposes of the revisionists and laid bare the core of their argument. The key to their interpretation was the con-cept of *dérapage*, and Mazauric argued that it was untenable, because the bourgeois component of the Revolution – headed by the assemblies – could not be considered to be a thing wholly apart from the popular components. The peasant and Parisian popular movements of 1789 had been both consistent with and essential to the revolution of the bourgeoisie. Despite the real independence of the four component movements of the social interpretation, their coming together in 1789 *was* a single revolu-tion, and not three revolutions 'telescoped'; 1789 was a liberal bourgeois revolution supported by the people. The bourgeoisie relied upon the people against counter-revolution, and 1792 was no *dérapage*, but was necessary to maintain this unity of the nation.[12]

Mazauric failed to take seriously enough the fact which he himself suggested – that Furet and Richet did not accept the opposition of 'aristocratic' and 'bourgeois' as in any real sense a *fundamental* conflict. In their analysis, it was not the objectives of the Revolution which were in real contradiction with the counter-revolutionaries, but the positions of power assumed – and sought after – by the revolutionary groups. Furet made this clear in his attack on the 'neo-Jacobin' 'catechism' of the Marxists. He argued that structural crisis caused by growth had opened a social rupture which gave play to the political dynamics of ambitious 'elites', including the 'micro-elite' of the Paris sections; but that otherwise this course of political development had no social basis. Indeed, as Lucas has noted, the fervor with which some revisionists – notably Chaussinand-Nogaret and Doyle – have embraced the idea that the Revolution was the product of a single but heterogeneous elite of the propertied makes it hard to understand what the revolutionary work of the Constituent Assembly was all about. Notwithstanding this tendency, it is because the revisionists have so successfully demonstrated that no significant social frontier existed between *noblesse* and *bourgeoisie* that the bourgeois revolution against feudalism today stands challenged.

The difficulty for the French Marxists has been that, as even they have freely admitted, it is simply not true that the bourgeoisie was a well-defined capitalist class which rose up to overthrow an unproblematically feudal society and its fetters, as a straightforward reading of the *Manifesto* might suggest. The social interpretation which sought to express the underlying 'truth' of bourgeois revolution had once been attacked only by reactionaries, and as a whole; it now had to withstand an exacting liberal criticism of its constituent parts, based upon a wealth of detailed research. Since the evidence did not immediately support the simple interpretation of a capitalist bourgeois class overthrowing a feudal nobility, a major reversal of the balance between history and theory was called for. Where once the history of the Revolution stood in testimony to the strength of Marxist social theory, now it would have to be theory that buttressed and 'clarified' Marxist history. Recent years have in fact seen a significant amount of theoretical debate among French Marxist historians, debate which has been impelled and inspired by a general resurgence of Marxist theorizing in the wake of the many New Left movements.

The New Approach to Bourgeois Revolution

A new theoretical direction was announced in 1970 by Régine Robin, with her publication of *La Société française en 1789: Semur-en-Auxois.*[13] Hardly appreciated for its ground-breaking and suggestive theoretical contributions, this book offered a historical overview of the ancien régime that *agreed* with, and added to, the evidence that the revisionists had mustered, but combined it with an extremely sophisticated, structuralist version of Marxist class analysis based upon the *articulation of modes of production.* The fundamental methodological problems of this analysis – which draws heavily on the work of Nicos Poulantzas – will be addressed in a subsequent chapter. Yet, simply as a Marxist analysis that accepted much of the revisionist case against the social interpretation, it is a significant work, and it necessarily had an effect upon the arguments of Albert Soboul and the other Marxists who rejected the revisionist claims outright. Robin's work has demonstrated that it is not only liberals who have recognized the weaknesses of the orthodox interpretation.

Robin opens her book with a chapter that outlines a methodology for the historical analysis of social relations and class structure, more rigorously than one might expect from even a Marxist historian. She acknowledges that the central issue in coming to terms with the society of the ancien régime is understanding the class character of the *noblesse* and *bourgeoisie.* This understanding must, however, be *scientific*, by which she means that the real structure of social relations – in terms of the *constitutive modes of production* of that specific 'social formation' – must be distinguished from the superficial *appearance* of social relations, the *ideological* form in which they are known by contemporaries.[14] On these grounds, she insists upon a distinction between the 'bourgeoisie' as a strictly defined class of the capitalist mode of production – the capitalist class – and the *'bourgeoisie d'ancien régime'.* The latter she takes to be a much broader class peculiar to the social formation of the ancien régime, created through the *articulation* of social relations of the capitalist mode of production within the structure of social relations of the ancien régime, originally characterized by the *feudal* mode of production.[15] Although the terms with which Robin makes this distinction will be rejected on methodological grounds, it does point in the direction of a distinction which ultimately must be made, in quite different terms, between a *capitalist class* and the French *bourgeoisie*.

Robin's argument draws upon Poulantzas's insistent and complex elaboration of the structuralist conception of 'mode of production'.[16] In these terms, it is argued that the ancien régime was a social formation *in transition* between feudalism and capitalism: a unique, dynamic, and transitory structure of social relations – predominantly characterized by the feudal mode of production, but increasingly *penetrated* by relations of the capitalist mode of production.[17] This penetration involved the transformation over time of many elements of the social formation, increasingly giving a new character to its social relations, but not restructuring it in any systematic way. The structural unity of the society lay precisely in this transitional character, a dynamic unity born of the transforming penetration of the old by the new. Most importantly, the modes of production are not seen merely to coexist, in confrontation. From the point of view of the articulation of modes of production, it is essential that the modes not be taken to be merely overlapping or opposed, but fundamentally discrete, configurations of productive relations. The penetration is not a juxtaposition of modes of production, but an *interaction*.

In seriously addressing the need for a systematic and consistent correspondence between Marxist social theory and historiography, Robin raises a number of profoundly important issues which must be considered in detail in later chapters. Her own approach to these issues is informed by a structuralist conception of 'mode of production'. The difference between the capitalist and feudal modes of production does not coincide with a vulgar distinction between 'feudal' agriculture and 'capitalist' development in industrial enterprise. Nor is it to be attributed to those differences in social relations which are apparent at the 'surface' of society, differences between the *bourgeoisie* and the *noblesse* simply as they were manifested in the ancien régime. Neither, however, are the surface relations of the social 'superstructure' to be taken as mere ideological trappings, by which the underlying 'real' class relations are disguised. Instead, for Robin, the differences between the capitalist and feudal modes of production lie precisely in the fundamental differences that exist in the characteristic structural relationship between juridical, political, and ideological relations, on the one hand, and directly 'economic' relations of production, on the other, as they are specific to each.

In offering this analysis, Robin draws upon Marx's extremely important discussion of pre-capitalist surplus extraction, as found in Volume III of *Capital*, in the chapter on 'The Genesis of Capitalist Ground-Rent'.[18] Marx emphasized the profound difference between *capitalist* agriculture, in which land is – as capital – in the direct possession and control of the capitalist, and only worked by hired labor under his command, and pre-capitalist, peasant-based modes of production, in which individual peasant households or the peasant community are in possession of the land, and in control of its production.

As Robin makes clear, Marx's analysis locates the key difference in what appears to be the strictly *economic* character of capitalist surplus extraction: in capitalism, contractually purchased labor-power is employed to produce *surplus-value* – the excess of the value produced through the purchase of labor-power over the value of the wages that purchased it. The appropriation of surplus takes place *immediately*, at the point of production: all of a day's production belongs immediately to the capitalist as it is produced, by mutually agreed economic contract. Because the producer has been completely separated from the means of production, there is no need for non-economic coercion *within* capitalism's fundamental exploitive relationship of wage-labor. (Note, however, that the social context in which the preponderant wealth of one class is produced by another' through 'purely' economic relations is itself predicated upon the existence of extra-economic coercion: both historically, in the 'primitive accumulation' by which the producers as a class were deprived of the means of subsistence in the first place; and in the ongoing social relations of property law and the state which are necessary for 'purely' economic relations to operate.)

It is very often assumed, as Cobban assumed, that 'class' is *in general* – in all societies – a category of 'the economy', as it appears to be in capitalism. In pre-capitalist societies, however, the extraction of surplus from peasant producers is necessarily conditioned by the fact that the peasants remain in direct possession of the means of production. Exploitation, then, must either take place through compulsory *corvée*, or take place *after* production. In either case, this necessitates an extra-economic element of coercion – juridical, political, military – *directly* in the exploitive relationship:

> Under such conditions the surplus-labour for the nominal owner of the land can only be extracted from them by other than economic pressure, whatever the form assumed may be.[19]

Marx's observations on the relationship of labor-rent and pre-capitalist ground-rent to the structure of political relations and state power are of central methodological significance in the analysis of pre-capitalist class relations, and, as will be considered later, they offer a key to understanding his historical materialism generally.

For Robin, the conclusion to be drawn from these passages of Marx has been that the *extra-economic* character of feudal surplus extraction is manifested in the juridico-political and ideological categories of *Estates* and *orders* In Robin's conception, 'it cannot be maintained that there is on one hand the superstructure, a simple juridical mask, and on the other the profound reality, class'.

> If 'ordre' is superstructure, it is in a mode of production where the superstructural plays a fundamental role.[20]

Therefore, in the feudal mode of production, unlike the capitalist mode, class is most definitely *not* an 'economic' category, not even in its surface appearance. In the ancien régime – understood as a social formation characterized both by the feudal mode of production and by increasing articulation of capitalist social relations – the fundamentally *contradictory* nature of 'class' in its feudal and capitalist forms made for an extremely complex articulation of their social intersection, and for a dynamic transition.[21]

This structuralist elaboration of the class relations belonging to particular modes of production, and their articulation, provided Robin with the grounds for an original reconciliation of the revisionist historical challenge with a Marxist analysis. Robin accepted that the picture of the bourgeoisie and nobility of the ancien régime that emerges from historical evidence differs greatly from the impression given by the established Marxist interpretation. Emphasizing this departure from 'orthodox' Marxism, she elaborated upon her method of analysis in a subsequent article, and brought her argument to fruition as a fully differentiated *new* Marxist analysis in a 1976 article written with Michel Grenon.[22] The essence of the argument is that one must base Marxist historical analyses on a 'proper' reading of Marx's theory, not on common-sensical or vulgarly 'empiricist' distortions of it, and that only through a proper (structuralist) reading of Marx can the Revolution be situated in the transition from feudalism to capitalism.

38

To summarize: Grenon and Robin agree with the revisionists that the bourgeoisie (*d'ancien régime*) and the nobility were *both* involved with both commerce and 'seigneurial' agriculture – with the rentier economy in general; that they intermarried and freely exchanged status; and that both were coming to share, in a variety of sometimes conflicting forms, in the ideology which corresponded to the increasing 'articulation' of capitalist social relations in the social formation.[23] The ancien régime was still primarily feudal in character; but being *in transition*, it increasingly both accommodated, and was dislocated by, the penetration of capitalist relations. Capitalism as such – the full complement of social relations of the capitalist mode of production, requiring the dissolution of corporative restrictions in production, free and general commodification of labor-power, and free and general circulation of capital – did not and could not as yet exist. Capitalism was the society *towards* which the ancien régime was in transition. On these grounds they also argue, following Engels here instead of Poulantzas, that the absolutist state was neither feudal nor capitalist, but, again, *transitional*. The state did not simply balance the nobility and the bourgeoisie – who were not in simple opposition – but corresponded to the specific, complex whole of the social formation's transitional social relations. In every sense, they emphasize, the feudal and capitalist modes of production were interactively conflated, not 'juxtaposed'.[24]

The transition had proceeded during the course of the eighteenth century through the penetration of *merchant* capital into formerly feudal relations:

> This development undermining the very foundations of feudalism meanwhile had specific effects at the level of superstructure which appeared, from the second half of the century, in an organic crisis of all ideological apparatuses, in a crisis of the state apparatus, in short, in a crisis which touched all the elements of *the superstructure*.[25]

This, then, was the origin of the Revolution: the crisis of a superstructure in transition. Not, they argue, a contradiction between an obsolete feudal preponderance in the superstructure, on one hand, and the growth of capitalist forces of production in the base, on the other, as has been suggested in 'mechanical' Marxist theories. Rather, they insist, it is the *conflation* of the relations of feudalism and capitalism which is central to transition, and which necessitates the transformation of the *entire* superstructure in the Revolution:

> We see . . . that it is not enough to suppress feudalism to let ideo-
> logical apparatuses that were *already* there but fettered burst
> forth and develop. The revolution suppressed or transformed radi-
> cally all the ideological apparatuses of the social formation, and not
> solely those which were tied by nature to the feudal mode of produc-
> tion.[26]

The Revolution was the specific form taken in resolution of the
superstructural crisis of transition, according to Grenon and
Robin; whereas the transition itself took the form of what Marx
described as the *less revolutionary* of two possible paths to capitalism.[27] This path of the transition itself, which has come to be
called 'Way 2', involves the ascendancy of *commercial capital*
over the production process; whereas, in 'Way 1', the 'really
revolutionary' path of transition, 'the producer becomes merchant and capitalist'.[28] While less revolutionary in its social form,
Way 2 still required a resolution of the contradictions between
the entrenched feudal forms of the superstructure and the needs
of capitalist economic liberalism.

Yet, continue Grenon and Robin, it was not intrinsically
necessary in the development and spread of commercial capital –
Way 2 – that the superstructural crisis of the ancien régime
should take the specific form that it did. Nor was it 'necessary' for
resolution of this crisis to take the form of a revolutionary shift
from Way 2 to Way 1. This shift occurred as a result of the
historically *specific* process of resolution, which emerged in the
form of the French Revolution, by which capitalist producers –
above all, the 'rural bourgeoisie' of the *fermiers* and *laboureurs*
(wealthy peasants) – became mobilized to undertake the transformation of society themselves.

Though the transition in dominant mode of production
implicit in the idea of 'bourgeois revolution' is historically
necessary, it is *not* necessary for that transition to take the
specific form of *social revolution*:

> This passage to economic liberalism . . . did it necessitate the
> economic or social dispossession of the nobility? Did it necessitate *a
> fortiori* the subordination of merchant capital? Put otherwise, did it
> necessitate the decisive intervention of the direct producers, both on
> the economic level and on the political level? What explains the
> specific role of the latter in the French Revolution is the overdeter-
> mination of the contradictions of the social formation in 1789, and

not, we hold, a necessity inscribed in the actual evolution of merchant capital in eighteenth-century France.[29]

Though this accentuates the historical specificity of the French Revolution, it does so by making the process of transition more important than bourgeois revolution, eliminating altogether the *necessity* of a bourgeois social revolution. Grenon and Robin claim that it is essential to shift the terrain of research on the Revolution, to situate it in the 'problematic' of transition. The 'strategic place of *bourgeois revolution*' would be maintained in the form of 'the key political moment in the phase of transition'.[30]

This elaborate structuralist analysis not only claims to be itself Marxist, it denies in turn that the 'orthodox' interpretation had ever been Marxist. Grenon and Robin insist that Soboul and the other 'established' Marxists have joined in an error which is precisely symmetrical to that of the revisionists – for all have failed to read Marx in terms of the structure of his analysis. The revisionists, failing to recognize the social revolution of Way 1 as being as much a part of the 'problematic' of transition as the gradual liberal reform of Way 2 (which they greatly prefer), can only conceive of the course of the Revolution as *dérapage*. The established Marxists, failing to recognize the character of the transition which had already been underway through Way 2, tend to *venerate* (*sacraliser*) the social revolution and its Jacobinism, without acknowledging the *specificity* of its 'really revolutionary' character or recognizing that it was not intrinsically 'necessary'.

In essence, Grenon and Robin argue that both the revisionist challenge and the orthodox interpretation have misunderstood Marx, that what they have each struggled either to disprove or to maintain was in fact no more than a *mechanistic* reading of Marx's analysis. They go so far as to assert that the revisionists' empiricism confronts no more than a 'Marxism' 'inventé de toute pièce, pour la mieux disqualifier'.[31] Yet at the same time, they realize that it is only with a 'double political risk' – both of being accused of neglecting the class struggle, and of alienating the Marxist 'establishment' – that they dare oppose this mechanistic reading. Robin's analysis of the ancien régime had already been severely criticized by Elizabeth Guibert-Sledziewski for its 'failure' to juxtapose the feudal and capitalist modes of production in contradiction to one another, in a form that necessitated a *revolutionary* transition from one to another.[32] This criticism, they agreed, was symptomatic of an insufficiently theorized Marxism which accorded 'la première place à la société capitaliste'. In their view, this error regrettably drew attention away from and minimized the importance of the actual transitional process of 'economic revolution'.

Where the revisionists have pounced upon the orthodox interpretation as an authentic expression of Marxism – and therefore as a perfect cautionary example of the supposed historical distortions produced by its 'polemical' conception of class struggle – the structuralist account denies that the orthodox interpretation is an expression of Marxism at all. The revisionists, understandably, have not accorded much attention to this new wrinkle. Furet, however, did credit Robin with 'the merit of taking Marxism seriously', and Geoffrey Ellis has recognized in Grenon and Robin's article an 'ingenious' effort to rescue a Marxist interpretation from the evidence.[33] Yet both argue that the undeniable rigor and consistency of the structuralist argument does not improve its 'operative value' in dealing with concrete historical processes; they argue that though *this* Marxism may agree with the facts, it does so only by means of an arbitrary method. Structuralist Marxism, they assert, offers an artificial means of reconciling the predetermined Marxist conception of historical development – which is said to be too global in perspective to offer concrete and short-term analyses – with the actual historical evidence; as such, it can only interpretively follow history, not *engage* it. Furet and Ellis both accuse the structuralist analysis of simply attempting to rescue the basic concept of bourgeois revolution by finding for it a place in the articulation of class forces in transition. This, they hold, ignores the fact that the socioeconomic structures of both the Empire and the Restoration were *fundamentally the same* as that of the ancien régime.[34]

There also remains the fact that the structuralists are ultimately trying to save Marx from himself. For – irrespective of other readings of Marx – the orthodox interpretation of the Revolution simply cannot be fairly viewed as a distortion of Marx's own analysis. There can be no doubt that Robin's structuralist argument does displace bourgeois revolution from its truly central position as the condition which made the 'economic revolution' of transition possible; nor that Marx himself *did* place it in that central position, 'bursting asunder' the feudal 'fetters' on productive forces. There is equally little doubt that Marx described the relations between aristocracy and bourgeoisie – feudalism and capitalism – in terms of confrontation, 'juxtaposition': *class struggle* between feudal and capitalist classes over political ascendancy.

As previously noted, Marx did come to accept that a bourgeois social revolution was less than strictly *necessary* for the emergence and development of capitalist society. Yet he never doubted that the social revolution in France had been based upon the fundamental conflict of capitalist bourgeois and feudal aristocrats, nor did he abandon this general paradigm of opposed bourgeois and feudal class interests. Certainly not in the case of Prussia, despite its default of bourgeois revolution; and though he acknowledged that a great part of the English aristocracy had gone over to bourgeois social relations, this did not change the necessary character of the struggle, in his analysis. Quite aside from the validity of its methodology, therefore, it might be asked if the structuralist analysis does not beg as many questions as it answers in claiming to oppose only a mechanistic 'distortion' of Marxism.

Reformulation of the Orthodox Account

Before 1976, Albert Soboul simply refused to credit the revisionists with having presented a serious challenge to the social interpretation. In a 1974 review of the 'classical historiography' of the Revolution and its recent criticism, Soboul dismissed the revisionist argument as no more than an ideological denial of the concept of bourgeois revolution.[35] He maintained that the absurd and ideological nature of this denial was revealed by the fact that the Revolution had been conceived in these terms in an unbroken line that stretched back from Lefebvre, not only to Aulard, but to the liberal historians of the Restoration, and even to Barnave in 1792. This was the line of 'classical' historical thought, from which only an ideologically motivated interpretation could dissent. Aside from Guibert-Sledziewski's cautionary rejoinder to Robin, it seemed that the established Marxist interpretation could be upheld without concern. With the growth of structuralist Marxist theorization, however, culminating in a depiction of the established conception as at best untheorized, and possibly a vulgar distortion, it became necessary for Soboul not only to reply seriously, but to demonstrate the conceptual grounding of his orthodox analysis in Marx's social theory.

The year following publication of the article by Grenon and Robin, therefore, brought a reformulation of the orthodox inter-

pretation by Soboul, wholly in terms of 'the transition'.[36] Soboul
went to precisely the same texts as Grenon and Robin – and even
took account of the substantial Marxist debate over the transition which had been based on these texts – in order to argue that
it was the supposedly 'vulgar' Marxism of the theory of bourgeois
revolution that offered the true Marxist theory of transition.

The key to Soboul's analysis was the way in which he
addressed the question of the bourgeoisie and capitalism. Soboul
had always insisted that the bourgeoisie was not a homogeneous
class – a fact to which he attributed the political differences of the
Feuillants, Girondins, Jacobins, etc. – and he had further taken a
very broad definition of the bourgeoisie, including master
artisans and shopkeepers (who constituted as much as *two-thirds*
of the heterogeneous whole he described).[37] In restating his
interpretation, Soboul now emphasized the difference between
the *haute bourgeoisie* of commercial capital, closely tied to
the absolutist state and always ready to compromise with the
aristocracy, and the productive 'industrial' capitalists of the
lesser and petty bourgeoisie.[38]

This distinction seems to parallel that made by Robin. Soboul,
however, not only carried this to a different conclusion, he
immediately differed from Robin by his less restrictive conception of 'capitalist producers' (Robin's 'bourgeoisie' proper), for
he included the artisans and the whole of the economically
independent peasantry. In addition, despite the assimilation of
the *haute bourgeoisie* to the society of the aristocracy, Soboul
maintained that seigneurial feudalism was still vital, still feudal,
still the dominant fact of agrarian life, and still the foundation of
the aristocracy:

> The problem of feudal survivals and of the seigneurial regime is at the
> heart of the society of the ancien régime: it remains at the heart of the
> French Revolution.[39]

Within the framework of the theory of transition and the 'really
revolutionary' route to capitalism, Soboul made precisely the
same arguments he always had, but shifted his emphasis down-
wards to the petty bourgeoisie in general, and the better-off
peasantry in particular.

Soboul argued that 'the transition' is precisely the historical
emergence of the capitalist economic order from the feudal
economic order; consequently, each nation's transition to capitalism is distinguished by the *specific* process by which its feudal

agrarian relations come to be dissolved and the means by which, in the process, its peasant producers are differentiated.

> In other words, the structure of modern capitalism has been determined, in each country, by what were, in the course of the phase of transition, the internal relations between the decomposition of feudal landed property and the formation of industrial capital.[40]

The focus of this analysis, drawing on the ideas put forward during the important debate sparked by publication of Maurice Dobb's *Studies in the Development of Capitalism*, is the actual transformation in the social relations of production, rather than abstract consideration of whether commercial or 'industrial' capital was socially predominant overall.[41] In the transition from feudalism to capitalism, the feudal extra-economic extraction of surplus – and the purely commercial forms of 'capital' which are involved in the post-production redistribution of surplus through profitable trade – must give way to the very different production of *surplus-value*, which is peculiar to the 'industrial' form of capital characteristic of the capitalist mode of production, even in agriculture.

The dominance of profit-making merchant capital over actual producers, which is the central condition of 'Way 2', does not constitute by itself a transition to capitalism, however large the scale of capitals. Genuine transformation of the fundamental relations of production is required, by which *production itself*, and not merely the producers, is subordinated to capital. As the means of production are themselves transformed into capital, the definitive form of capital becomes the means of production, rather than the commercial consignment: wage-labor and 'industrial' capital are born. One of the major advances in the theory of transition, as Soboul observed, was recognition of the role of *agrarian* capital in this development – a recognition, facilitated by the fact that the English Civil War had been led by a landed gentry, that was inspired by the need to identify an *intrinsic* dynamism within the transition from feudalism to capitalism.

From this theoretical perspective, Soboul disagreed entirely with Robin's analysis of the 'articulation' of capitalist social relations in a social formation conflating the two modes of production. He argued that, while it was true that the commercial capital of the *haute bourgeoisie* was indeed allied to the feudal agrarian regime, it was not through the *gros fermiers* or *fermiers généraux* of that regime that capitalism was emerging, but from among the 'paysans du type *yeoman, laboureur,* ou *kulak'*.[42] Indeed, Soboul went on to argue, drawing on the work of the Russian historian A. Ado, that the later weakness of capitalist growth in France was largely due to the persistence of large-scale property, preventing a sufficient restructuring of agriculture in favor of dynamic small- and medium-scale peasant capitalism.[43] This is a suggestive reformulation, marking a notable departure from the usual assumptions of the classic conception of bourgeois revolution – particularly striking in its application to this archetypal bourgeois revolution. Yet its novelty has been little appreciated, or explored, because it occurs in the context of Soboul's reaffirmation of long-standing Marxist claims about bourgeois class revolution.

For Soboul, then, the coming together of *haute bourgeoisie* and *noblesse* was not an aspect of the transition by Way 2 at all, but a characteristic aspect of the original *feudal* structure of the ancien régime. The French route to capitalism lay with the direct producers, and with the fundamental restructuring of society *from below* to remove the barriers to productive growth (if, unfortunately, only incompletely), in the 'really revolutionary' way. Soboul thus insisted that the orthodox interpretation of a *necessary* bourgeois-capitalist social revolution – requiring popular radicalism and mobilization to be realized – was entirely sustained, though with a more pronounced emphasis on the petty rural bourgeoisie. The complex political struggle which arose against the ossified feudal and corporatist ancien régime was nuanced by the ambiguous position of the commercial and rentier bourgeoisie, but driven forward by the numerous proto-capitalist *laboureurs* and artisans, with their organic ties to the popular masses. Transition to capitalism by way of compromise between feudal aristocracy and capitalist bourgeoisie, Soboul held, might occur where, as in Italy, there were no grounds for the alliance between urban bourgeois and peasant masses that made possible a true bourgeois social revolution.[44] In France such a non-revolutionary compromise was not possible; the cutting edge of capitalist development – in cottage industry as well as agriculture – lay with the lesser 'rural bourgeoisie', below the plane of compromise, in contact with the masses and directly in conflict with feudalism.

Social revolution, Soboul maintained, is in fact a necessary development wherever capitalism emerges from petty bourgeois production and challenges the feudal order – which for its part is able only to tighten the screws of the seigneurial regime to sustain itself. In his last major statement of this interpretation, Soboul emphasized that real revolution is necessarily *social* revolution; that in revolution, fundamental social relations of the old society are necessarily destroyed in the crucible of violent class struggle, to be replaced by new relations corresponding to the 'level of productive forces'.[45] Revolution is to be distinguished not only from *coup d'état*, but especially from mere *reform*:

> Reform is not a revolution stretched out in time; reform and revolution are not distinguished by their duration, but by their content. Reform or revolution? It is not a question of choosing a longer or shorter route leading to the same result, but of specifying an end: to wit, either of the establishment of a new society, or of superficial modifications to the old society.[46]

The very heart of *revolution* is the destruction of the old order to clear ground for the new, and the concept must not be 'diluted' by the notion of transition through gradual reform. It goes without saying that if a revolution was indeed necessary for the transition, the French Revolution must have been it. Seen in this light, the orthodox interpretation seems both Marxist and uniquely correct, while the structuralist version stands accused of failing to draw the profound distinction between revolutionary change and reform. As she and Grenon had anticipated, Robin is charged with forgetting the class struggle: Soboul asserts that her perspective approaches that of Richet, denying the essential character of the Revolution and conceiving of it only as a reformist reorganization of the superstructure, rather than as the very means and substance of social transformation.

The Balance of Challenge and Response

Important issues have been raised by this Marxist debate over interpretation of the Revolution, and both sides have made new and serious approaches to Marx's thought as well as to the historical evidence. There are still further grounds for challenge and counter-challenge between the structuralist and established Marxist positions, each making a claim for its own 'orthodoxy'. Yet it is instructive to view this sophisticated theoretical infighting from the perspective of the revisionist critics, who have successfully shattered the general approval once enjoyed by the social interpretation. The unmistakable impression is one of

Marxists desperately clinging to Marx, searching for a means to salvage Marx's historical account. Perhaps Soboul has undertaken an intellectual *restoration*, while Robin an intellectual *reclamation*; but both are more concerned with 'validating' Marxism than with testing it.

Both Robin and Soboul, as Marxists, take as *given* that the Revolution was a bourgeois revolution situated in the transition from the feudal mode of production to the capitalist mode of production. Since this has been a central element in Marxist thought, and Marx himself unquestionably held to it, they – as Marxists – have presumed the fundamental necessity of maintaining this point; they have taken for granted that it is in some sense true. Each, then, defines what they believe to be *Marxist and true*, taking first this premise and then considering the historical evidence regarding the Revolution and the emergence of capitalism. They differ in the way they propose to 'read' Marx and this evidence, but each takes for granted that whatever is 'essential' to Marx's analysis will be retained.

Two questions need to be raised here. In the first place, are either of these Marxist interpretations *historically correct*: are they consistent with the evidence, do they adequately take account of enough of the evidence, are they not merely logical constructions but also methodologically sound? In the second place, can *either* of these interpretations truly be said to be *Marxist* in conception?

With regard to the first question, there is on the one hand little doubt that, despite Soboul's defense of the established interpretation, the ample evidence and observations adduced by the revisionists as to the character of society between 1787 and 1815 pose a substantial challenge to the Marxist orthodoxy. Robin's interpretation, on the other hand, draws its strength precisely from incorporating the damaging evidence. Aside from the methodological issues that remain to be explored, however, the criticism which Colin Lucas made of the revisionist interpretation clearly applies to Robin as well: if social revolution was not fundamentally *necessary* to the transition, which was already proceeding through penetration of the social formation by merchant capital, how is the sustained revolutionary transformation carried through by the Constituent Assembly – which had no discernible connection with the 'capitalist producers' of a more revolutionary Way 1 – to be explained?

The second of these questions has of course already been asked by Soboul and Robin of each other. On the surface it would seem to require some preliminary agreement as to what in fact constitutes a Marxist analysis. The specific character of Marx's methodology will be addressed in a later chapter. There are, however, immediate historical reasons for doubting whether *either* 'Marxist' interpretation, or for that matter Marx's own account of 'bourgeois revolution', is really consistent with the theoretical principles which Marx put forward.

The structuralist and 'orthodox' positions sharply disagree on how to appropriate Marx's analysis of bourgeois revolution and the transition to capitalism. Structuralist Marxism claims to be grounded in the logic of Marx's system of analysis; an elaboration upon the *fundamental* concepts of Marxism, in terms of a logically structured whole, with the purpose of 'clarifying' the analysis and allowing its application to other contexts. This structuralist approach emphasizes that experience is appropriated only through concepts – not 'directly', as empiricists presume – and that Marxism is distinguished by the rigorous and *scientific* character of its concepts. The key to Marxism, it is argued, is that its concepts critically penetrate the veils of ideological distortion, including both 'common sense' and formal bourgeois ideology. The orthodox Marxists prefer to take their account of bourgeois revolution straight, without the methodological preoccupations of the structuralists. They are, however, no less certain that Marxism represents scientific knowledge employed to counter bourgeois ideology.

Yet, it must be asked whether the ideas which both positions take to be central to a Marxist analysis of the French Revolution – bourgeois-class social revolution as part of the epochal transition from feudalism to capitalism – actually have the critical character of Marx's social theory, piercing the veils of liberal ideology. This question cuts across the issue of which camp can more correctly interpret and apply Marx's own historical assertions – assertions which in any case will be seen to conflict with his analysis of *class* – to ask whether these 'central' concepts can be said to be *Marxist* at all. There are, it will be seen, three sets of reasons for questioning the theory of bourgeois revolution put forward by Marx: it is not consistent with the methodological principles which Marx himself worked out in his studies; it is not consistent with the historical evidence in even the two major cases for which it is claimed; and it is in its origins actually a *liberal* conception – one which reflects, not criticizes, bourgeois ideology.

Putting aside the methodological issue for the moment, the

historical problems faced by the idea of bourgeois revolution have long been obvious. In terms of evidence, Cobban's challenge retains the greatest force. Its thrust has been somewhat obscured by the revisionists' insistence that there had been a single propertied 'elite', with no substantial basis for struggle between opposed social groups. Yet even if this virtually non-conflictual interpretation could be rejected out of hand, Cobban's original challenge would still stand: the Revolution was not a *capitalist* transformation of society.

The impact of the evidence, Cobban realized from the first, precisely paralleled the explosion of the 'myth' of bourgeois revolution in the case of the English Revolution. Here too, Marxist historians had sought to fill in the social history of bourgeois revolution, conforming to the description contained in the *Manifesto* and embellished upon slightly in other texts. At first, again, the analysis and class categories were seen to be unambiguous, even though English Marxists were faced with a revolution led by landed gentry, in an even more profoundly agrarian society than eighteenth-century France. These Marxists, however, were able to draw upon more of Marx's own analysis to provide nuance, because of his familiarity with English economic history. The relations of the bourgeoisie and the lesser members of the landed class, the capitalist tendencies of the latter – such issues were given a more theoretically informed treatment by Christopher Hill and other Marxists in 1948 than were comparable issues in the context of the 'classical' French bourgeois revolution.[47] Still, it was the 'new gentry' which were seen to be joining with the *bourgeoisie* – and their alliance would always be abbreviated as 'the bourgeoisie', not 'the gentry'. The assumption was always made that however rural industry might be, and however important the capitalist agriculture of the gentry, there was indeed a *bourgeoisie* behind the revolution.[48]

Yet over the next two decades it came to be realized that the evidence did not clearly support this classic account. While still regarded as a bourgeois revolution, its specific class alignments increasingly were blurred over, while particular aspects were given selective emphasis. When Hill produced a major history of the era of the Civil War in the late 1960s, he avoided any clear statement on the bourgeois class character of the revolution. Instead, he suggested only that 'the civil war which began with a revolt of the nobles ended with a struggle between opposed social classes'.[49] In context, this apparently refers to the emerging struggle between the propertied and the small producers. Although this may suggest a parallel with the course of the French Revolution between 1787 and 1795, and perhaps suggests the emergence of capitalist society, it is quite unrelated to the dynamics of bourgeois revolution as such. It simply was no longer possible to make a stronger claim for class struggle – as Cobban had noted, the idea of an English bourgeois class revolution had already been discredited.[50]

Indeed, the evidence that there was *no* struggle between self-conscious classes, and certainly no meaningful sense in which a bourgeoisie can be said to have made a social revolution against a ruling class of feudal aristocrats, has only grown. Robin, in fact, actually justified her novel analysis of the ancien régime by noting that the 'bourgeois revolution in England was able without paradox to be led by a part of the nobility'.[51] Hill himself has even more recently argued that the concept of bourgeois revolution does *not* mean a revolution 'made by or consciously willed by the bourgeoisie', but rather one which creates the conditions necessary for the development of capitalist society.[52] Robert Brenner has even suggested that the evidence instead indicates that the conflict of the Civil War first arose between virtually the whole of an agrarian capitalist landowning class and the vestigially feudal and parasitic monarchy, and that only through the differentiation of radical and conservative positions *within* the ruling class, associated with the growth of radical *popular* participation, did the war itself occur.[53]

All the evidence, taken together, clearly poses a challenge to any interpretation of the two revolutions as bourgeois revolutions in the orthodox sense – although perhaps more indicatively than conclusively. There are still more substantial grounds, however, for outright rejection of the concept itself as *non-Marxist*, in both its origins and implications. For, simply stated, the concept of bourgeois revolution did not originate with Marx and Engels – as they themselves clearly acknowledged. It was earlier liberal historians and the bourgeois revolutionaries themselves who developed the concept of class revolution against feudal aristocracy, even if Marx may have put it more emphatically and in greater detail. This fact has always 'been known' – certainly by Marxists – but its implications have never been appreciated, and the point has been virtually ignored at least until recently.

Yet it is a matter of profound importance. It is not that Marx and Engels merely adopted a historical truth, rather than discovering it. It is that the theory of bourgeois revolution which they accepted was in fact a central expression of liberal-bourgeois ideology, one which is intrinsically at odds with Marx's own concepts of historical materialism. Indeed, in the following chapters, a thorough examination of the liberal ideological character of the concept of bourgeois revolution will lead to a fundamental criticism of much of what has been taken to be Marxist historical theory.

Notes

1. Alfred Cobban, *The Social Interpretation of the French Revolution*, London 1968, pp. 129–31.
2. François Furet, *Penser la Révolution française,* Paris 1978.
3. Hal Draper offers a thorough and insightful discussion of Marx's thought as it developed, in *Karl Marx's Theory of Revolution*, 2 vols, New York 1977, 1979.
4. Ibid., vol. II, chs 7, 8, and 9.
5. Ibid., pp. 169–74, 182, 192, 219.
6. Ibid., ch. 10.
7. Draper quite systematically sorts through the issue.
8. Hobsbawm, *The Age of Revolution, 1789–1848*, New York 1962, 'Introduction'.
9. Cobban, 'The Myth of the French Revolution', in *Aspects of the French Revolution*, London 1968.
10. Review of 'Myth of the French Revolution', *Annales historique de la Révolution française*, xxviii (1956), 337–45.
11. Claude Mazauric, *Sur la Révolution française. Contributions à l'histoire de la révolution bourgeoise*, Paris 1970; for a discussion of the debates set in motion by the revisionists, see Geoffrey Ellis, 'The "Marxist Interpretation" of the French Revolution', *English Historical Review*, xciii (1978), 353–76, as well as A. Gerard, *La Révolution Française: Mythes et Interprétations*, Paris 1970.
12. Mazauric, *Sur la Révolution*, pp. 54–5.
13. Régine Robin, *La Société française en 1789: Semur-en-Auxois*, Paris 1970.
14. Ibid., pp. 17–18.
15. Ibid., p.48.
16. Nicos Poulantzas, *Political Power and Social Classes*, London 1968; *Classes in Contemporary Capitalism*, London 1974.
17. Robin, *La Société française*, pp. 33–41.
18. Karl Marx, *Capital* (3 vols, Moscow 1954, 1956, 1959) vol. III, ch. XLVII, pp. 782–813; Robin, *La Société française*, pp. 28–32.
19. Marx, *Capital* vol. III, p. 791.
20. Robin, *La Société française*, p. 33. (my translation)
21. Ibid., p. 39, p. 53.
22. Robin, 'La nature de l'état à la fin de l'ancien régime: Formation sociale, Etat et Transition', *Dialectiques*, 1–2 (1973), 31–54; Michel Grenon and Régine Robin, 'A propos de la polémique sur l'ancien régime et la Révolution: pour une problématique de la transition', *La Pensée*, 187 (1976), 5–30.
23. Grenon and Michel, 'Transition', pp. 9–12.
24. Ibid., p. 26.
25. Ibid., p. 21. (my translation)

26. Ibid., p. 26. (my translation)

27. Ibid., pp. 16–22; *Capital* vol. III, p. 334. See also the discussion of the two 'ways' in the original transition debate, collected in Hilton, Sweezy, Dobb, *et al.*, *The Transition from Feudalism to Capitalism*, London 1976.

28. *Capital* vol. III, p. 334.

29. Grenon and Robin, 'Transition', p. 21. (my translation)

30. Ibid., p. 30.

31. Ibid., p. 12.

32. Elizabeth Guibert-Sledziewski, 'Du féodalisme au capitalisme: transition révolutionnaire ou système transitoire?', *La Pensée*, 173 (1974), 22–36.

33. Furet, *Penser*, p. 159; Ellis, 'Marxist Interpretation'.

34. Furet, *Penser*, p. 159; Ellis, 'Marxist Interpretation', p. 376.

35. Soboul, 'L'historiographie classique de la Révolution française', *Historical Reflections/Réflexions historiques*, I (1974), 141–67.

36. Soboul, 'Du féodalisme au capitalisme: la Révolution française et la problématique des voies de passage', *La Pensée*, 196 (1977), 61–78.

37. Soboul, *A Short History of the French Revolution, 1789–1799*, Berkeley 1965, pp. 16–20; *The French Revolution, 1787–1799*, London 1974, pp. 44–51.

38. Soboul, 'Du féodalisme au capitalisme', p. 64.

39. Ibid., p. 66. (my translation)

40. Ibid., pp. 63–4. (my translation)

41. Maurice Dobb, *Studies in the Development of Capitalism*, New York 1963; Hilton, Sweezy, Dobb, *et al.*, *Transition*.

42. Soboul, 'Du féodalisme au capitalisme', p. 64.

43. Ibid., pp. 70–71.

44. Ibid., pp. 71–2.

45. Soboul, 'Qu'est-ce que la Révolution?', *La Pensée*, 217/218 (1981), 33–45.

46. Ibid., p. 44. (my translation)

47. Christopher Hill, 'The English Civil War as Interpreted by Marx and Engels', *Science and Society*, xii (1948), 130–56; Historian's Group of the Communist Party, 'State and Revolution in Tudor and Stuart England', *Communist Review*, July 1948, pp. 207–14.

48. Hill, 'English Civil War', pp. 137–9; Historian's Group, pp. 210–11.

49. Christopher Hill, *Reformation to Industrial Revolution*, Harmondsworth 1967, p. 131.

50. Cobban, *Social Interpretation*, p. 9.

51. Robin, *La Société française en 1789*, p. 42.

52. Christopher Hill, 'A Bourgeois Revolution?', in J. G. A. Pocock, *Three British Revolutions*, Princeton, NJ 1980, p. 110.

53. Robert Brenner, Colloquium at Vanier College, York University, March 10, 1982.

3

Bourgeois Revolution: A Liberal Concept

Bourgeois Revolution Before Marx

In recent years, both Albert Soboul and Raphael Samuel made a point of the fact that the idea of bourgeois revolution originated with early liberal historians of the French Revolution.[1] Each stressed the continuity of this interpretation from these early origins to the present. Soboul traced it back to Barnave, Robespierre, and Sieyès in the period of the Revolution (the political ideology of which will be considered in a later chapter), while Samuel highlighted the debt owed by Marx to the French historians of the Restoration period, Thierry, Mignet and Guizot.

In 1948, Christopher Hill alluded to Guizot's class analysis of the English revolution of the 1640s; yet as Samuel has noted, in keeping with the general tone of Marxism at the time he left the impression that the concept of bourgeois revolution – and the linking of the French Revolution with the English – was an innovation by Marx.[2] Soboul also, early in his career, had credited 'the most clear-sighted of the doctrinaire apologists of the middle class' in the nineteenth century with recognition of the historical 'creation and rise of the bourgeoisie'. He had argued, however, that they were incapable of shedding light on the fact that

> the Revolution is to be explained in the last analysis by a contradiction between the social basis of the economy and the character of the productive forces.[3]

53

The apologists, he continued, had been so preoccupied with the rise of the bourgeoisie 'that they barely concerned themselves with a detailed study of the economic origins of the Revolution or of the social classes which brought it about'. Therefore, in those years before it became important to establish the long continuity of the 'classical' historiography of the Revolution, Soboul maintained that the class character of the Revolution had been *uniquely* described by Marx and Engels.

Hill and Soboul were not alone, of course, in downplaying Marx's debt to the liberal historians. It was, in fact, generally ignored by Marxist historians (and unknown to the majority of Marxists) that Thierry and Mignet, even more than Guizot, had had fully developed *liberal* conceptions of bourgeois class revolution, long before Marx, which they applied to both England and France. This *impression* of Marx's innovation was understandable, considering the importance of bourgeois revolution to Marxist historical theory. It was, ironically, only the effectiveness of the revisionist challenge which subsequently made it necessary to bolster Marx's authority with extensive references to similar ideas held by earlier, and presumably respectable, liberal historians.

If mid-century Western Marxists were perhaps influenced by the desirability of attributing so widely accepted an idea as bourgeois revolution to Marx, such considerations had not worked upon G. V. Plekhanov. An important chapter of Plekhanov's *In Defense of Materialism* is devoted precisely to the subject of the bourgeois materialism of the French Restoration historians.[4] Moreover, while recognizing that this materialism embodied a conceptual advance, Plekhanov emphasized its imperfect and ideological character.

The Restoration historians categorically maintained the class character of the revolutionary struggle of the bourgeoisie against the aristocracy on materialist grounds. Even more, they recognized that the struggle had been based on *property relations*. As Guizot had stated generally:

> In order to understand political institutions, we must study the various strata existing in society and their mutual relationships. In order to understand these various social strata, we must know the nature and the relations of landed property.[5]

In his emphasis on the determining influence of property relations upon, first, the classes, and, second, political relations,

Guizot 'is directly opposed to the view of Vico',[6] and represents a new development in bourgeois materialism as it was influenced by the French Revolution itself.

Thierry and Mignet, Plekhanov observes, also shared this perspective. All identified the importance of the *conquest* of landed property in the development of European political history, which created class conflict between the aristocracy and 'the people' or the bourgeoisie.[7] The full significance of this line of materialist thought will be better appreciated at the end of this chapter.

Yet, as Plekhanov critically notes, this materialism failed to account adequately for the origins of property itself, beyond reference to 'human nature' in the tradition of Locke. These liberal historians were capable of comprehending the developmental character of opposed social relations and resulting class conflict in the sphere of agrarian property, but the origins of this social dynamic were lost in a haze of speculation. Precisely reflecting the ideological purposes of bourgeois history, as will be seen, Guizot, Thierry and Mignet supported the justice and necessity of overthrowing the order of feudal exploitation *without* calling into question the legitimacy of property itself.

It is clear that Plekhanov saw this bourgeois ideological materialism as an important but flawed precursor to the materialism of Marx and Engels. Marx and Engels themselves were in fact the first to acknowledge the debt they owed to the Restoration liberals – and their acknowledgements did not even hint of criticism. These acknowledgements were noted by both Soboul and Samuel, but the lack of criticism has passed without comment. The relevant passages are in fact from well-known letters, and they are often quoted, but not usually in connection with the theoretical and historiographical issues of the French Revolution.

In 1894, Engels wrote to H. Starkenberg:

> While Marx discovered the materialist conception of history, Thierry, Mignet, Guizot and all the English historians up to 1850 are evidence that it was being striven for, and the discovery of the same conception by Morgan proves that the time was ripe for it and that it simply *had* to be discovered.[8]

More than forty years earlier, Marx himself had been still more modest in a famous letter to Joseph Weydemeyer:

And now as to myself, no credit is due to me for discovering the existence of classes in modern society or the struggle between them. Long before me bourgeois historians had described the historical development of this class struggle and bourgeois economists the economic anatomy of the classes.[9]

Marx would only take credit for proving 'that the *existence of classes* is only bound up with *particular historical phases in the development of production*' (original emphasis), and tying this class struggle to the creation of *classless* society through proletarian revolution (making an exceedingly rare reference to 'dictatorship of the proletariat').

The whole of this chapter will be devoted to revealing just how true it was that Marx's work followed upon and was influenced by a substantial body of bourgeois-liberal materialist history and political economy. Yet one of the central points of this book as a whole is that Marx was far too generous to the liberal historians, and that he seriously underestimated the originality of his own method of social analysis – historical materialism. Historical materialism was specifically developed through Marx's critical confrontation with liberal political economy. Its theoretical thrust was also wholly incompatible with the class analysis of liberal *history*, but Marx's own historical observations – and particularly those on bourgeois revolution – unfortunately incorporate this liberal class history in an uncritical manner. As a result, they frequently are factually incorrect, ambiguous and contradictory in a manner that his critique of political economy, *Capital*, is not.

Bourgeois Revolution Under the Restoration

Stanley Mellon's *The Political Uses of History* offers the definitive analysis of the way in which the political liberalism of Guizot, Mignet, and Thierry permeated the history they produced.[10] Guizot was the most conservative of these three liberals, and after the overthrow of his Orleanist ministry in 1848 his conservatism became even more pronounced. Marx (who had been expelled from Paris by Guizot's government) not only reviled Guizot's politics, but heaped scorn upon his frustrated lament that the French 'character' was the cause of the collapse of constitutional monarchy, whereas given the English character it thrived.[11] Yet even at this time, Marx felt obliged to pay full credit to the historian Guizot had once been.

Guizot had been a historian of the *progress of civilization* – itself a characteristically liberal pursuit – and he had seen the history of this progress in the development of representative government, with constitutional monarchy its supreme achievement. Yet his was not merely a history of ideas, for it was filled with *class struggle*. While Marx was still only a child, Guizot had argued in his lectures that 'Modern Europe was born from the struggle of the various classes of society', and all his subsequent historical work was illuminated by this idea of the conflict of class interests.[12]

None the less, for Guizot it was the *cessation* of class struggle, and the assimilation of classes through representative government, that was the hallmark of social progress.

> The classes have incessantly struggled; they detested each other; an utter diversity of situation of interests, and of manners, produced between them a profound moral hostility: and yet they have progressively approached nearer, come to an understanding, and assimilated; every European nation has seen the birth and development in its bosom of a certain universal spirit, a certain community of interests, ideas, and sentiments, which have triumphed over diversity and war.[13]

In his later history of France, he argued in the same vein that though France alone had known a complete and far-reaching victory of the bourgeoisie in their Revolution of 1789, this had in fact been an over-stepping of purpose. Guizot saw in Sieyès's claim that the *Tiers Etat* had been 'nothing', and must become 'something', not a historical truth – for the bourgeoisie had always been a force – but a programmatic demand that the bourgeoisie should become *all*.

Guizot found this over-reaching bourgeois egoism regrettable, but peculiarly in keeping with the French character. The French bourgeoisie had been 'destined' to overtake that of England, which had instead satisfied itself with alliance to a part of the aristocracy, forming with it the preponderant chamber of government. France alone would know the 'outburst of bourgeois pride' which led to the exclamation: 'Qu'est-ce que le tiers état? Tout.'[14] In Guizot's analysis – true to his conservative liberalism – the reforms and social progress that were associated with the Revolution were basically desirable and an expression of civilization's general progress. The excesses, however, were unfortunate. The significant difference between Guizot and later conservative liberals, of course, was that under the Restoration, with liberal politics still frustrated in its goals, Guizot *embraced* (in his weak way) the idea of class struggle. This concept of class struggle by the bourgeoisie would become, through Marx, a fixture of the left-liberal/socialist interpretation of the Revolution.

If Guizot recognized the existence of class struggle between the bourgeoisie and the aristocracy, François Mignet put forward a concise history of the Revolution itself, published when Marx was only six years old, which describes the character of bourgeois revolution in terms that sound remarkably like those of the *Communist Manifesto*:

> I am about to take a rapid review of the history of the French Revolution, which began the era of new societies in Europe, as the English Revolution had begun the era of new governments. This revolution not only modified the political power, but it entirely changed the internal existence of the nation. The forms of the society of the middle ages still remained. The land was divided into hostile provinces, the population into rival classes. The nobility had lost all their powers, but still retained all their distinctions: the people had no rights, royalty no limits; France was in an utter confusion of arbitrary administration, of class legislation and special privileges to special bodies. For these abuses the Revolution substituted a system more conformable with justice, and better suited to our times. It substituted law in the place of arbitrary will, equality in that of privilege; delivered men from the distinction of classes, the land from the barriers of provinces, trade from the shackles of corporations and fellowships, agriculture from feudal subjection and the oppression of tithes, property from the impediments of entails, and brought everything to the condition of one state, one system of law, one people.[15]

The parallels between this summary and the brief polemical account in the *Manifesto* are indeed many and striking. Marx and Engels of course had a very different perspective upon the ultimate consequences of the Revolution – for they saw in these progressive steps the creation of capitalist class rule – but their account of the social transformations themselves is virtually identical.

Mignet based his analysis of the Revolution on an examination of social interest and economic life. He described the material conditions which had led to the Revolution:

> Under the regency, the third estate acquired in importance, by their increasing wealth and intelligence, all that the nobility lost in consideration, and the clergy in influence;[16]

and,

> The nobility, on its side, while it resumed a political independence long since lost, was aware that it would have to yield more to the people than it could obtain from royalty. It was almost entirely in favour of the third estate, that the new revolution was about to operate, and the first two orders were induced to unite with the court against the third estate, as but lately they had coalesced with the third estate against the court.[17]

Mignet in fact cast the whole history of the Revolution in terms of a *class* revolution:

> The 14th of July had been the triumph of the middle class; the constituent assembly was its legislature, the national guard its armed force, the mayorality its popular power.[18]

The 'patriot party' of Duport, Barnave, and Lameth, basing itself on the far left of the assembly, reached out to the clubs, 'putting itself at the head of those who had no leaders', until the flight to Varennes; after which the three leaders withdrew, to stand with 'the mass of the assembly and the middle class' against 'the multitude'.[19]

Mignet was less conservative a liberal than Guizot, and he unreservedly approved of the bourgeois revolution of 1789. Still, he closely identified with the constitutional monarchists. Severely critical of the Montagnards, he admired the Girondins while lamenting their willingness to defend the Revolution through extra-legal means.[20] For Mignet, it was *faction* that undermined the work of the Constituent, which was attacked by the aristocracy and invaded by 'the multitude'. In keeping with his liberalism, however, it was particularly the opposition and emigration of the aristocracy which was the tragedy of the Revolution, for it made the involvement of 'the multitude' necessary:

> The latter would not have become sovereign, had not civil war and the foreign coalition called for its intervention and aid. To defend the country, it became necessary that it should govern it; then it effected its revolution, as the middle class had effected its own.[21]

It was scarcely possible that the bourgeoisie, which had been strong enough to overthrow the old system and the privileged classes, but which had reposed after that victory, could resist the emigrants and all Europe. For this there was needed a new shock, a new faith; there was need of a numerous, ardent, inexhaustible class, as enthusiastic for the 10th of August, as the bourgeoisie had been for the 14th of July.[22]

As Soboul noted in asserting the continuity of interpretation of the Revolution, while Mignet greatly regretted revolutionary violence, he saw it as *necessary*; and he saw the Revolution itself as a historical necessity not only in its origins, but throughout its violent course.[23] Mignet's conception of bourgeois class revolution clearly belongs to the line of 'classical' historiography, and clearly figures in Marx's understanding of the Revolution. Yet, in all its details of class analysis, it remains a thoroughly liberal conception.

Even before Mignet, Augustin Thierry had interpreted the English Civil War from the perspective of the immediate aftermath of the Revolution in France.[23] Thierry particularly emphasized that English history had been marked by the long struggle between a conquering nobility and the expropriated native English people, which finally had been ended by the bourgeois revolution of the Civil War. In this, Thierry was refracting the historical perspective of his principal source, David Hume, through the experience and ideology of France after the Revolution.[25] In the earlier period of English history, Thierry emphasized the process whereby the English 'bourgeoisie', despite the miserable state to which they had been reduced by the Norman conquest, made themselves indispensable to the monarchy of the conquerors through their great 'industry' – eventually leading the king to *compel* them to attend upon him in his council. Over time, the 'lower ranks' of the conquerors became assimilated and, in losing their alien status, joined with the 'bourgeoisie' to stand together as the Commons against the king and peers.

Thierry contrasted the growing wealth and importance of the industrious Commons with the parasitic indolence and cruel exploitation of the conquerors:

It was in their property, in their industry, that the conquered were concerned with emancipation: on all sides their industry was hindered; prohibitions held up their undertakings; monopolies discouraged work and overturned sound establishments. . . . When the *subjects* arrived at the point of appreciating the relations between independence and wealth, of appreciating the lines of interest by

which they were tied together, by the need for the liberty of all, they
rallied together; they became a nation, they became a power.[26]

One could say that the rallying cry of the two armies were, on one
side, *idleness and power*, and on the other, *industry and liberty*:
because the idlers, those who wanted no other occupation in life than
pleasure without pains, of whichever caste, enlisted with the royalist
troops, to defend interests conforming to their own; whereas those
families from the caste of the former conquerors that had been won
over to industry joined the party of the commons.[27]

Here, then, are themes which will be seen again and again in the
liberal historical tradition: middle-class 'industry' has been the
progressive force of civilization, though for long it had been
hampered by parasitic wealth and indolence; by tradition, privilege, and ignorance; by special interests and arbitrary injustice.
The heroic history of modern, bourgeois progress since the
Renaissance has been the overcoming of these hindrances in
politics, society, the economy, and culture – pushing aside the
entrenched but decadent old order of things.

All the versions of liberal history have accepted that the old
order had to be changed and room made for the new. The
differences which have emerged have concerned the degree to
which the old order was itself ready to change; how immediate
and pressing was the need for change; whether conflict was
integral to the change; and how far violence could be excused in
the process. Where the more conservative liberals disagreed with
the less conservative, in short, was on the extent to which progress necessarily coincided with *class struggle*.

After the Revolution, continental liberals understandably
tended to recognize the existence of class struggle, something
perhaps less visible in the case of the 'English character' envied
by Guizot, which had been 'conciliatory' – at least since early in
the eighteenth century. David Hume, however, had expressed
the more conservative sort of liberalism, apologizing for the
English Revolution, but also for the Stuarts. By 1720, both
Tories and Whigs, with greater or less conservatism, had come to
share a common, fundamentally liberal ideology, creating a very
different political context than Restoration France. Though a
serious examination of eighteenth-century liberalism is beyond
the scope of this work, it will be seen that whereas in Britain it led
to the development of political economy, and in France to the
history of class struggle, in both cases it was founded on a *liberal
materialist* conception of progress.

In a very much less conflictual form than Thierry's, this liberal materialism is revealed by Hume's treatment of both 'progress' and social interests in *The History of England*, written at the same time as Adam Smith's *The Wealth of Nations*:

> The habits of luxury dissipated the immense fortunes of the ancient barons. . . . The landed proprietors also, having a greater demand for money than for men, endeavored to turn their lands to best account with regard to profit; and, either enclosing their fields or joining many small farms into a few large ones, dismissed those useless hands which formerly were always at their call in every attempt to subvert the government or oppose a neighboring baron. By all these means the cities increased; the middle rank of men began to be rich and powerful; the prince, who in effect was the same with the law, was implicitly obeyed; and *though the further progress of the same causes begat a new plan of liberty, founded on the privileges of the Commons*, yet in the interval between the fall of the nobles and the rise of this order the sovereign took advantage of the present situation, and assumed an authority almost absolute.[28]

The struggle was not between classes, for Hume, but between court and Commons. Yet the classes are there, rising and falling. The role of class interest is there as well, as is apparent in the account of the struggles that began under James I:

> The spirit and judgement of the House of Commons appeared, not only in defence of their own privileges, but also in their endeavor, though at this time in vain, to free trade from those shackles which the high exerted prerogative . . . of Elizabeth, had imposed upon it. . . . While the Commons were those attempting to give liberty to the trading part of the nation, they also endeavored to free the landed property from the burden of wardships, and to remove those remains of the feudal tenures under which the nation still labored.[29]

Though this is far from the histories of class struggle which French liberals produced after the Revolution, it is not without conflict. Not only does Hume embrace the concept of progress, but also the specific idea that it was the growth of free trade as the basis of rising urban middle-class wealth which forced fundamental changes in the old order – that there was a sea change in social life, capped by the emergence of a liberal political order. This more conservative historical perspective – very different from a truly reactionary condemnation of the rise of liberalism, however much it might oppose *further* change – forms something of a middle element in materialist liberal ideology, encompassing much of the perspective of bourgeois revolution, yet inclining more towards the reconciliation of interests implicit in classical political economy.

The Unity of Liberal Ideology

It can be seen, then, that with regard to 'bourgeois revolution', taken in the broadest sense, liberal history has offered one consistent line of thought, *within* which there has been more specific debate reflecting several political differences. There has been a wide range of opinion among liberals as to the legitimacy, the necessity, the wisdom – or even the very existence – of bourgeois class struggle to achieve economic liberalism and representative government. Yet there has been general liberal agreement, not only about the desirability and necessity of these modern social forms, but also about their underlying socio-economic causes.

This broad liberal perspective clearly includes the whole of the 'classical' historiography of the French Revolution, which accepted – in a range of interpretations stretching from Guizot, through Aulard, to Soboul – the idea of bourgeois class revolution. It also, however, includes the quite different line of conservative-liberal interpretation that *rejects* the category of class struggle, yet embraces the idea that progress towards modern liberal capitalist society was the inevitable product of economic growth, rational organization, and intellectual 'enlightenment' – a conservative tradition that comprises not only Tocqueville and Brinton, but also Doyle and Richet. The very fact that the social interpretation was taken for granted for so long by the majority of established academics must be seen as evidence of its compatibility with liberal ideology. Within the liberal perspective as a whole, the social interpretation has essentially been an expression of center-left opinion.

It might be wondered, even without further investigation, how a supposedly Marxist analysis could be found in such a context. The liberal ideological content of the concept of bourgeois revolution is derived, in fact, from the same ideas about progress, social development, and human nature that produced liberal political economy – which was the very focal point of Marx's *criticism*. What has been supposed to be a Marxist analysis of the Revolution, of such power that even bourgeois academics were forced to accept it, is in fact only a radical version of the general liberal interpretation – as expressed first in the political discourse of the bourgeois revolutionaries themselves – which Marx incorporated into his early thought and never subsequently criticized.

Marx, in fact, never made *any* systematic, original study of history. As a result, he incorporated quite a number of significant liberal historical errors or distortions into his ideas about pre-capitalist societies. In a subsequent chapter, the development of Marx's own original method of social analysis – *historical materialism* – will be traced from his early radical appropriation of the liberal politics descended from the Revolution. It will then be appreciated that though Marx created historical materialism specifically through the *criticism* of liberal social theory, in the form of a critique of political economy, his political purpose of socialist revolution in capitalist society did not lead him to make a similar criticism of liberal history. This later discussion will lead into an analysis of the method of historical materialism itself, as developed by Marx in confronting capitalist class society. It will then be possible to describe how historical materialism might finally be applied to the class analysis of pre-capitalist societies. First, however, it is essential to examine in greater detail the liberal ideology that lies behind *both* the idea of bourgeois revolution and the concepts of political economy, in order to consider the ways in which this stream of ideology has been mistaken for Marxist theory.

The Currents of Liberal Materialism

In early- and mid-nineteenth-century European social thought, the main currents of history and political economy bore an ideological perspective closely associated with – and intellectually legitimizing – political liberalism. This liberalism was preoccupied with progress: in history, the progress of politics and social forms; in political economy, the progress of national prosperity based on division of labor and trade. In Britain, experiencing explosive capitalist growth, the political economists loomed larger than Whig historians; in France, the vital political and ideological issues of the Revolution and its aftermath gave preeminence to the historians of progress through bourgeois civilization. In both liberal history and political economy, the apologists of progress were confronted by the issue of class struggle in social development, making these the essential intellectual currents with which Marx had to come to terms.

Both of these strains of social ideology were descended from a line of liberal materialist thought that had developed within that loose movement of ideas which collectively were known as the Enlightenment. Not every thinker attributed to the Enlightenment was a liberal, as will be seen; neither were they all materialists. Yet, on the whole, its secular rationality, taken in combination with individualism and an appreciation of material progress, was strongly inclined towards materialism. Plekhanov, indeed, cited Hegel's authority to assert that 'the writers of the Enlightenment who rose up against materialism were themselves only *inconsistent materialists*'.[30] From within the broad spectrum of Enlightenment thought, it is particularly through the development of a 'stages' theory of social development that liberal materialism can be traced through history and political economy to its influence upon Marx's work.

The stages theory was conceived in its classic form in the mid eighteenth century by Turgot and Adam Smith, independently, it appears. Each of them developed the concept through consideration of the moral philosophy of progress, and for each it provided a foundation for the development of political economic ideas. The intellectual history of this stages theory has been closely studied by Ronald Meek, who emphasizes that the key to it was the role attributed to *modes of subsistence* as the basis for social development – citing, for example, William Robertson, in 1777:

In every inquiry concerning the operations of men when united together in society, the first object of attention should be their mode of subsistence. Accordingly as that varies, their laws and policy must be different.[31]

This view was directly derived from the central conception of the stages theory: that human social life has been determined in each of four more or less distinct epochs by a prevailing means of winning subsistence – respectively, hunting, pasturage, agriculture, and commerce – and that these epochs have constituted the successive stages, marked by the advance in mode of subsistence, through which humanity has passed in the 'natural' development of the species. Each mode of subsistence, by this theory, determined a social way of life to which, in Meek's words, 'there corresponded different sets of ideas and institutions relating to law, property, and government, and also different sets of customs, manners, and morals'.[32]

Meek observes at one point that this concept of mode of subsistence can be distinguished from Marx's conception of *mode of production* on the grounds that the latter 'embraces not only the kind of living that men get but also the relations they enter into with one another in order to get it'.[33] In some of its expressions, however, the liberal stages theory does give considerable attention to social relationships, such as in the observations upon the origins of law and government offered by Lord Kames in 1758:

> The life of a fisher or hunter is averse to society, except among the members of simple families. The shepherd life promotes larger societies, if that can be called a society, which hath scarce any other than a local connection. But the true spirit of society, which consists in mutual benefits, and in making the industry of individuals profitable to others as well as themselves, was not known till agriculture was invented. Agriculture requires the aid of many other arts. The carpenter, the blacksmith, the mason, and other artificers, contribute to it. This circumstance connects individuals in an intimate society of mutual support, which again compacts them within a narrow space. . . . The intimate union among a multitude of individuals, occasioned by agriculture, discovered a number of social duties, formerly unknown. These behoved to be ascertained by laws, the observation of which must be enforced by punishment. Such operations cannot be carried on, otherwise than by lodging power in one or more persons, to direct the resolutions, and apply the force of the whole society. In short, it may be laid down as an universal maxim, that in every society, the advances of government towards perfection, are strictly proportioned to the advances of the society towards intimacy of union.[34]

What is striking is not the difference, but the *similarity* of these observations to certain passages in Marx's work – though mainly, as will be seen, to passages in *The German Ideology*. For not only does Kames's analysis identify *relations* of production as the determining basis for politico-legal development, but specifically relations attendant upon the division of labor in production. Yet it remains true that this liberal materialism contains a largely mechanistic conception of social development, founded on 'technique'. As will be seen in a later chapter, this differs fundamentally from Marx's historical materialist conception of class societies developing on the basis of social relations of production and exploitation. Indeed, the difference between the economic and technological determinism of liberal materialism, and the specific form of determination by social relations of production which Marx uncovered through the critique of political economy, is essential to understanding historical materialism. It will, however, also be seen that Marx and Engels were in fact influenced, in a number of unfortunate ways that they never entirely repudiated, by the simplistic liberal materialism represented by 'mode of subsistence'.

In Meek's presentation of the history of the liberal four stages theory, its development from idea to full-fledged ideology is strikingly clear. His *Social Science and the Ignoble Savage* focuses on the origins and pervasive influence of the novel idea that 'in the beginning all the World was *America*'.[35] The roots of the idea appear to lie in the problem presented to the European world-view by discovery of native Americans. The historical origins of the Americans presented a challenge to biblical interpretation, because of the vast ocean barriers which separated the New World from Eden, and because there was no account of the Americans in the book of Genesis. Since the Americans knew none of the arts known to Noah's family; nor for that matter the herding and farming known to Cain and Abel; nor even the rudiments of the Jewish religion, it had to be presumed that they had *forgotten* them, perhaps as a consequence of their isolation and 'idleness'.[36] Once it became possible to dispense with biblical scripture in social analysis, or to give it no more than formal acknowledgement, this 'reversion' of the Americans offered a suggestive state of simple humanity, stripped of civilization, from which social philosophers could deduce the first principles of human progress. The speculations of early 'theorists' of American origins therefore prepared the way for a line of equally speculative theorists of the *origins of property* in the seventeenth century.

The growth of a secular conception of social progress, as the unintended but providential result of human action, contributed to the emergence of a materialist social theory. At the same time, societies which were distinguished on the grounds of their significant material attributes – which frequently included climate but always included mode of subsistence – came also to be seen as corresponding to different 'levels' of development. As the Enlightenment's secular 'origins myth' of social progress developed, the theorists of the age imbued it with a speculative and anachronistic history of the origins of certain contemporary social relations. Particularly important was the speculation by such seventeenth-century thinkers as Grotius, Hobbes, and Locke as to the origins of government, law, and – especially –

property.[37] It is to these political philosophers of the seventeenth century, and specifically to their *ideological* accounts of the origins of property, that the immediate sources for the liberal stages theory of social development can be traced.

It is precisely in the integration of the idea of social development with the speculations of political philosophers upon the 'state of nature' and the origins of property and law, that the transformation of materialist social concepts into liberal ideology is revealed. Neither the Americans themselves nor the problematic accounts of Genesis were directly of interest to Locke. He made reference to America in his *Treatises of Government* only to harness its image of pristine early society to an explanation and vindication of *modern* social relations. Locke did not offer a clearly worked-out idea of definite social stages. The logic of his argument implied social development, however, in stating that America was 'a Pattern of the first Ages in *Asia* and *Europe*' because the primitive Americans had not advanced beyond hunting to the combination of labor with nature, and so knew no property.[38] If Locke and the Enlightenment thinkers generally came to see that 'in the beginning all the World was *America*', the point was that in the *end* – except where unfavorable circumstances might intervene – all the World would be *Europe*.

Though Montesquieu somewhat anticipated the four stages theory in his profoundly conservative, yet eminently 'enlightened' defense of *The Spirit of the Laws* (natural enough a topic for a wealthy aristocrat who owned a presidency in the *parlement* of Bordeaux), the theory itself only emerged a year or two later, around 1750 – and nearly simultaneously in France and Scotland.[39] All at once, the idea was 'in the air' – expressed first by Turgot and Adam Smith, and then by many others – that society had progressed by moving through successively more productive modes of subsistence, impelled by population pressures, and that basic social relationships had developed through the growing division of labor.

It is striking that, whatever other material conditions were sometimes considered, it was the superficially 'natural', mechanistic force of population growth which provided the essential impetus of social development for liberal materialism. Without pressing the point too far, it should be noted that this suggests a very old lineage indeed for the perspective of 'demographic history' within liberal ideology. This non-conflictual interpretation of social development, emphasizing the 'natural', impersonal, and ultimately *beneficial* character of 'scarcity' and inequality, preceded the emergence of a liberal concept of class struggle. While there already were those who unfavorably compared Europeans to Americans, Turgot, as Meek points out, argued that 'savage' humanity, far from enjoying a 'superior' condition of equality, was *inferior*, precisely because inequality is necessary to the development of division of labor and commerce, and therefore to all the social benefits which modern Europe enjoyed through them.[40]

In the still rosy light of the four stages theory, commerce figured unproblematically as the motive force of progress since the dawn of agriculture. Ultimately, from the perspective of political economy, this optimism would have to be tempered by some recognition that economic and social development was accompanied by misery, want, even class struggle – but Malthus would come only at the end of the century. At the same time, because commerce developed alongside agriculture, and did not *replace* agriculture even when fully mature, it was not quite parallel to the earlier modes of subsistence. This lack of parallelism between agriculture and commerce would also become associated with class struggle, from a historical perspective. As a world-view, the four stages theory incorporated *progress* as a determined function of human nature, and identified property, division of labor, and thus social inequality as *integral* to this nature; it therefore provided the essential intellectual groundwork for development of both political economic and historical liberal thought.

The four stages theory is liberal ideology in classic form. Situated in Lockean materialism; taking 'utility' – or the pursuit of pleasure and avoidance of pain – as a basic social principle; presuming that human arts develop in response to necessity; seeing progress in individual capacities as more significant than the disruption of the social whole: the four stages theory could be carried so far as to become the very embodiment of Pangloss's world unfolding as it must, in this best of all possible worlds. Yet this neat synthesis of ideological currents into one ideology of social development, while contributing to the materialist foundations of modern social anthropology, was less important in itself than as the seedbed of political economy.

This relationship with political economy is quite obvious, not least because it was Turgot and Smith who first developed the stages theory, aspects of which each then incorporated into the political economy which became their main work. (While Meek, for one, is aware of the fundamental difference between Turgot's view of agriculture as the *unique* source of social wealth, and Smith's view of labor as the general source of value, he sees this merely as an error by Turgot, and not – as will be argued in the conclusion – a reflection of the different social realities of France and Britain.[41]) Several other authors also followed this pattern of turning to political economy only after having elaborated a scheme of development stages (a pattern Meek would apply even to Marx, although it will be seen that Marx in fact began by *criticizing* the speculative histories of the origins of property, and continued by *criticizing* political economy). Even more to the point, political economy can be seen to be essentially an elaboration upon the attribution of general social and economic benefits to growth in the division of labor and the exchange of commodities under 'commerce'. Variations of the stages theory continued to play a role in works of political economy well into the nineteenth century.

Meek has offered a substantial account of the stages theory and its development, locating it within the materialist perspective which emerged with the Enlightenment. What Meek has not considered, up to the point at which the stages theory gives way to political economy, is the ideological character of this intellectual current. Beyond its role in the emergence of political economy and its influence upon history, this paradigm unquestionably made a real contribution to the development of sociological and anthropological thought; but it remained deeply imbued with the ideology of its underlying premises.

Where Meek does take account of ideology is in the way political economy itself developed from the stages theory. The whole point of the stages theory had been social progress, which naturally had included the growth of *wealth*, and political economy now identified the source of (modern) wealth in the growth of division of labor and commodity exchange, and the accumulation of capital.

> When political economy as the study of 'the nature and causes of the wealth of nations' began to separate itself out from jurisprudence, sociology, and historiography, therefore, it was only natural that the economists, when they looked back at the earlier stages of society, should tend increasingly to project back into them, as it were, these three crucial categories of labour, commodity exchange, and capital. We now begin to hear that even in the earliest stage the savage hunter possessed 'capital' in the form of his bow and arrows and fishing net. There was an increasing tendency, in other words, for the economists

to interpret development in the pre-commercial stages in terms of the economic categories appropriate to contemporary capitalism.[42]

In this way, the sense of development through a series of qualitatively different stages of mode of subsistence gave way to an emphasis upon the 'eternal truths' of capitalist production. This anachronism, in fact, is central to the ideology of political economy, and the significance of Marx's criticism of it will be more fully explored in a later chapter.

If the main thrust of the four stages theory contributed directly to the largely non-conflictual ideology of political economy, it was immediately of far less service to those concerned with explaining actual political history. In both Britain and France, the inescapable issue of political history was the conflict between the rights of unprivileged property and talent, on the one hand, and aristocracy and royal prerogative, on the other. Liberal history was no less founded on the concept of progress than was liberal political economy; and it is clear that Hume – writing at the same time as Smith – and the French Restoration historians were in agreement that the source of modern historical progress was the growth of commerce.

If, however, progress was to mean the rise of liberal society, then from the historian's point of view it had to mean not only the passing from simple agriculture to commerce, but also passing from the aristocratic to the liberal state. Implicit in the liberal conception of progress was a connection between the growth of prosperity and economic power through the rise of 'commerce' – and hence, of course, the rise of the bourgeoisie – on the one hand; and the development of political liberalism – individual liberty, representative government, and the rational pursuit of the 'general interest' – on the other. In the case of Britain, this connection was relatively unproblematic and non-conflictual: the conflict between the House of Commons and the Stuart monarchy needed to be accounted for, but by the mid eighteenth century it had been replaced by a broad constitutional consensus. There was correspondingly little need for a British historian to focus on class struggle.

After the Revolution, however, social progress through the rise of commerce necessarily presented a very much more conflictual process for French historians. Conflict over the state had emerged specifically between bourgeois liberalism and aristocratic privilege, which meant that the rise of commerce had to be very much more clearly restricted to the bourgeoisie *as opposed* to the nobility. The development of the modes of subsistence and the development of political relations had to be integrated in such a way as to explain why such sharp conflict accompanied the rise of commerce. As has already been seen, the underlying connection between political relations and the modes of subsistence had in the first place been presumed to have been based upon *property*.

It has also been noted that there was a lack of parallelism between the stage of commerce and the previous stages, because commerce had not actually supplanted agriculture as a mode of subsistence. The most explicit linkage of the class conflict between bourgeoisie and aristocracy with the stages theory of development was made precisely on the basis of this disjuncture by Barnave, in his *Introduction à la Révolution française*, written while imprisoned and awaiting execution during the course of the Revolution.[43] Barnave proposed that 'commercial property' was a new and qualitatively different social form, fundamentally opposed to the power of concentrated landed property that had arisen during the epoch of 'agriculture'. Landed property was the basis of aristocracy and decentralized political power, while commercial property supported the bourgeoisie and democratic unity. For Barnave, it was through the victory of the bourgeoisie that 'commerce' was to replace 'agriculture', and it was this struggle which formed the basis for the Revolution.[44]

Meek therefore brings the historical development of property (and class struggle) together with the stages theory through Barnave, and goes so far as to credit Barnave with pointing the way towards the transformation by Marx of the methodology of mode of subsistence into that of *mode of production*. However, Meek sees the problem being addressed as essentially one of logical inconsistency: if commerce develops alongside agriculture without replacing it, how can it be presented as a new and separate *stage* of social development?[45] Surely, however, it was Barnave's need to come to terms with the raging conflict of the Revolution that led him to the confrontation of aristocratic and bourgeois property, not simply a logical inconsistency in the four stages theory.

What is required, once again, is a recognition that the methodology of the four stages theory, and in this case the historical offshoot of its theory of bourgeois revolution, belongs to liberal ideology. It is the ideology of bourgeois progress which explains how and why the stages theory passed into liberal history. In this regard it must be pointed out that, notwithstanding the origina-

lity and power of Barnave's *Introduction* – which in 1792 offered
a clear conception of bourgeois revolution and an account of the
development of civil society that anticipates *The German Ideology* – it was not published until 1843.[46] By that time, the generation living the 'bourgeois revolution' had already given way to a
generation of its historians. Liberals such as Guizot, Mignet, and
Thierry had by then long since recognized the critical determining role of property in history, and particularly the conflict
between aristocratic and bourgeois property, as emphasized
earlier in this chapter. It also has been seen that Hume had
anticipated much of Barnave's line of thought in dealing with
England's less conflictual historical development. While Marx
was familiar with the work of these thinkers, he apparently was
unaware of Barnave's *Introduction*.[47] Neat as Barnave's synthesis is, then, it must be seen as simply one expression of the
development of liberal ideology through the stages theory.

A further point which underscores the ideological character of
the adaptation of the stages theory to the theory of bourgeois
revolution is that the French liberal historians – who were presumably familiar with essential social facts of the ancien régime –
juxtaposed aristocracy and agricultural property, on the one
hand, to the bourgeoisie and commercial property on the other,
in a way that implied mutual exclusion. While this is central to
the idea of a necessary bourgeois revolution, the revisionists
have conclusively demonstrated it not to have been the case. It
certainly is true that aristocratic property was overwhelmingly
agrarian; and likewise true that commercial property was overwhelmingly bourgeois; but only by rhetorical sleight of hand can
the property of the bourgeoisie be presumed therefore to have
been overwhelmingly commercial. For the early liberals this
logical inversion clearly served an ideological purpose, identifying the political movement of revolutionary liberalism with the
ineluctable force of commercial progress. That it was bourgeois
who led the Revolution against aristocrats, and for liberalism;
and that, even before Marx, this was *interpreted* to be the
'natural' consequence of the rise of commerce, cannot be
doubted. It in no way follows that the Revolution actually was a
'bourgeois revolution' in the usual sense, as liberal ideologists
chose to portray it.

Before leaving this liberal ideological background to the concept of bourgeois revolution, it must be noted that political
economy did not remain entirely non-conflictual, nor did it
ignore the subject of 'class'. Yet political economy, unlike either

the liberal historians or Marx, did not accord class *struggle* an integral role in social development. Within political economy, classes were determined by the 'natural' operation of the system of commercial exchange – they simply followed from the natural inequality of property and the necessary effects of the division of labor. Some conflict between the classes might be seen as inevitable in the commercial system of capitalism, but these classes were certainly not defined by exploitation, and this 'class struggle' was not associated with historical development as such. For the historians, however, as Thierry most clearly demonstrated, it was precisely class struggle which was integral to development, because the aristocratic class had held back the bourgeois class. In this regard, Thierry closely followed Hume, freely associating aristocratic property with *conquest*. This historical element of struggle was entirely missing from political economy's conception of the development of property.

This thrust of liberal political ideology will be considered again in relation to the origins of Marx's thought. It should already be apparent that it was Marx who was uniquely responsible for bringing together ideas of political economy and economic development with the divergent liberal stream of the political history of class. What these two streams of thought had in common was the celebration both of 'commercial' or capitalist society and political liberalism, as the chief achievements of natural human progress. Marx would accept this as progress, but only as one side of the coin. In liberal political economy, specifically, he discerned an ideological rationalization of the *other* side, with which Rousseau had been concerned – the social *injustice* that was created through the development of property.

This will be seen to have been the essential starting point of Marx's historical materialism. What Marx did not appreciate, however, was that though liberal political history differed substantially from political economy in its recognition of class struggle, it was no less integral an expression of liberal ideology. The incorporation of such liberal historical concepts as 'bourgeois revolution' into his work, though not calling into question Marx's historical materialism as such, has had a profound and regrettable effect upon Marxist analyses of pre-capitalist societies.

Notes

1. Albert Soboul, 'L'Historiographie classique de la Révolution française', *La*

Pensée, 177 (1974), 40–58; 'Qu'est-ce que la Révolution?', *La Pensée*, 217/218 (1981), 33–45; Raphael Samuel, 'British Marxist Historians, 1880–1980: Part One', *New Left Review*, 120 (1980), 21–96.

2. Christopher Hill, 'The English Civil War as Interpreted by Marx and Engels', *Science and Society*, xii:1 (1948), 156; Samuel, 'Marxist Historians', p. 33n.

3. Soboul, *The French Revolution 1787–1799*, 2 vols, London 1974, vol. I, p. 21.

4. G. V. Plekhanov, *In Defense of Materialism*, London 1947.

5. Ibid., p. 41, quoting Guizot, *Essais sur l'histoire de France*, 10th edn, Paris 1860, pp. 75–6.

6. Ibid.

7. Ibid., pp. 41–51.

8. Karl Marx and Frederick Engels, *Correspondence, 1846–1895*, trans. Dona Torr, London 1934, p. 518 (preferred translation); cited also by Samuel, 'Marxist Historians', p. 33n.

9. Marx–Engels, *Correspondence*, p. 57; also cited by Samuel, 'Marxist Historians', p. 33.

10. Stanley Mellon, *The Political Uses of History*, Stanford 1958.

11. Marx, Review of Guizot's 'Pourquoi la Révolution d'Angleterre a-t-elle réussi?', Marx–Engels, *Collected Works* vol. X, New York 1978, pp. 251–6.

12. François Guizot, in Stanley Mellon, ed., *Historical Essays and Lectures*, Chicago 1972, pp. 206–7.

13. Ibid., p. 207.

14. Guizot, *L'Histoire de France, racontée à mes petits-enfants*, 5 vols, Paris 1877, vol. V, pp. 463–5.

15. François Mignet, *History of the French Revolution*, London 1913, p.1.

16. Ibid., p. 6.

17. Ibid., pp. 28–9.

18. Ibid., p. 65.

19. Ibid., pp. 65–6.

20. Ibid., pp. 129–30.

21. Ibid., p. 125.

22. Ibid., pp. 173–4.

23. Soboul, 'Qu'est-ce que la Révolution?', p. 39.

24. Augustin Thierry, 'Vue des révolutions d'Angleterre' (1817), in *Dix Ans d'Etudes Historiques*, vol. 6 of *Oeuvres Complètes*, Paris 1851.

25. David Hume, *The History of England*, London 1840 (the 1776 edition reprinted, with an update by Smollet).

26. Thierry, 'Vue des révolutions', p. 51, my translation.

27. Ibid., p. 64.

28. Hume, *History of England*, Appendix III, p. 810 (emphasis added).

29. Ibid., p. 496.

30. Plekhanov, *Materialism*, p. 40n.

31. Ronald Meek, *Social Science and the Ignoble Savage*, Cambridge 1976, p. 2, quoting William Robertson, *History of America* (1777), in *Works*, Edinburgh 1890. vol. II, p. 104.

32. Ibid., p. 2.

33. Ibid., p. 229n.

34. Ibid., pp. 103–4, quoting Lord Kames, *Historical Law Tracts*, Edinburgh 1758, vol. I, pp. 77–80n.

35. Ibid., pp. 37–67; the phrase is from Locke's *Second Treatise of Government*.

36. Ibid., p. 47, p. 60.

37. Ibid., pp. 12–23.

38. Ibid., pp. 21–2, citing John Locke, *Two Treatises on Government* (ed. Peter Laslett), New York 1965, pp. 328–9, p. 383.

39. Ibid., p. 68ff; Ronald Meek, *Turgot on Progress, Sociology and Economics*, Cambridge 1973.

40. Meek, *Social Science*, pp. 70–71, citing Turgot's letter of 1751 to Madame de Gaffigny, in G. Schelle, ed., *Oeuvres de Turgot*, vol. 1, Paris 1913, pp. 241–55.

41. Ibid., p. 221; Meek, *Turgot*, p.33.

42. Ibid., pp. 221–2.

43. A. P. J. M. Barnave, *Introduction à la Révolution française*, translated and edited by Emanuel Chill as *Power, Property, and History*, New York 1971.

44. Meek, *Social Science*, p. 228, citing Barnave [Chill], *Power*, pp. 79–80, 85, 93.

45. Ibid., pp. 227–8.

46. In his Introduction to *Power, Property, and History*, pp. 31–3, 56–70, Chill offers an analysis of the relationship between Barnave's ideas and Marx's. His discussion of the genre of 'philosophical history' is likewise quite germane.

47. Ibid., p. 65.

4

In Defense of History:
A Marxist Critique of Marxist Theory

The straightforward account of the French Revolution offered in the *Communist Manifesto* is a problem for Marxists. This fact was indirectly acknowledged even by Soboul, who turned to the Sweezy–Dobb transition debate in order to find some grounds for a re-situation of the classic social interpretation. When faced with the difficult task of defending the Marxist account of bourgeois revolution against damning evidence to the contrary, the understandable and wholly appropriate response has been to consider what Marxist theory has to say.

Unfortunately, Marxist theory has not so far proved very helpful. A good part of the historical observations contained within Marx's texts have been drawn from or influenced by historical accounts that are tinged with liberal ideology. Far from resolving this problem, Marxist theoreticians have only reproduced it at another level, for they have based their theoretical approaches to history on many of the conceptions which must in fact be called into question. While Marxist historians such as Soboul, Hobsbawm, and Rudé have made important contributions to our understanding of the lives and struggles of ordinary people in pre-capitalist and transitional periods, Marxist theory has been unable to deal adequately with the periods themselves.

Marx's work embraced many fields, but Cobban was not wrong in describing its central theoretical perspective as *historical sociology*: the historical study of social structure, and, above all, the study of history as *social change*. As will be seen,

77

historical materialism holds that history – specifically, the history of Western class society – is an integral whole: a developmental continuum, impelled by fundamental social forces in a dynamic historical process. Marxist theory, however, has so far recognized this continuum only in terms of the specific sequence of modes of production and the epochal transition of bourgeois revolution that Marx offered in several of his texts. This historical framework has been systematized in a number of ways, but they all have in common that they are based on a scheme of history, rather than an actual method of historical materialist analysis.

This chapter, then, will examine the ways in which Marxist theory, in both its orthodox and structuralist forms, has been hamstrung in approaching the historical process by its commitment to a preconceived structure of modes of production. It will be seen that, without a method to maintain the vital link between historical materialism and the historical process, aside from references to Marx's texts, Marxist theory has not been able to describe convincingly how the French Revolution figures in the history of class society. In the chapters that follow, an effort will therefore be made to recover and clarify Marx's method of historical materialism from his actual practice of it in the critique of political economy. The conclusion, finally, will offer some indication as to how this method may be applied to interpret the Revolution.

Orthodox Marxism

The term 'orthodox Marxism' will here be taken to comprise the whole range of quite divergent lines of Marxist thought that generally have tended to take Marx's textual assertions at face value, sufficient in themselves as expressions of historical materialism. In translating historical study into historical materialism, the point of reference for orthodox Marxism remains Marx's own work.

As previously noted, Eric Hobsbawm's *The Age of Revolution*, as a 'history' of bourgeois revolution, is a classic statement of orthodox Marxism: it straightforwardly argues for the dual bourgeois revolution – economic and political – that Marx described in the *Manifesto*, offering Lefebvre's work on France and the British industrial revolution in substantiation. Yet it is also Hobsbawm's work that best demonstrates that orthodox

Marxism need be neither untheoretical nor uncritical. Indeed, Hobsbawm's introduction to the volume of excerpts from the *Grundrisse* which was published as *Pre-Capitalist Economic Formations* offers a profound awareness of the difficulties presented by Marx's own historical observations.[1] The *Grundrisse* was then all but unknown to English-speaking Marxists, and Hobsbawm's explicit intention was to stimulate critical analysis of major problems in the theory of historical development, recognizing that existing Marxist interpolations had not proved adequate.

Hobsbawm argued that Marx's most essential historical conception was an *overview* of the process of historical development:

> Though particular social-economic formations, expressing particular phases of this evolution, are very relevant, it is the entire process, spanning centuries and continents, which he [Marx] has in mind. Hence his framework is chronological only in the broadest sense, and problems of, let us say, the transition from one phase to another, are not his primary concern, except in so far as they throw light on the long-term transformation.[2]

Hobsbawm reprises the central ideas of this essential historical perspective. History is social development, *progress* through successive class societies. Individual human capacities develop through the progressive transformation of productive relations. Development finally concludes with the elimination of class antagonisms and the reintegration of fully-realized individuals in communism's self-consciously *social* production, based on the achievement of human potential. This underlying Marxist conception of development is indeed central to historical materialism, as will be emphasized in the chapters which follow.

Hobsbawm goes even further, to distinguish between historical materialism as a whole and the specific historical categories which Marx put forward, whether taken individually or in series. He emphasizes that there were very real limits to Marx's historical knowledge – both in the limitations of his sources, and in the limited, sometimes negligible extent of his attention to *pre-capitalist* societies.[3] With regard to the 'classical' modes of production specified by Marx in the 'Preface' to *A Contribution to the Critique of Political Economy* – 'the Asiatic, the ancient, the feudal and the modern bourgeois modes of production' – Hobsbawm insists that there is no obligation to accept the list as given; that Marx and Engels tinkered with this list themselves; and that 'few parts of Marx's thought have been more revised by his most devoted followers'.

> The list, and a good deal of the discussion in the *Formen* which lies behind it, are the outcome not of theory but of observation. The general theory of historical materialism requires only that there should be a succession of modes of production, though not necessarily any particular modes, and perhaps not in any particular pre-determined order. Looking at the actual historical record, Marx thought that he could distinguish a certain number of socio-economic formations and a certain succession. But if he had been mistaken in his observations, or if these had been based on partial and therefore misleading information, the general theory of historical materialism would remain unaffected.[3]

This goes a long way towards escaping from the straitjacket of 'what Marx said', and Hobsbawm goes even further in making criticisms of the forms of analysis typically found in Marxist theory.

Indeed, Hobsbawm discusses the two main tendencies in orthodox Marxist historical thought since Marx, and reveals the weaknesses of each. One is the frankly simplistic 'war horse' Marxism, which reduces historical development in every case to a 'ladder' of successively ordered, necessary modes of production. The other – looking to attain greater flexibility and a closer correspondence to particular historical realities – freely dispenses with the inconvenient 'Asiatic' mode of production, and restricts the application of an ancient (slave) mode to Greece and Rome, filling in the gaps outside Europe with variations on the feudal mode (for example, 'semi-feudal' China). This tends both to blur the specific character of national histories and to obscure the specific historical form of European feudalism as a class society. Hobsbawm himself has no aversion to the revision or even rejection of a given mode of production; on the contrary, his objection is that these Marxists simply have not theorized the problem adequately.

As Hobsbawm has suggested, manipulation of a handful of allusive observations and standard historical formulas has not proved adequate to the task of historical materialist analysis of pre-capitalist society. If such study is to be taken seriously, it is necessary for Marx's whole conception of the modes of production to be thoroughly re-examined, on the basis of up-to-date historical information and a critical appreciation of liberal historical ideology. Indeed, two decades after Hobsbawm's observations, what is still required is an elaboration of the *method* of historical materialist inquiry, by which the stages and process of historical development are in each case to be revealed. Without such groundwork, the texts Hobsbawm brought forward have simply figured as more grist for the mills of interpretation. It is essential to get beyond clever dissection of Marx's extant texts, and the temptation to tinker yet again with the basic scheme of modes of production. Marx's many writings are too easily reduced to convenient fragments of analysis, to be pieced back together as needed, one fragment quoted against another in justification of the 'whole'. All of this has for too long been preferred to reopening the framework suggested by Marx's texts to new and serious investigation.

Perhaps the most revealing case in point is that offered by the debate over transition from feudalism to capitalism. The celebrated exchanges between Sweezy and Dobb, and subsequent interventions by Lefebvre, Hilton, and others, together constitute one of the outstanding instances of Marxist theoretical inquiry to date.[5] This debate has inspired several reinterpretations of the process of historical development, including Soboul's effort to find a capitalist bourgeoisie in the peasant *laboureurs* of the ancien régime. Yet the theoretically sophisticated analyses of this debate were advanced without addressing the problem of Marxist methodology. The divergent historical interpretations of the participants all attempted to follow the *sense* of what Marx meant in discussing the transition from feudalism to capitalism, and yet came to loggerheads over their mutually exclusive readings of identical texts. The debate therefore clarified the main issues of contention regarding several important points of Marxist historical analysis, but could not resolve them. (The extent to which this ultimately is due to real contradictions in Marx's work will be taken up in a later chapter.)

The underlying difficulty in the way orthodox Marxists have so far tended to theorize historical development lies in the need for correspondence between two bodies of knowledge which would *equally* be accorded the status of 'truth': Marx's texts, and history. This correspondence has in the event proved quite problematic. Most Marxists will acknowledge that Marx might have been wrong on this or that point – indeed they often must argue so in order to make sense of their own interpretations of his work – but they will naturally insist that his theory was correct as a whole. This commitment to Marxist 'theory', however, usually translates into placing a preferred version of what Marx meant *above* historical investigation, by including some particular combination of his historical categories among the indisputable 'givens' of historical analysis.

If, instead, historical materialism is to stand as a genuine *method* of historical conception, of which Marx's fundamental overview of historical development is an expression, then Hobsbawm's introduction must be taken as a call to set aside 'what Marx said' in favor of a real encounter with history, to put historical materialism first. It is to begin this task, to elucidate the method of historical materialism and suggest how it may be applied to pre-capitalist societies, that this book is ultimately devoted.

Structuralist Marxism

Other Marxists, however, have responded to the dilemma of Marxist historical theory by maintaining the orthodoxy of Marx's historical texts, but at the same time elaborating a 'scientifically rigorous' methodology through which they must be interpreted – giving rise to structuralist Marxism. Structuralist Marxism can in fact be seen as an effort to eliminate the ambiguous status of historical truth, in order to replace laxness and imprecision with theoretical rigor. This reconciliation of different orders of 'truth' has been attempted through a systematization of Marxist ideas as theory/method, as originally proposed by the philosopher Louis Althusser.

Central to the structuralist approach has been the dismissal of 'empiricist' modes of analysis that would appropriate historical knowledge without first processing it through the structuralist system of determinant modes of production. By rejecting even Marxist forms of 'historicism' as methodologically naive and tainted with bourgeois ideology, the structuralist approach effectively eliminates the possibility of contradiction between Marxism and history. Historical knowledge must descend in the first instance from Marxist 'scientific' theory. The fundamental scientific work is supposed to have been accomplished by Marx, and the structured form of class society revealed through his essential concept of mode of production. The characteristic practice of structuralist Marxism, therefore, has been the sustained – one is tempted to say endless – theoretical elaboration of the relations and contradictions of 'mode of production' in the 'social formations' of class society.

This is not the place for an exhaustive critical review of structuralist Marxism. The most fundamental criticism leveled against it has been that it is intrinsically ahistorical, and this has been forcefully argued by Edward Thompson.[6] What has not been sufficiently dealt with by the critics of structuralism is the extent to which a number of Marxist theorists have sought to adapt its theoretical categories – and especially the articulation of modes of production – precisely in order to engage history. Indeed, several theorists have even prided themselves on correcting earlier errors of 'structuralism'.[7] Althusser's work has in fact primarily served as a catalyst for adapting the structuralist conception of mode of production to those historical and Third World societies that appear not to conform to Marx's basic modes. It is particularly this development of structuralist Marxism that has figured in conceptions of the transition from feudalism to capitalism, and interpretations of the French Revolution.

The real point of departure for structuralist theory, then, is a particular conception of 'mode of production', specifically as a structure of *determination*. Althusser's original contribution was the 'recovery' of a Marxist conception of 'the relation between *determinant instances* in the structure-superstructure complex'.[8] On the basis of this conception of structured determination, the concept of mode of production has been construed to be a purely theoretical construct. A mode of production is a structure of social relations ultimately determined, as a whole, by particular relations of production, or more precisely by the contradictions of fundamental relations of production. In the actual historical world, however – and this is the key to this line of theoretical development – there are to be found no such pure modes of production. What exist instead are *social formations*, and it is through the elaboration of this concept that structuralist Marxists have attempted to translate the determination of theoretical structures into the determination of historical structures.[9]

By social formations, the structuralists mean 'societies', but societies as untidy combinations of modes of production, or fragments of modes of production. Not only may the instances determined by the constituent modes of production be said to exist in each social formation, but the combinations may be said to ramify, and thus create new levels and instances. This provides the theoretical grounds for describing a unique structure for each social formation at a given historical 'conjuncture'. The conception of modes of production as contradiction-ridden, but integral, abstract structures of determination allows virtually any social relationship to be described as determined by two or more of Marx's original modes, contradictorily combined in a given historical social formation. The whole of each social formation may then still be said to be determined by the relations of production, 'in the last instance'. It is for these reasons that Marxist anthropologists and historians of societies not directly studied by Marx have been drawn to the structuralist categories.

It is particularly through the concept of the *articulation of modes of production* that structuralist Marxism has been adapted to historical analysis. For, even if social formations can adequately be described as combinations of modes of production, the question of historical development remains: how is historical movement within a social formation, from dominance by one mode of production to dominance by another, to be described? The critics of Althusserian structuralism have repeatedly emphasized its inherently ahistorical character, arguing that in the end the system of abstract structures of determinant instances is left grandly rotating in an empty theoretical sky. Many Marxist theorists feel that such critics have failed to understand the efforts they have made to theorize the concept of articulation of modes of production as a real historical process.[10]

The concept of articulation has been derived from the notion that different modes of production dynamically *interact* through the historical combination of their social relations in particular social formations. The articulation of a mode of production, as indicated previously in the discussion of Robin's work, refers to the contradictory and interactive development of its social relations in a structure initially dominated by another, previous mode. If the concept of social formation allows structuralism to describe historical societies as structures of modes of production, the concept of articulation allows description of historical development in terms of these structures.

Criticisms of Structuralist Methodology

Precisely because the structuralist approach has been virtually alone in confronting seriously the issues of Marxist methodology, and because theorization in terms of the classic model of modes of production is so widely seen to be fundamental to Marxist practice, it is essential to establish without question that this approach is entirely incapable of resolving the theoretical issues raised by the history of the French Revolution. In the first place, therefore, the underlying structuralist methodology will be shown to be profoundly ahistorical, despite all insistence upon its 'historical specificity'. Then, the primary contribution of this approach, the concept of transition from feudalism to capitalism through a protracted articulation of the two modes of production, will be shown not only to be trapped by the circularity of its ahistorical foundation, but also to be at odds with the historical evidence.

To begin with, the theoretical model of articulated structures of modes of production remains incapable of providing any guidance as to *how* and *why* given modes of production, or fragments of their relations, coexist and come to interact in any given historical conjuncture. In applying the concept of articulation to history, only the *description* of development is possible, not explanation – the different levels of development represented by two modes of production must each be presumed in order for the process of development to be described by the articulation of one in the other. Structuralist 'theory' provides no more than the conceptual categories for filling in such a description, and the capacity to create additional categories, as needed, through specification of still more levels and instances. Instead of a theoretically informed explanation of historical process, there is only an endless proliferation of taxonomic categories between two structures presumed in advance.[11]

It can be said, for example, that the capitalist mode of production coexists with the feudal mode of production at certain times and places, that capitalist economic relations are 'articulated' in a structure characterized by feudal political relations, and that in their contradiction this articulation is dynamic. Yet no explanation is offered as to *how* this coexistence came about. How is it that some set of relationships that may be abstracted as the capitalist mode of production can be said to exist at all – even abstractly – in order to be articulated in the first place? The transition from one mode of production to another cannot be explained except by assuming that the two *coexisted from the start*. Thus the transition from feudalism to capitalism occurs because, in the coexistence of relations from both modes of production, the capitalist mode becomes dominant. Again, this is no more than a description of the event. How relations of the capitalist mode of production actually came to be present along-side those belonging to the feudal mode of production is a question that structuralist Marxism firmly begs, so that it recognizes no need to look to feudal relations themselves for a dynamic that might account for the emergence and development of such relations – let alone their dominance.

Structuralist Marxists have not been alone in conceptualizing away the problem of transition in this way, of course. It has been a staple of Marxist historiography to 'solve' the problem of transition by assuming that capitalism is already present in feudal society, waiting only for an opportunity to burst its fetters asunder. This is precisely where the Marxist 'debt' to liberal historiography is most apparent. With their conceptualization of mode of production and social formation, however, and especially their notion of 'articulation', the structuralist Marxists have provided a theoretical framework, a scientific legitimacy, for the begging of this fundamental historical question.

It must particularly be emphasized that no degree of insistence on a correspondence between taxonomic categories and historical events will impart the missing dynamism of *historical process* to the concept of articulation of modes of production. Many Marxists have found it appealing to conceive of historical social formations as determined in contradictory ways by relations of production that belong to more than one analytically distinct mode of production. Such a social formation may then be said to have two 'basic' classes – those of its dominant mode of production – but also classes belonging in one way or another to other, now subordinate, modes of production, as well as classes created by the secondary implications of fundamental relations of production in the context of this complex structured whole.[12] Régine Robin's analysis of the French Revolution, for example, takes particular advantage of the proposition that in periods of transition the social formation is *not* primarily determined by a dominant mode of production. In arguing that the articulation of modes of production does not mean their overlapping, but rather their organic interpenetration, she is able to argue for the existence of class forms in the period of transition which are different from *either* the feudal or capitalist sets of classes. It is just this degree of descriptive flexibility that makes structuralist analysis so attractive to Marxists working in difficult historical epochs and the contemporary Third World.

In all such analyses, it is insisted that class struggle is the 'motor' of history. The 'motoring' of such complex and historically specific structures through unique sequences of historical conjuncture might seem at first to be a qualitative improvement over Althusserian structuralism. Nevertheless, much as Geoffrey Ellis observed, despite their ingenuity and detail in labeling what happened in history as what 'had' to happen, the structuralist accounts simply cannot engage the historical process itself.[13] 'History', in this sort of analysis, is still no more than a ghostly reflection of the structures of theory.

As Robert Brenner argues, the fundamental objection may be expressed in quite simple and concrete terms: an analysis of history which takes for granted the appearance of a given mode of production *assumes* precisely that which most needs to be explained – the *origin* of those social relations of production by which the mode of production is defined.[14] If the transition from one mode of production to another is based upon the articulation of relations of production which will then be fundamental to the second mode, what causes the appearance of these transformative relations in the first place? In Robin's conception of articulation, the capitalist mode of production seems to call *itself* forth, as *its* relations penetrate the previous social formation and cause contradictions which then drive the transition *towards* capitalism. What then is the source of the specific and characteristic social form of *surplus-value* – which does not exist in simple commodity exchange – through which the production and appropriation of social surplus becomes governed by the logic of capital accumulation? Are these fundamental social relations of capitalism somehow always 'in the air'?

With regard to the sequence of modes of production, what characteristics of human development might be responsible for the order of their succession? If the different modes of production follow each other only contingently, there would seem to be no grounds for Marx's conception of a logic of human historical progress through social development. It has often been said of the more abstract forms of structuralism that they cannot account for the transition from one mode of production to the next. Describing historical development as the articulation of one mode of production in another does nothing to account for their sequence, does not explain why one mode of production emerges to replace another.

In practice, it seems as if the historical sequence of modes of production is implicitly taken to be based on some logic of 'progress' in productive technique and the division of labour –

certainly the structuralist framework puts forward no other grounds for the development of social production. Quite apart from the fact that this sort of technological determinism is itself an expression of liberal ideology (as will be argued in a later chapter), it must be asked what becomes of *class struggle* as the motor of history if progress in the division of labor becomes the prime determinant of both mode of production and class?

Furthermore, any technological conception of historical progress, whether implicit or explicit, faces the problem that there is very little in the capital relation, as analyzed by Marx, which presupposes any necessary level of technology, beyond the systematic capacity to produce social surplus through instruments of labor. As will be seen, Marx explicitly argued that while the *social* division of labor by class or occupation precedes capitalism, significant growth in the *technical* division of labor within production is generated by capitalism, and not the reverse.[15] No doubt capitalism could not take form in a hunting society. Yet the fact that English capitalism first developed through agriculture is now becoming widely accepted, and is the central point of Brenner's important articles. Why then, since ancient Greece and Rome both had widespread commercial agriculture (with specialization and cash crops), as well as large-scale and even standardized manufactures, did *they* not experience capitalist relations of production (as Max Weber, among the many others who understand capitalism to mean only 'profit making', would argue they did)? If feudalism was no more than the passive recipient of the 'seeds' of capitalism, then on what grounds can it be held that there is any sequential relationship between the modes of production, or any particular moment which is 'ripe' for transition? If the articulation model equally accounts for the development of capitalism in feudal society and the Third World, why then did it *not* emerge in ancient society?

In short, what is the dynamic behind the historical processes of class society which has led it from the ancient Greek *polis* to the modern capitalist industrial nation? The inherent logical flaw of the articulation of modes of production framework is a function of its ahistorical nature: modes of production can be elaborated in all their structuralist particulars, but no *process* exists to link and bridge between them. Locating the modes of production in historically detailed social formations, complete with complex 'articulations', in no way addresses the issue of *what* leads from one mode of production to the next.

A final problem comes to the fore in actually applying structuralist Marxism to historical interpretation. Despite all the criticism there has been of the abstract edifice of determined relations which Althusser erected upon the concept of mode of production, there is little disagreement that modes of production may in fact be said to exist; that theoretically coherent systems of exploitive reproduction can be recognized in social relations. Yet when applied to the real historical world, structuralist Marxism must leave behind 'mode of production' as an abstract concept, and deal with Marx's own handful of modes.

It is, of course, precisely because of this limitation that the concept of social formation was put forward in the first place. Nonetheless, a serious conceptual problem exists. Is it really to be maintained that Marx's modes of production make up the entire vocabulary of fundamental relations of exploitation – exhausting all the modes of exploitive production which might ever be identified in social formations? If so, on what grounds? By what intrinsic logic is class exploitation limited to these forms? And if not, how then might other fundamental relations of exploitation be identified? How is it to be known what the 'true' modes of production really are? For, if the articulation of modes of production is used to explain the lack of congruence between Marx's straightforward historical assertions and the evidence actually presented by concrete social formations, it remains a mystery how these original modes can then also be claimed to have been reliably and scientifically described by Marx.

Yet in order to justify the structuralist approach it must in fact be claimed that, whatever the appearances, Marx did adequately and scientifically work up all the 'raw material' of knowledge that will *ever* be required. The work need not be checked or repeated; indeed, no method of reproducing it will even be considered. *Only* Marx's texts, and only certain fragments of them, are necessary. This structuralist enshrinement of Marx's *dicta* should by now be clear. Robin, it is true, offered the hint that it is the specific relations of exploitation existing in any society that constitutes the basis for its mode of production, through her appropriation of Marx's argument from Volume III of *Capital* – and this is indeed suggestive. But she has *reversed* the logical direction of this relationship by starting with the mode of production as the given. On what grounds can it be presumed in advance that a scientific investigation of the relations of exploitation in some society will reveal one (or more) of Marx's modes?

The problem is not that the categories themselves are abstract:

after all, a logical structure may be abstracted from history for purposes of analysis, so long as it is actually rooted in historical reality. The structuralist theoretical framework of modes of production, however, has been entirely elaborated in the abstract. Above all, the modes themselves have been conceived *a priori* – their structures have been 'abstracted' from social relations before those social relations are themselves studied, solely on the basis of Marx's word. Ultimately, Marxist structuralism is no more than a clever descriptive system that takes a predetermined scheme of historical development and finds a way to apply it to history.

If it must be admitted with Hobsbawm that Marx, like any other investigator, at least *might* have been wrong, then there can be no justification for basing the theoretical apparatus of historical analysis directly on the modes of production Marx thought he observed. More to the point, it can clearly be demonstrated that Marx *was* wrong. It has also been seen that it was liberal ideology that first introduced both the stages theory of history and the concept of bourgeois revolution; that the liberal ideological conception of 'modes of subsistence' influenced Marx's concept of mode of production; and that liberal materialism regrettably remained a palpable influence on Marx's thought. Indeed, the extent to which specific elements in his conception of pre-capitalist modes of production were derived directly from liberal ideology will be considered in a later chapter.

Structuralist Marxism and 'the Transition'

The articulation of modes of production approach to historical analysis has gained credibility with a considerable number of Marxists, who seem to find in it both a general methodology of social and historical analysis, and a specific link between Marx's texts and inconvenient social formations. The remainder of this chapter, therefore, will consider in some detail the real inability of this approach to deal with the issues raised by the French Revolution. In the first place, it will be argued that Régine Robin's global application of the method of articulation of modes of production to the Revolution is both logically insupportable and fundamentally in conflict with Marx's own work. In the second place, the somewhat different work of Pierre-

Philippe Rey and Gilles Postel-Vinay will be considered – for, between them, they seem to offer a uniquely detailed historical account of the actual articulation of the capitalist mode of production in the agrarian sector of the ancien régime. It will be seen, however, that far from vindicating the structuralist approach, their work actually offers specific evidence that relations of ground-rent show *no* sign of a transition to capitalism.

It must again be asserted that the underlying purpose of the structuralist reformulation of Marxist analysis – whatever the intentions of its individual practitioners – has *not* been to underwrite a wholly fresh theoretical encounter with historical knowledge. Its purpose has been to lend support and theoretical rationalization to Marx's account of the modes of production, while making them applicable to social formations Marx never addressed. This has been accomplished through a sublimation of vulgar determinism into structuralist determination in 'the last instance', and the transformation of mode of production into a hidden source of structure. As a result, economic determination has been at once both affirmed and, for all practical purposes, removed from the scene. On the one hand, this has very properly shifted the focus from crude indicators of economic development, such as spinning jennies or steam engines, to the analysis of social relations of production. On the other hand, it has presented the opportunity of ascribing a mode of production to a society purely on the basis of theory, even if the 'social formation' *appears* not to conform to it.

The rationalizing character of this structuralist methodology is apparent in Robin's work. Defending and validating Marx's 'history' of the Revolution becomes not merely a thankless, but indeed an impossible task once the evidence cited by the revisionist historians is acknowledged and the lack of simple capitalist/feudal class struggle is admitted. In order to make some sense of Marx's account, Robin has had to raise the level of analysis to the theory of *transition*. By applying the concept of articulation of modes of production, she makes it possible to describe a complex class structure – the product of *both* the feudal and capitalist modes of production, inextricably combined in the social formation – comprising 'feudal' classes, 'capitalist/transitional' classes, and eventually 'residual' classes.[16] This allows Robin to give full play to the *contradictions* of the feudal and capitalist modes – contradictions to which the Revolution may then be attributed – without actually having to identify a

92

feudal-capitalist class conflict, as bourgeois revolution would ordinarily demand. Then, in the revolutionary restructuring which is but *one* path to completing the transition, the 'feudal' classes break up, recombining to form 'capitalist/transitional' classes (which have themselves been transformed) and the new 'residual' classes. The whole structure can then develop as a capitalist social formation.[17]

This salvage operation is perfectly circular. The lack of supporting evidence for Marx's interpretation is met with an appeal to the theory of *transition* through articulation of modes of production. This in turn presumes that the relations of the feudal and capitalist modes of production will be identified, and in fact found to be in contradiction – after which it is a relatively minor quibble whether or not 1789 was specifically a bourgeois class revolution.

The problem begins precisely with Robin's attempt to build upon Marx's fragmentary remarks on pre-capitalist history. Quite apart from his questionable appropriation of the liberal concept of bourgeois class revolution – which, it must be remembered, he turned against the liberals – Marx only considered the emergence of capitalism ('the transition') *retrospectively*, from the point of view of capitalist society. In his critique of political economy, Marx revealed and analyzed the constitutive elements of capitalism. To this end, he particularly sought to clarify the specific and peculiar character of the apparently 'universal' capitalist relations of production and exchange, through retrospective consideration of their pre-capitalist antecedents. This is particularly apparent in Marx's very loose usage of the concepts of 'capital' and 'capitalism' in the historical sections of *Capital*, in contexts where he clearly does not mean the capitalist mode of production. It is the lineage of the specifically *capitalist* social forms that Marx is interested in – not the pre-capitalist forms as such – and his whole discussion is predicated on an understanding of these specific capitalist forms, with which *Capital* begins.

In the *Grundrisse*, Marx explicitly considered this problematic relationship between the political economic categories of capitalism – exchange value, labor, money, etc. – and their 'antediluvian existence' as categories of earlier societies, recognizing it as an important issue in the exposition of his critique of political economy.[18]

In the succession of the economic categories, as in any other historical, social science, it must not be forgotten that their subject –

here, modern bourgeois society – is always what is given, in the head
as well as in reality, and that these categories therefore express the
forms of being, the characteristics of existence, and often only individual sides of this specific society, this subject, and that therefore this
society by no means begins only at the point where one can speak of it
as such . . . .[19]

Capitalism, therefore, will figure not only in the economic
categories of 'capitalism as such', but also in the retrospective
'histories' of these categories as they are written with conscious
reference to the development of capitalist society. Far from
being anachronistic, the conscious purpose of this exercise is to
reveal the 'perfection' in capitalism of social forms which are, in
fact, as such *unique* to capitalism – despite apparent historical
antecedents. Considering an earlier social form (for example,
'merchant capital') in light of the peculiarly capitalist social form
it appears to become (for example, capital) intentionally sacri-
fices the real historical characteristics of the 'pre-historic' form in
order to highlight what is distinctive about capitalism. It is always
necessary to remember that the history presented in *Capital* is
part of the critique of political economy, the critical analysis of
capitalism as such, and is not presented as the history of other
societies in their own terms.

This at least in part explains the apparently teleological
character of Marx's historical observations in the critique of
political economy. He *is* in fact anticipating capitalism, which is
his real subject. Actually to project the impact of capitalist social
relations back into the history of pre-capitalist societies, as Marx
did not, is precisely to fall into teleological error. The fact that
pre-capitalist relations of commodity production and exchange
seem naturally to give rise to capitalism in *Capital* does not mean
that it emerged so simply in history. Appropriation of Marx's
historical observations must be tempered by more than an
awareness of the *external* limits to his historical knowledge: Marx
nowhere even *attempted* a history of pre-capitalist society in its
own terms. His retrospective consideration of the broad historical circumstances from which capitalism emerged, its social
and legal antecedents, etc., is perfectly valid as a means to better
understanding of the historical *specificity* of capitalism itself. It
must not be taken as a representation of the actual historical
processes by which men and women created their changing social
existence in pre-capitalist societies, nor treated as an account of
historical causation. If Marx himself at any given time con-

founded these different uses of history – which he did not, on the whole – then he was simply mistaken.

Marx did, of course, from time to time *sketch* an overview of class society's history, as in the Preface to *A Contribution to the Critique of Political Economy*. These sketches differ from the retrospective view proper to the critique of political economy, for they subsume capitalism as one class society in a sequence. These sketches are thus in principle more historical than the retrospective 'history' viewed through the prism of capitalist categories; but there is very little historical detail in the sketches.

For Robin, however, the anticipation of capitalism is everything. Capitalist relations emerge unproblematically and without prior cause in feudal society, because their ultimate cause in fact lies in the future consequence of the 'transition'. Relations of production acquire a progressively 'more capitalist' character (articulation of the capitalist mode of production) until the entire structure – led by contradictions of the *superstructure* – must finally become decisively capitalist, with or without revolution.

It must, finally, be said of Robin's conception of the transition that neither class struggle nor class relations of exploitation play any observable role; they are, at best, 'offstage'. Given the liberal origins of the concept of bourgeois revolution, of course, it is unsurprising that relations of *class exploitation* do not figure in even its 'Marxist' accounts. Bourgeois revolution does embrace a kind of 'class struggle', but only in the form of a struggle between the competing *ruling classes* of feudalism and capitalism. Since the evidence does not support even this straightforward feudal/capitalist class conflict, the structuralist analysis substitutes for it the development of 'contradictions' between the social forms of the respective modes.

This removes class conflict of any kind from the field of historical behavior, and leaves only the *implicit* exploitation and 'struggle' which can be abstractly attributed to the structures of the given modes. Indeed, despite alleging that in a transitional social formation the classes are determined by specifically exploitive modes of production in complex combination, Robin's analysis offers no consideration at all of this structure as an *exploitive class society*, rather than just a society with 'classes'. Aside from the final Marxist judgement that modes of production must by definition be exploitive, there is little to distinguish Robin's structuralist analysis from Richet's revisionist account of the transition.

Class Relations and Articulation of Modes of Production

Robin's interpretation, then – approaching historical development through a global application of the concept of articulation of modes of production – is quite as ahistorical as the Althusserian structuralism which wholly neglects history. The interpretive essay which sets out her ideas at the start of her main work, in fact, has almost nothing to do with the solidly researched historical monograph that follows. The respectively theoretical and historical contributions of Pierre-Philippe Rey and Gilles Postel-Vinay, however, have attempted to pursue the concept of articulation more rigorously, and apparently more historically, in terms of the actual development of class relations of production during the transition.[20]

Rey's *Sur l'articulation des modes de production* was written from the point of view of Marxist anthropology, and has received attention from a somewhat broader audience than Robin's work has enjoyed. It is also a polemic written in support of the class struggle of exploited peoples through class alliances, modeled on the Chinese and Vietnamese revolutions. Rey in fact argues a revolutionary 'peasant Marxism' that goes so far as to consider that the German Peasants' War of the 1520s might have ended feudal class exploitation had Thomas Munzer only had the time to learn a strategy of class alliances from the dialectic of class struggle![21] While it is beyond the scope of this book to deal with all of Rey's arguments, which range from the highly questionable to the remarkably insightful, it is necessary to consider – and reject – his conception of the transition from feudalism to capitalism in France (on which Postel-Vinay based his own historical work).

Rey raises the issues of transition through his argument that 'underdevelopment' in the Third World refers specifically to development of the capitalist mode of production, to which indigenous modes of production have offered greater resistance than did European feudalism.[22] His point is that the original transition from *feudalism* to capitalism is only *one* form which the general process of articulation of the capitalist mode of production may take – while at the same time it may be said that pre-capitalist modes of production and class struggle will universally *persist* in the social formations undergoing articulation.[23] Rather than simply sweeping away the existing social relations of production, the process of articulation will in each instance preserve certain specific pre-capitalist relations as a condition of the survival and growth of capitalism – making a strategy of class alliance generally necessary. Rey even cites, from this point of view, the persistence of millions of peasants in France as a measure of 'underdevelopment'.[24] It is to argue that this persistence is a general effect of the articulation of the capitalist mode of production that Rey turns to the case of its indigenous development – and so to the analysis of capitalist ground-rent in Volume III of *Capital*.

Rey's central point is that Marx was wrong to treat ground-rent wholly in terms of the social relations of the capitalist mode of production. He notes that whereas in Volume I Marx proceeds from absolute surplus-value to the more complex idea of relative surplus-value, in Volume III he begins with the complex idea of differential capitalist rent and concludes with absolute rent. Rey dismisses differential rent as the specific agrarian form of surplus profit which accrues to capitalists producing under specially favored conditions in any branch of production.[25] (It is Postel-Vinay's evidence on differential rent that, contrary to Rey's opinion, will be seen to point up the absurdity of seeing a transition to capitalism in the ancien régime.)

Rey follows Marx in asserting that the source of absolute rent is the relatively labor-intensive character of agriculture, which yields proportionately more surplus-value than the industrial average – value which but for the monopoly in land would be shared out in the averaging of rates of profit across sectors of production. He contends, however, that according to Marx's strictly capitalist analysis, absolute rent must equal the slight increase in market price by which marginal land is brought into production.[26] Since land yields nothing until rented, however, he concludes that this rent is not merely small, as Marx held, but *vanishingly small*, approaching zero. Citing Marx's own evidence that historically observed levels of absolute rent were actually quite high, Rey concludes that Marx was simply unable to explain absolute rent because he viewed rent exclusively from the perspective of capitalism.

On the basis of the 'Trinity formula' (capital/profit, land/ground-rent, labor/wages), by which landlords and capitalists are treated as separate classes, the rent relation cannot be a social relation of *production* – existing as it does between two non-producing classes – and must instead be a relation of *distribution*. Examining the role Marx attributed to landed property in the rise of capitalism, Rey argues that it clearly operated within a *pre-capitalist* mode of production, in that it was *peasants*, not workers, who were separated from the means of production by landed property.[27] From this follows the central point upon which Rey hangs his view of the 'transition':

> 'Capitalist' ground-rent is a relation of *distribution* of the capitalist mode of production, and this relation of distribution is the effect of a relation of *production* of a different mode of production in which capitalism is articulated.[28]

It is here that Rey makes a claim that seems to imply the historical process which has been missing from the theory of articulation of modes of production: that the transition is both an expression of the necessity of developing capitalism, *and a necessity of the pre-capitalist mode of production*.[29] Rey cites Marx – 'Rent can develop as money-rent only on the basis of commodity-production, in particular capitalist production'[30] – in order to claim that 'it is the reproduction on an extended scale of the fundamental relation of production of the feudal mode of production, ground-rent, which creates the conditions of development of the capitalist mode of production'.[31] If this indeed were the case, Rey would have resolved the fundamental problem of how and why capitalism emerged from feudalism, decisively establishing the articulation model of transition.

On the basis of this analysis, one would expect ground-rents in the ancien régime to reflect the development of capitalism – as Gilles Postel-Vinay claims in his study of ground-rents in the Paris basin – which would set the stage for the sort of 'bourgeois revolution' through protracted transition for which Robin argued. Indeed, Rey and Postel-Vinay tend to go beyond Robin in echoing Richet's revisionist view of a long wave of economic transformation, for the French Revolution itself plays an entirely subordinate role in their work. Postel-Vinay, in fact, has written a Marxist history of *agrarian class relations*, explicitly focused on the transition from feudalism to capitalism in eighteenth-century France, that makes only passing mention of the Revolution![32] Even then, he simply echoes Rey: that in the ancien régime there was a primary convergence of interests between landlords and the capitalist bourgeoisie; and that contradiction developed between them only at a secondary level, based on deduction of surplus-value from the bourgeoisie for rents to the owners of landed property.[33] It was on the basis of this secondary contradiction that bourgeois capitalists became for a time the 'champions' of the peasants against landed property. Yet after the

Revolution they re-established similar relations of production, carrying through the same 'transitional' functions – exploitation and eviction of the peasants – for their own benefit.

In the first place, it is striking that Rey does not shrink from identifying the bourgeoisie as *capitalist*, in precisely the same terms by which Marx refers to industrial capitalist entrepreneurs. At the same time, the only concrete social relations which Rey discusses for this capitalist bourgeoisie are those which they re-establish with the peasants. No working class actually appears which might produce surplus-value for the 'capitalist' bourgeoisie from which rent might be deducted.

In the second place, it should be clear that except for two points – the identification of a pre-capitalist logic for the emergence of the capitalist mode of production, and Postel-Vinay's claim of historical verification – Rey's argument is subject to precisely the same criticisms as Robin's. Rey, too, has *presumed* that in Europe generally and France in particular, it is the transition from feudal to capitalist modes of production – as defined by Marx – which is at issue. Rey's argument, moreover, is even more explicitly derived from Marx's critique of political economy – reflecting fully-developed capitalist society – and his analysis is just as clearly projected backwards: from capitalism, through the logic of transition, to arrive at pre-capitalist society. Indeed, to an even greater extent than one might have expected, Rey's 'historical' material is simply drawn from the retrospective sections of *Capital*, with all its inherent anticipation of capitalist development intact.

Furthermore, without delving too deeply into the complexities of ground-rent in capitalist society, it must be said that Rey has completely misread Marx with regard to the 'vanishingly small' magnitude of absolute rent. Marx's main point with regard to absolute rent, in fact, is that *however* large it might be, it cannot interfere with the determination of differential rents.[34] Indeed, the minute amount that Rey describes as absolute rent is actually the level of *differential* rent necessary to bring new land into production, rent which would be in *addition* to whatever level of absolute rent had already been established on land previously in production. Absolute rent is in this sense *prior* to differential rent, to which it is unrelated – absolute rent is a sort of rent-threshold, defined by the monopoly of landed property. Only where there is *no* absolute rent will the rent on additional land brought into production be vanishingly small.

Ironically, while Rey has thus completely misconstrued the

issue, his argument that absolute rent must be a pre-capitalist holdover is not necessarily invalidated. Since there are in fact no grounds *within* capitalism for establishing a level for absolute rent, and it is logically *prior* to capitalist differential rent, ground-rent may well be viewed as having roots in pre-capitalist surplus extraction. In considering the genuinely transitional period of English agrarian capitalism, from roughly the mid sixteenth through eighteenth centuries, the transformation of rent relations and rise to dominance of specifically capitalist differential rent may well be informed by this insight. But this is very different from attributing important class implications to the persistence of absolute ground-rent in the period of developed capitalism. Even more to the point, as will be seen, there are no grounds for attributing any comparable period or similar development of social relations to France.

Rey repeats this pattern of misconstruing Marx's critique of political economy, and applying it to France whether or not it fits the historical context. With regard to the proposed *dual* historical logic of the transition, based on both the feudal and capitalist modes of production, for example, it must again be noted that the capitalist mode of production first must be *presumed* to exist in order to be articulated. Rey explicitly carries his analysis back from Marx's analysis of developed capitalism, presuming that there is a 'transitional' social formation with capitalism on the agenda. Rey never appreciates the fundamental difference between using the concept of articulation to describe the interaction of two contemporary social systems, and using it to describe a process of indigenous historical development. The parallel pre-capitalist logic which Rey claims to have identified is in the event no less problematic: the passage which he cites to establish that *feudal* rent relations provided their own logic for capitalist development is in fact taken from a discussion of 'the nature of capitalist production' and *its* development.[35] The anachronism of Rey's citation of this passage is reinforced by Marx's opening to the chapter in which it appears:

> The analysis of landed property in its various historical forms is beyond the scope of this work. We shall be concerned with it only in so far as a portion of the surplus-value produced by capital falls to the share of the landowner. We assume, then, that agriculture is dominated by the capitalist mode of production . . . .[36]

Beyond all this anachronism and illogic, Rey, in his eagerness to establish landowners as a continuing pre-capitalist class holdover, downplays the extent to which Marx's critique of political economy *was* a criticism of the 'Trinity formula'. Rey's over-emphasis of Marx's view that the Trinity of land, labor, and capital expressed a necessary mystification of capitalist social relations leads him to conclude that the class of landlords must be comparable to those of the workers and capitalists – while at the same time he neglects Marx's emphasis on the fundamental relation of extraction of surplus-value.[37] As will be seen in a later chapter, Marx recognized in even his earliest work that landlords and capitalists had effectively – and ever more completely – joined together as an integral ruling class based on capitalist property. His reference to the Trinity formula was specifically conditioned by the history of *English* capitalism – with its strong agrarian capitalist legacy – and even more by his criticism of vulgar political economists, for whom the Trinity formula formed both point of departure and intellectual horizon. In describing capitalism, therefore, Marx was torn between the historical specificity of the Trinity formula – expressing the social reality of a branch of production which had once been dominant – and his critique of this formula as an ideological mask for the fundamental opposition of capital and the working class. Rey's argument that landlords formed a genuine class based on survival of pre-capitalist social relations might perhaps be put forward for the agrarian capitalism of Stuart or even Hanoverian England – but Marx certainly never intended to suggest that it held for mid-Victorian capitalism.

Rey particularly goes astray in treating Marx's analysis of capitalist ground-rent without recognizing the specifically English historical context which informed it – an error he compounds by presuming that the analysis applied equally to France. Precisely because ground-rent cannot be fully comprehended through the logic of capitalism alone, it is essential to understand the specific historical circumstances in which capitalism develops. One would expect French agrarian capitalism to have developed similarly to England's only if, at the time of capitalist development, pre-capitalist agrarian relations were also similar. While Rey and Postel-Vinay do seem to recognize that differences in starting point explain the eventual differences of development in the agriculture of Britain and capitalist France, they never even question whether a logic for capitalist development in fact existed in the ancien régime.

Here, indeed, emerges the most striking argument against the whole analysis proposed by Rey and Postel-Vinay. Rey initially presumed that the class relations of rent which he deduced from *Capital*, based on British development, applied equally to France. In the wake of Postel-Vinay's work, however, Rey criticized his earlier formulation, and in particular his unquestioned acceptance of Marx's analysis of differential rent. Rey argues that Postel-Vinay has shown that the generally superior land of the large 'capitalist' farms of the Paris basin did not pay higher rents than the poorer land of peasant plots, but actually paid *lower* rent.[38] This certainly is not consistent with capitalist differential rent, as described by Marx, based upon the 'industrial' form of farm production typical of English agrarian capitalism.

On the basis of this evidence, Rey would conclude with Postel-Vinay that Marx's error was even greater than previously suspected – that there is in fact no such thing as differential rent in agriculture! This is a truly stupefying reversal, which would now take *France* to stand as the general model of capitalist relations, ignoring England, and would reject Marx's whole analysis of capitalist ground-rent for failure to conform to that model. This flies in the face of all the evidence which demonstrates that differential rent *did* exist in British agrarian capitalism, and in fact played a major role in the development of political economy. Postel-Vinay's evidence is certainly not a proof that differential rent does not exist; it does, however, demonstrate that France did not develop capitalism in the same way that Britain did. Even in the region of France whose agrarian relations were most apparently similar to English capitalist farming, French agriculture did not produce a capitalist structure of rents. Now this does not absolutely bar the logical possibility that capitalism might somehow have been developing in the ancien régime – introduced from somewhere else than French agriculture – but it certainly means there are no grounds for *presuming* capitalism to have been developing. Clearly, capitalism developed in France eventually, and from somewhere – and when it did, it left French agriculture with a different character than England's. Yet this development can no longer simply be taken for granted. In light of Postel-Vinay's evidence, it very much remains to be shown whether any development towards capitalism had emerged in the ancien régime, and whether in fact capitalism developed indigenously in France at all.

The implications of Postel-Vinay's findings will be considered again in the conclusion. Indeed, in the short sketch of the class relations of the ancien régime that is offered there, a wholly different interpretation of rents and French historical develop-

ment will be suggested. First, however, having established that
neither orthodox nor structuralist Marxism has adequately
theorized Marx's method of historical materialism, it is necessary
to turn to the sources and course of development of his work in
order to clarify the intellectual basis for his thought, and the
explanation for the contradictions that he failed to discern.

Notes

1. Eric J. Hobsbawm, 'Introduction' to Karl Marx, *Pre-Capitalist Economic Formations*, New York 1965. See also Hobsbawm, 'Karl Marx's Contribution to Historiography', *Diogenes*, 64 (Winter 1968), reprinted in Robin Blackburn, *Ideology in Social Science*, London 1972, pp. 265–83.
2. Hobsbawm, 'Introduction', p. 14.
3. Ibid., pp. 20–27.
4. Ibid., pp. 19–20.
5. R. Hilton. P. Sweezy, M. Dobb, *et al., The Transition from Feudalism to Capitalism*, London 1976. See Chapter 6 below.
6. For the key structuralist work, see Louis Althusser, *For Marx*, New York 1970. Although it has been severely criticized by a number of Marxists, E. P. Thompson's 'The Poverty of Theory', in *The Poverty of Theory and Other Essays*, London 1978, remains the most important treatment of Althusserian structuralism. It is a virulent polemic, in the best tradition of Marx's own; but it also presents the essential logic of structuralism with great care – the better to criticize it. Where Thompson may be faulted is in attributing *Stalinist* politics to Althusser, which is a greal deal more than demonstrating that his structuralism replaced vulgar 'official Marxism' without fundamentally engaging it.
   Also important is the debate engaged in by Ralph Miliband, Nicos Poulantzas, and Ernesto Laclau: Ernesto Laclau, 'The Specificity of the Political', *Economy and Society*, 1 (1975), reprinted in Laclau, *Politics and Ideology in Marxist Theory*, London 1977, pp. 51–79; Ralph Miliband, 'Reply to Nicos Poulantzas', *New Left Review*, 59 (1970), reprinted in Blackburn, *Ideology in Social Service*, pp. 253–62, 'Poulantzas and the Capitalist State', *New Left Review*, 82 (1973); Nicos Poulantzas, 'The Problem of the Capitalist State', *New Left Review*, 58 (1969), in Blackburn, pp. 238–53, 'The Capitalist State: A Reply to Miliband and Laclau', *New Left Review*, 95, 1976.
7. Nicos Poulantzas, *Classes in Contemporary Capitalism*, London 1978, p. 13; Pierre-Philippe Rey, *Matérialisme historique et luttes de classes*, in *Les Alliances de classes*, Paris 1973 (1978).
8. Althusser, *For Marx*, p. 111. Thompson carefully works through Althusser's difficult arguments in 'Poverty of Theory', pp. 272–5.
9. The essential texts remain those of Nicos Poulantzas: *Political Power and Social Classes*, London 1968, and *Classes in Contemporary Capitalism*.
10. On the articulation of modes of production, see Robin, *La Société française en 1789: Semur-en-Auxois*, Paris 1970; Grenon and Robin, 'A propos de la polémique sur l'ancien régime et la Révolution: pour une problématique de la transition', *La Pensée*, 187 (1976), 5–30; and Pierre-Philippe Rey, *Sur l'articulation des modes de production*, published with the critical postscript *Matérialisme historique et luttes de classes*, in *Les Alliances de classes*.
11. Miliband first criticized this purely descriptive and formalistic character of

structuralism as 'structuralist abstractionism'; Laclau later terms the same defect 'taxonomy' without recognizing Miliband's point.

12. Poulantzas, *Classes in Contemporary Capitalism*, pp. 14–24, 207–8, 224. In a different but comparable vein, see Robin, *La Révolution française*, pp. 48–54.

13. Geoffrey Ellis, 'The "Marxist Interpretation" of the French Revolution', *English Historical Review*, xcii (1978), 353–76.

14. Colloquium at Vanier College, York University, March 10, 1982.

15. Karl Marx, *The Poverty of Philosophy*, in *Collected Works* vol. VI, New York 1976, p. 186.

16. Robin discusses the developments among the various classes by type, *La Révolution française*, pp. 48–54, but she does not use these labels, which have been added for ease of reference.

17. Ibid., pp. 53–4.

18. Karl Marx, *Grundrisse*, Harmondsworth 1973, pp. 100–108.

19. Ibid., p. 106.

20. Gilles Postel-Vinay, *La Rente foncière dans le capitalisme agricole*, Paris 1974; Rey, *Sur l'articulation des modes de production*.

21. Rey, *Matérialisme historique et luttes de classes*, p. 199.

22. Rey, *Sur l'articulation*, p. 11.

23. Ibid., pp, 20–22, 70–71.

24. Ibid., p. 22.

25. Ibid., pp. 37–8.

26. Ibid., pp. 43–5 (citing Marx, *Le Capital*, 8 vols, Editions sociales, Paris 1960, liv. III, tom. III, p. 142, corresponding to *Capital* vol. III, Moscow 1959, p. 757).

27. Ibid., pp. 48–58.

28. Ibid., p. 60 (my translation).

29. Ibid., p. 70.

30. Ibid., p. 71 (citing Marx, *Le Capital* 1. III, vol. III, p. 29, corresponding to *Capital* vol. III, pp. 637–8, which is reproduced here).

31. Ibid., p. 73 (my translation).

32. Postel-Vinay, *La Rente foncière*, pp. 92–3, p. 109; Postel-Vinay refers readers to Rey 'once and for all' on the question of articulation of modes of production, p. 10n.

33. Rey, *Sur l'articulation*, pp. 60–61.

34. Marx, *Capital* vol. III, pp. 748–9.

35. Ibid., pp. 637–8.

36. Ibid., p. 614.

37. Rey, *Sur l'articulation*, pp. 52–8; Marx, *Capital* vol. III, pp. 825–30.

38. Rey, *Matérialisme historique*, pp. 213–14.

5

Liberal Ideology and the Politics of the Revolution

The difficulty Marxists have had in explaining the French Revolution is only symptomatic of a more general theoretical problem. While Marxists have made seminal contributions to history – *as historians* – the historical process itself, and its class dynamics in pre-capitalist societies, have so far eluded the practice of Marxist theory. It is only for specifically capitalist societies that a convincing Marxist analysis has been put forward – and Marx himself provided the analysis.

The problem, as we have seen, is that Marxists have looked to Marx's limited and unsystematic historical observations as a guide to his historical materialism. They are not – they are qualitatively different from the fully developed social analysis of capitalism in *Capital*, as is most clearly demonstrated in the case of the French Revolution. Marx's remarks on pre-capitalist history are not merely based upon liberal histories, but they incorporate a significant amount of uncriticized liberal historical ideology. In fact, much of what has been taken to be fundamental to Marx's thought has instead been drawn from an offshoot – an offshoot which, unlike his essential historical materialist thought, is directly based on liberal ideological conceptions.

In the chapters which follow, an effort will be made to distinguish between these two contradictory lines of thought in Marx's work; to clarify that it is the *criticism* of liberal ideology that is central to historical materialism; and finally to elaborate an actual method of historical materialist analysis. Virtually all of what will be said about historical materialism is based upon the logic of Marx's analysis in the *Grundrisse* and *Capital*. But instead of simply counterposing one reading to another, as has so often been done in the past, it will be argued that Marx's mature analysis of capitalist class society belongs to a coherent and continuous line of theoretical development that dates from his earliest work.

In order, then, to escape from endless abstract re-theorization of the modes of production and their transitions, and to establish instead the real basis for Marx's practice of historical materialism, and how it may be appropriated for pre-capitalist history, we must first return to the sources of his thought and the logic through which it developed. This means, in the first instance, the liberal social and political ideology against which Marx's own thought was both defined and sharpened. Because our ultimate purpose is to make sense of the French Revolution as a social phenomenon, we must eventually consider it anew, in the terms of a fresh historical materialist analysis. Yet before we attempt to determine its underlying social origins, we must consider the contemporary political and intellectual impact of the Revolution. It is clear that from the start the Revolution was linked to the issues of political liberalism, and further that its conflict was the crucible of nineteenth-century liberal politics. Conservative liberalism, radical liberalism, and popular radicalism came to be problematically linked in their common, sometimes joint, struggle against aristocratic reaction – for whatever reasons – and Marx's ideas were born of the politics of this time. Therefore, though the issue must again be taken up in our conclusion, it is necessary now to turn to the liberalism which went into, and emerged from, the French Revolution.

Liberal Ideology and the Ancien Régime

In most respects, the content of liberal ideology is too familiar to require much elaboration, and the ideological origins of liberal history and political economy have already been considered. At the heart of liberal ideology is a commitment to *modern* society – a social order based on the free, competitive play of individual industry and intellect – and to the political order necessary to enshrine, reflect, and advance it. Liberalism is most clearly recognized in its conflict with 'aristocracy' and the old order founded upon tradition and privilege. Liberalism, in fact, does not emerge from a vacuum: its 'liberality' is essentially defined *against* the old order of things, aristocracy and/or monarchical 'tyranny'. The absolutist ancien régime naturally, and in fact by definition, offered a considerable range of targets for liberal opposition.

It must immediately be acknowledged, however, that the ancien régime of the eighteenth century was by no means un-relievedly 'aristocratic'. Many aspects of liberal ideology were already widely – even generally – shared by persons of property, regardless of their status. The pastiche of ideas known as the Enlightenment comprised such widely divergent thinkers as Voltaire, Montesquieu, and Rousseau; and Chaussinand-Nogaret is surely correct in holding that *some* 'enlightened' ideas found as much favor among nobles of all ranks as among members of the bourgeoisie.[1] Yet the conflict between 'bourgeois' liberals and 'aristocrats' – specifically recognized as such – was unmistakably the central political fact of the French Revolution, and of European politics generally well into the nineteenth century. It was, indeed, through the differentiation of certain specific 'bourgeois' liberal political positions from equally specific and fundamentally opposed 'aristocratic' reactionary positions that the political conflict of the Revolution took form.

That there were opposed *social interests* behind the revolutionary conflict is of course the essential point to be made by a historical materialist analysis; and this is clearly what remains to be proved. The existence of an opposition between ideologies in the ancien régime, however, is well established, Chaussinand-Nogaret notwithstanding. In the decades prior to the decisive confrontation over the constitutional issue of calling the Estates, conflicting principles of political ideology had tended to be blurred – even conflated, as in the case of Montesquieu – by their expression in the common idiom of Enlightenment. The fundamental differences that existed between the liberals and 'aristocrats', who chafed equally under the absolutist regime, were as a result disguised. They remained unrecognized even among the politicized, until – following the polarization and open conflict brought about by the Revolution itself – the aristocratic ideology was reformulated in highly traditional terms of natural hierarchy, hereditary prerogative, and racial superiority. None the less, it is important to recognize that the existence of this ideological conflict was not simply a product of the Revolution, and that the broad mantle of the Enlightenment had in the first place disguised two fundamentally opposed political perspectives.

Nannerl Keohane has considered the development of these conflicting political philosophies in *Philosophy and the State in France*.[2] She traces their development in the French context to the existence of an earlier and significantly different political conflict between the centralizing policies of royal absolutism – for which support could often be found among the bourgeoisie – and the centripetal pressures of the princes and greater noble families, which had been expressed in the terms of 'aristocratic traditionalism'. In the course of the recurring eighteenth-century struggles over absolutism, these positions underwent a significant transformation: the ideology of royal absolutism increasingly became influenced by liberal conceptions of the nation state, and even the aristocratic ideology was influenced by the Enlightenment – as witness Montesquieu. The consequences were, on the one hand, the growing development of *constitutional liberalism* among the most 'National' of the great aristocrats and a limited circle of 'patriots'; while on the other hand an *aristocratic constitutionalism* emerged that was particularly strong among the *parlementaires*. Though they briefly came together in 1787–8 in the overthrow of absolutism, these ideologies remained in fundamental opposition, and came into open confrontation in the final crisis of the ancien régime.

In fact, the most essential point about the aristocratic/liberal conflict of the Revolution is precisely that it arose *directly* out of the constitutional issues that were raised by the fall of absolutism: as has so often been noted, the heated antagonists of 1788–9 had been united in 1787–8 by their opposition to the absolutist monarchy. Any effort to explain the conflict between *Aristocrates* and *Nationaux* in social terms must account for the priority of this constitutional issue in the revolutionary confrontation. For whatever reason, then, political liberalism can clearly be seen to have been central to the outbreak of the Revolution.

Liberal Politics in the French Revolution

If political liberalism figured centrally in the substance of the revolutionary conflict, the ongoing political processes of Revolution in turn led to the differentiation of a whole range of liberal political and ideological positions, through a series of struggles over the character and policies of the revolutionary liberal state. The extent to which the Revolution in this way laid the foundations for nineteenth-century Continental politics is perhaps best revealed in the development of the concept of *class*, which came to figure in liberal ideology from the outset of the conflict.

The pamphlets of the liberal constitutional propagandists such as Sieyès politicized 'the Nation', demanding the calling of the Estates General through new, liberal procedures, rather than through the traditional constitutional forms that the *parlement* of Paris specified in September 1788. The 'aristocracy' that continued to insist upon the traditional forms were castigated as a class apart from the Nation, preying upon the productive Third Estate – not least through their privileged monopoly of 'all the best posts' for personal profit.[3] The development of this concept of class in the politics of the Revolution, from this point through the Jacobin accession to power, has been traced in detail by Shirley Gruner. She has shown that within the year – by the autumn of 1789 and the outbreak of a rancorous debate over application of the *marc d'argent* – a full spectrum of liberal class analysis, including a line of popular-radical criticism, had already emerged.[4]

The *marc d'argent* was the electoral property qualification proposed for the constitution of the new, liberal French state which it was the recognized task of the Constituent Assembly to establish. In classically liberal terms, the *marc* was to distinguish between 'active' and 'passive' citizens on the basis of property. As Gruner points out, the proponents of this property qualification put forward in its justification the idea of *la classe mitoyenne*: the new, hardworking, and virtuous class of commercial prosperity; the *responsible* class, situated between the opulent and the poor.[5] In response to this decidedly conservative liberal position (which none the less belonged to the revolutionary movement) two distinct tendencies of democratic politics emerged in opposition: *constitutional democracy*, and *direct democracy*.

Brissot, the future Girondin leader, put forward what would remain the basic Jacobin position: the *marc* was an insult to 'the people', who had actually made the Revolution. His *constitutional democratic* argument was that the people should be sovereign in a representative republic, the achievement of which would properly bring popular revolutionary activism to a close. The more radical proponents of *direct* democracy, however, took merely representative government to be itself a form of

'aristocracy'. Marat exemplified these popular-radical ideologues, whose ideas came in time to achieve common currency in
the Parisian sections, asserting that *all* the rich were enemies of
the people. By 1791, long before the Terror, Marat was arguing
that the Revolution was in fact a *loi agraire*, being made by the
people through the rightful, direct exercise of their sovereignty.[6]
Thus, from the start of the Revolution, a series of quite different
positions were demarcated among the revolutionaries in relation
to the issue of popular sovereignty.

After installation of the new constitution in 1791, the
conservative-liberal supporters of constitutional monarchy, the
constitutionnels, struggled to bring the Revolution to an end.
They were opposed not only to the recalcitrant aristocracy, but
also to both the constitutional-democratic Jacobins on their left,
and to the *monarchiens*, the less than virulently counter-
revolutionary supporters of royal prerogative, on their right. The
constitutionnels argued that they represented the 'overwhelming
majority', who were truly the people: the *middle* class of the
bourgeoisie – beset on one side by the selfishness of the opulent,
and on the other side by the 'poor and ignorant', stirred up by
crafty agitators. In defense of this conservative liberalism,
Duquesnoy wrote:

> Thus, neither the magnates nor the brigands are the people; it is
> composed of the *bourgeoisie*, that throng of busy, virtuous men who
> are corrupted neither by opulence nor poverty; they truly are the
> nation, the *people*.[7]

As Gruner argues, the *constitutionnels* adopted the position that
as a result of the achievements of the Revolution there were
no longer classes in the proper sense: only the 'majority' who
were satisfied with the work of the Constituent, and the *selfish
minorities*.

Such a denial of antagonistic class interests is an enduring
feature of conservative liberalism in power. In criticizing this
position, Pétion, mayor of Paris, gave a new sense to the term
'bourgeoisie'. He argued that the rich bourgeoisie – the *constitutionnels* – were raising themselves above the rest of the Third
Estate, and aspiring to the level of the nobility. Indeed, in what
Gruner suggests may have been the very first allusion to bourgeois class revolution (in a sense apart from the rightful progress
of the middle class *as* the people), Pétion and Robespierre wrote
a pamphlet that emphasized the idea that the bourgeois class,
believing that they had been delivered from the nobility and

despotism, now were eager to take advantage of the new order without sharing its fruits with the people.[8]

The *constitutionnels* responded by charging that, in so distinguishing between the bourgeoisie and the people, Pétion was only attempting to resurrect and inflame class divisions, when all such distinctions had been settled by the Revolution and had no place in the new society. In defense of Pétion, however, Brissot declared that it was the *constitutionnels* who in fact sought to divide 'the people'. They did so, he alleged, by differentiating 'the multitude' as a group apart from the properly bourgeois 'people' – a dangerous error, which would debase the one part and ultimately subject the remainder to their insurrections, or to despotism. On these grounds, he supported Pétion's position in the interest of the *harmony* of classes, against the destructive self-interestedness of the *constitutionnels*.[9] The Jacobin left as a whole – still including the Girondins – shared to one degree or another the ideals of democratic republicanism, and stood for a 'classless' democratic unity, against the false and discriminatory 'unity of the people' which the conservatives would impose through the effective exclusion of 'the multitude'.

Yet again, however, there were two different critical conceptions of bourgeois exclusivity. On one hand, when used negatively by Jacobin radical-liberals, the 'bourgeoisie' referred to the *haute bourgeoisie*, who separated themselves from the mass of the people, bourgeois and sans-culottes, who formed the Nation. On the other hand, the usage of the proponents of *direct* democracy – which came increasingly to be understood by the sans-culottes themselves – implied an opposition between *les prolétaires*, as the people, and the whole of a broader bourgeoisie, who threatened to become another form of 'aristocracy'.

Subsequently, as Gruner shows, the Girondins and the Montagnards each in turn rose into power, on the basis of popular support, while making this radical-liberal argument. Each charged the previous revolutionary leadership with representing the bourgeois 'aristocracy of property' through their refusal to carry the democracy of the Revolution any further. Yet each then in turn wished to limit the Revolution to the realization of their own policies, and prevent further moves to the left. Brissot, once in power, actually put forward a class analysis which was very much like that of the deposed *constitutionnels*: he argued that the people, the middle-majority, had now achieved their just goals, and were opposed only by a few selfish aristocrats and the clamorous 'multitude'.[10]

Marat therefore attacked the new leadership in the same terms as the old, and he was joined in this by Robespierre and the Montagnards. After yet another year of contention, the Mountain in their turn displaced the Girondins. Yet *its* relations with the popular movement were no less problematic, as Soboul and Rudé have amply demonstrated.[11] (Indeed, the popular movement is the one area of Marxist analysis of the Revolution – since it is not concerned with the opposition of feudalism and capitalism, but with the sans-culottes as a specific category of the ancien régime and Revolution – which has not been called into question by the revisionist challenge, despite the effort made to transform perception of the popular role through the concept of *dérapage*.)

In keeping with the political role played by the popular movement from the start of the Revolution – refined over time by the growing development of an autonomous popular ideology – the Jacobins in their turn rose into power with the support of the sans-culottes.[12] The fundamental contradictions in interests and ideology between the bourgeois Montagnards and the popular movement, however, ultimately meant that no greater popular base of support existed for Robespierre's pursuit of the society of 'virtue' than for any previous revolutionary leadership. Robespierre occupied the extreme left of the *constitutional*-democratic spectrum; but despite the genuinely 'social' aspects of his own radical beliefs, a gulf separated his politics from that of the popular movement and the propagandists of direct democracy and the *loi agraire*. Indeed, the Jacobin Revolutionary Government was in its turn attacked from the left – but with the essential difference that there was no longer a *bourgeois liberal* left-opposition available to join with the Hébertistes and other popular radicals of the left and rise into power upon the support of the sans-culottes.

In the development of these internal liberal political positions of the Revolution, then, there is to be discerned the successive emergence of *three* conceptions of class. The conservative liberals saw class as an anachronistic category, dangerously revived without reason by agitators and wreckers. Implicitly, however, they recognized a middle class in the 'majority' who were virtuously situated between the aristocrats and 'brigands' – a classically liberal conception of the progressive bourgeoisie. The republican left liberals *also* believed in 'classless' harmony, but saw it as frustrated by the group in power. They too put forward an implicit three-class conception – but from the obverse side imposed by their role in opposition. They recognized the ultimate enemy in the aristocracy, but also recognized an enemy within, in the *haute bourgeoisie* who sought to end the Revolution in order to serve their own interests. Both the aristocracy and the bourgeoisie, then, were classes, wrongly separating themselves from the Nation.

Yet once in power, even Robespierre translated this opposition conception of class into the governing view, calling for the repression of both Right and Left. The popular movement differed significantly. With increasing clarity, they put forward a conception which recognized only *two* classes. On the one hand, there was the *aristocracy*, which came to include all bourgeois – who by their wealth, opinions, or political power (arrogation of popular sovereignty) stood apart from the sans-culottes; on the other hand, *the people*, who were in just possession of no more than the necessities for life and work, and who directly exercised their democratic sovereignty without need for representation.

It can be seen, then, that through the politics of the Revolution, and in close association with the developing concept of class, the essential ideological expressions of nineteenth-century liberalism emerged: conservative, radical-democratic, and petty bourgeois social-radical. Initially, the National Assembly had comprised the full spectrum of bourgeois liberal positions; indeed, when they were united as an opposition to the aristocratic politics that had blocked concessions to liberalism in 1788–9, the various liberal positions were hardly to be differentiated. Not all liberals, however, were easily reconciled to actual revolution, and still less to democratic radicalism. Popular revolutionary activism and the threat of popular sovereignty therefore drove away successive groups of increasingly less conservative liberals, while the revolutionary leaders were increasingly forced to choose between being radical or ineffectual.

The conservative victory over the issue of the *marc d'argent* had helped to keep the badly divided Constituent Assembly together; but the political context – above all the persistence of implacable aristocratic and royal opposition, and the ongoing war – precluded the creation of a stable conservative-liberal government. It proved impossible to effectively mobilize in defense of the Revolution while attempting to contain the threat of its opening towards popular sovereignty. The revolutionary dynamic of successive moves to the left in conjunction with the popular movement was set in motion: on the one hand to preserve the Revolution, on the other hand to extend it. This was no *dérapage*. Rather, this progressive radicalization of the Revolution is a fact integral to any conception of it as a political whole, expressing the necessity and willingness of a more and more limited and radical leadership to take increasingly audacious steps to preserve and carry through the liberal national renovation that *was* the Revolution.

The liberal bourgeois of the Revolution remained internally divided as well as caught between the threats of counter-revolutionary conquest and popular insurrection. Even after the Revolutionary Government had forged a national instrument capable of keeping these threats at bay, the political differences between supporters of royal prerogative, constitutional monarchists, moderate republicans, and democratic Jacobins made any real reconciliation impossible. In the end, despite their Thermidorean counter-coup, the conservative liberals were never able to provide a stable regime that was secure against both monarchical and Jacobin opposition. Meanwhile the most progressive ideas brought forward by the social revolution crystallized in the conspiracy of Babeuf. Each of these varied political tendencies – including the Bonapartist imperialism which finally imposed a form of dictatorial liberalism to resolve the internal political dynamic of the Revolution – was carried forward into the mid nineteenth century.

It is precisely the coherence of this line of political development, and the persistence of the polarization that underlies it, that offers the clearest evidence that the Revolution actually did constitute a 'bloc'. The very structure of the political struggle demands recognition that some truly revolutionary issue was engaged in 1789 – an issue of sufficient substance that the political polarization of liberals and 'aristocrats' would survive such violent internal conflict *among* the liberals as the Terror and the Thermidorean reaction. The persistence of a fundamental struggle between liberal *Nationaux* and the *Aristocrates*, whatever its underlying cause, is certainly clear. That was how the revolutionaries themselves conceived the struggle; and, despite the great violence and disruption engendered by conflict within the new liberal nation, not even the very moderate liberals who prevailed after Thermidor could unite with their perpetual opponents, the aristocracy, in order to end the Revolution.

Yet to identify the issue as liberalism is not to explain it. If it is clear that there was a real revolutionary struggle between bourgeois liberals and aristocrats, it is a different matter entirely as to *why*. If the Revolution was not a conflict between capitalists and

feudal lords, then who in fact were these bourgeois and aristocrats (assuming, of course, that they were not merely those who
were comprised by the *political* categories of revolution and
counter-revolution, as Cobban had it)?[13] It is this question that
requires a new and serious historical materialist inquiry into the
ancien régime and the origins of the Revolution, some anticipation of which will be sketched in the conclusion to this book.
The essential fact remains, however, that a long, virulent, and
consistent political conflict *was* unleashed in 1788–9; and that,
through a struggle which was from the start consciously directed
against an aristocratic opposition, groups holding successively
more radical liberal politics successively came to power from
within an increasingly well-defined spectrum of liberal ideological positions.

It was the course of the Revolution itself that gave definition to
these various liberal positions, just as the politics which led to the
Revolution defined the basic opposition of aristocracy to
liberalism as a whole. Real aristocratic opposition to liberalism
endured long after the Revolution had passed – as did the need
for further revolutionary advances to achieve basic liberal goals.
In fact, the endurance of the whole political spectrum defined by
the Revolution is striking. More than half a century later, in
1848, not only the objectives, but even the political terms of the
great revolution still served for reactionaries, conservatives,
liberals, and radicals – only the communists were to declare for a
new struggle, in new terms.

There was no fundamental reconciliation of the essential
parties to the struggle of 1789, liberal bourgeois and reactionary
aristocrats, comparable to that reached between British Whigs
and Tories: not after Thermidor, not after the Restoration – in
truth, not ever. The Revolution did not end in reconciliation; its
democratic republicanism, its raising of the 'social question', and
the anti-democratic opposition it engendered, all remained lively
issues long enough to acquire new meaning through the emergence of a socialist workers' movement. And so, in the sense that
M. Furet would have the Revolution be 'over', it has really only
been over since the Liberation, or perhaps since the *Fifth*
Republic finally cleared the field.[14]

If liberals were not wholly secure in their political power until
the second half of the twentieth century, they were not even
united in defense of a regime until the Third Republic. That their
partners in an ambivalent alliance would then be a socialist
workers' movement, in the place of the popular movement of the

sans-culottes, is an indication of the fundamental changes France had undergone between the 1780s and 1880s. Yet the continuities of political polarization were real, and they revolved about the establishment, extension, and ultimately the limitation of the liberal democratic state. It is this political context which must be understood when considering the development of Marx's critique of liberal ideology and politics. The real challenge, then, will be to uncover the social foundations for this multi-party political conflict, both in the Revolution and as it endured into the nineteenth century.

Class, History, and Liberal Ideology

As conflict within the ranks of the revolutionaries differentiated conservative-liberals, radical-liberals, and popular-radicals, their differing conceptions of democracy and social policy came to be expressed in different conceptions of *class*. Yet the underlying concept was not itself the product of this internal revolutionary conflict. It was derived from the broader liberal social-historical ideology of *progress* – which was implicitly progress against the 'old order'. Class, in this sense, was just as central to liberal ideology as progress itself.

Liberal ideology took it to be both a historical necessity, and a true expression of the 'general interest', that the social order should actively embrace the cardinal liberal virtues. This particularly implied, of course, that as a matter of natural justice and social progress the state should cease to recognize significant forms of social and political privilege. Liberal policies and ideology strongly identified with the *active* element in society, as was so clearly expressed in the liberal histories. To a great extent, what liberalism stood for was simply allowing the 'active' a free hand to accomplish what they could: freedom of intellect, enterprise, and of course property, would naturally lead to progress in every field.

On the whole, however, as liberal thought took form in the old regimes of Europe, it tended to identify a basic class struggle – certainly a divergence of conditions and interests – between the idle aristocracy of the old order of privilege, and the active 'middle' class of society. Even the non-conflictual British ideology of political economy, long after the struggles of 1640–1715 were resolved in favor of a more or less conservative liberalism, retained a suggestion of this opposition in its conception of

landlord and capitalist classes. As Marx and Engels said, it was
the liberals who first discerned the existence of classes – but did
so in a sense far different from that which Marx would come to
mean.

Within this broad liberal ideology, class *conflict* specifically
belonged to the field of history. Political economy, instead,
brought the classes together, as factors of production. Class
conflict figured as a historical, and all too regrettable, deviation
from that 'national unity' which was a central feature of the
liberal ideological conception of society. Historical progress
therefore corresponded to a triumph of the active, national
element over the divisions of class. In making its case for progress, liberal history looked to class struggles as far back as the
classical age of Greece and Rome.

Liberal interest in ancient society was to a certain extent
directly ideological. In part, the attraction of the classical age was
the cult of *citizenship* and *statesmanship*, the cult of the *polis* or
res publica translated into the cult of the liberal nation. In liberal
England, this cult of the classical merely found expression in
public school education. In France, a more militant cult was
required:

> Camille Desmoulins, Danton, Robespierre, Saint-Just and
> Napoleon, the heroes of the old French Revolution, as well as its
> parties and masses, accomplished the task of their epoch, which was
> the emancipation and establishment of modern *bourgeois* society, in
> Roman costume and with Roman slogans,

as Marx observed.[15]

Yet the real early horizon for the liberal historical conception
of social development was the interregnum of the Dark Ages.
While all of known history fell within the epoch of the agricultural mode of subsistence, classical antiquity was seen to have
been something of a dead end. It was followed by the relatively
primitive agrarian society of the barbarian invaders, strongly
marked by its military organization and conquests. Consequently, the real thrust of liberal history was a continuum of
progress from the barbarism of the Dark Ages.[16]

The essential classes of this continuum were the aristocracy
and the bourgeoisie: the idle and decadent descendants of the
feudal order of Germanic conquerors, and the productive, in-
novative, and virtuously 'active' elements who sprang from the
indigenous people. The 'multitude', 'lower orders', or perhaps

even 'the people' were also, frequently, recognized as a class –
although *the people* was usually taken to be a positive and inclu-
sive term which (as with Duquesnoy and Brissot during the
Revolution) really meant the bourgeoisie. When 'the multitude'
or 'the people' *were* distinguished as a separate class, it was
always in negative terms: the ignorant, irresponsible, and 'un-
productive', in contrast to the active bourgeoisie.

Usually, in fact, when the people were distinguished as a class,
it was through their much-lamented 'intrusion' into public affairs,
as in revolution, or through the need to educate them. It might be
proposed, therefore, to 'tutor' them in citizenship through admis-
sion to primary electoral bodies. In any case, they certainly
would have the opportunity to 'raise' themselves to a level of
responsible participation – for which they would demonstrate
their readiness by acquiring adequate property. This was, of
course, the perspective taken by the Constituent Assembly in
differentiating between active and passive citizens on the basis of
the *marc d'argent*. Yet this liberal conception can also be discerned in Robespierre's very different and genuine belief in
popular education for the good of the Nation.[17] It likewise
appears in Mignet's more conventional view that the intrusion of
the people into the Revolution, while perhaps inevitable and
necessary, was no less *tragic* for that fact.[18] Finally, this conception is of course inherent in that conservative liberal position,
now again in vogue, which holds that the popular movement was
neither necessary nor desirable after all.

In the liberal historical conception, class was primarily a function of social rank, privilege, political position, and means of
securing a living: active, idle, or 'passive'. Classes were *not*
defined in terms of fundamental relations of exploitation, need-
less to say. Class struggle was a clash of interests, but in the form
of one class holding back another; not a confrontation between
the producers and appropriators of social surplus. It was with this
basic meaning, then, that 'class' came to play a major role in the
conflict of liberal and radical ideologies among supporters of the
Revolution. Even in popular ideology, the opposition of two
fundamental classes was in essence political: the 'aristocracy'
oppressed the people, but did not directly *exploit* them.

The predation of the 'idle' upon the active, which liberals such
as Thierry later asserted to be a cause of revolution, might seem
to suggest class exploitation, but it is very different from Marx's
conception of fundamentally exploitive class relations of production. The same is clearly true of the monopolization of 'all the

best posts' against which Sieyès agitated in *What is the Third Estate?*. These were instances of *liberal* 'class struggle', of the bourgeoisie battling with the aristocracy for rightful social ascendancy. That Marx *also* referred to the conflict between bourgeois and aristocrats as class struggle is certainly true; but this is precisely a manifestation of the incorporation of liberal ideas into his thought. The conflict between the bourgeoisie and aristocracy as rival *ruling* classes is a very different thing from the struggle of peasant against lord, or proletarian against capitalist.

What, then, is not to be found in liberal ideology is Marx's original contribution of a concept of class struggle that is based on exploitation. The *paired opposition* of fundamental classes – as distinct from 'ranks' of classes – was the essential difference in the way that Marx came to conceive of class. It is inherent to the direction of his early work, and clearly stated in the *Manifesto*: 'Freeman and slave, patrician and plebian, lord and serf, guild-master and journeyman, in a word, oppressor and oppressed'.[19] Above all, capitalist and proletarian. Regardless of the specific classes in this list, it is this *form* of class struggle which is the key to Marxist social analysis, and which creates the indissoluble difference between Marxist class analysis and the liberal recognition of 'classes'. For Marx – as not for Guizot, nor for Furet, nor Brissot, not even for Robespierre – there could be no reconciliation or assimilation between the fundamentally opposed classes of producers and appropriators of surplus.

Early in his work, Marx came to reject merely liberal politics and ideology, and instead embraced and developed the concept of fundamental class conflict between capitalists and workers. Through the central concept of historical materialism – that the history of all hitherto existing societies is the history of class struggles – Marx cut through the screen of bourgeois conservative-liberal ideology that denied liberal society was *class* society in any sense except that of the 'natural' expression of division of labor in 'economic classes'.

Equally, however, Marx cut through the ideological misconceptions of merely *social-radical* opposition to the capitalist order – especially the widespread belief that a redistribution of wealth was sufficient to end social injustice. Such social radicalism had developed to some extent during the Revolution: among some Jacobins, and particularly Robespierre; among the most popularly oriented journalists and ideologues, such as Marat; in the sectional assemblies of the sans-culottes; and, in its fullest expression, in Babeuf's Conspiracy of Equals. All of these views were in the end based upon merely political conceptions of class and revolution. This radical-social ideology entered nineteenth-century politics through utopian socialism and Bunoarroti's resurrection of *babouvisme*, finding its way into both the Parisian and English workers' movements, and into Proudhon's philosophy. Not until Marx and Engels, however, were the limitations and contradictions of such merely radical social movements – as extreme forms of petty bourgeois, socially-concerned radical-liberalism – systematically revealed, through an analysis of the specific class character of bourgeois economic liberalism and property relations.

It was Marx who brought together the conclusion he arrived at through critical study of liberal philosophy, politics, and history – that bourgeois class revolution was not the key to human emancipation and social justice, only a victory for particular class interests – with the lesson that *Engels* formulated through his early study of political economy and exposure to the English working class – that capitalism *created* working-class misery, and that its development would lead to revolutionary struggle between the working class and the propertied capitalists and landlords.[20] From this intersection of the critique of liberal political ideology and the critique of political economy, Marx grasped the central historical materialist concept of the dynamic of class history, as early as 1844. He then continued to develop his historical materialist analysis of specifically capitalist class society, and the politics of working-class struggle, through the critique of political economy (though without entirely eliminating the contradictory liberal historical ideas that he incorporated alongside his own). Marx gave a wholly original social and political interpretation to class in society; but he did so specifically through his response to the social and political ideology of liberalism which dominated the European thought of his youth.

Notes

1. Guy Chaussinand-Nogaret, *La Noblesse au xviiie siècle. De la féodalité au lumieres*, Paris 1976.

2. Nannerl O. Keohane, *Philosophy and the State in France*, Princeton, NJ 1980.

3. E. M. Sieyès, *What Is the Third Estate?*, London 1963, pp. 54–7, p. 177n.

4. Shirley Gruner, 'Le concept de classe dans la révolution française: une mise à jour', *Histoire Sociale-Social History*, ix (18) 1976, pp. 406–23.

5. Ibid., p. 410.

6. Ibid., pp. 412–15.

7. Quoted by Gruner, ibid., p. 415, citing Duquesnoy, 'De l'influence de la révolution sur les moeurs domestiques', *L'Ami des Patriotes*, xvi, March 1791. (my translation)

8. Ibid., p. 416.

9. Ibid., pp. 415–17.

10. Ibid., pp. 418–20.

11. Albert Soboul, *The Parisian Sansculottes and the French Revolution, 1793–4*, Oxford 1964, pp. 251–9; George Rudé, *The Crowd in the French Revolution*, Oxford 1959, pp. 128–41.

12. For a discussion of the development of popular ideology both in general and in the French Revolution, see George Rudé, *Ideology and Popular Protest*, New York 1980.

13. Alfred Cobban, *The Social Interpretation of the French Revolution*, London 1968, p. 162.

14. For Furet's polemical argument that the Revolution is 'over', directed against the Marxist 'catechism' to the contrary, see *Penser la Révolution française*, Paris 1978.

15. Marx, *The Eighteenth Brumaire of Louis Bonaparte*, in the Vintage Marx Library, *Surveys From Exile*, New York 1973, p. 147.

16. See Guizot's 'The History of Civilization in Europe', in Stanley Mellon, ed., *Historical Essays and Lectures*, Chicago 1972.

17. For Robespierre's genuinely social-radical liberalism, see George Rudé, *Robespierre, Portrait of a Revolutionary Democrat*, London 1975.

18. François Mignet, *History of the French Revolution. From 1789 to 1814*, London 1913, p. 124, pp. 184–93.

19. Marx–Engels, *Manifesto of the Communist Party, Collected Works* vol. VI, New York 1976, p. 482.

20. It is not often enough acknowledged that Engels dealt with these ideas in his 'Outlines of a Critique of Political Economy' (*Collected Works* vol. III, pp. 418–43) *before* Marx had expressed the idea of a proletarian revolution in any form, and for the journal which Marx edited. See the discussion of Marx's early thought in the chapter which follows.

6

Marx's Early Thought

The politics of the French Revolution without question remained the pre-eminent focus of European politics in the era of Marx's youth. Here, aristocratic reaction was in power. There, conservative liberals warily eyed republicans. Everywhere, *democracy* was a subversive force. In 'backward' Germany, the French Revolution had loomed large, and in the Rhineland of Marx's birth it had left a tangible legacy which contrasted starkly to the freshly imposed rule of ascendant Prussia. Jean Bruhat, in two articles devoted to the impact of the French Revolution on Marx's thought, particularly emphasized this strong liberalism of homeland and family as a background to Marx's studies.[1]

Yet, as Marx and Engels were to contend, social conditions in Germany were not such as to have produced a real bourgeois liberal *movement*. Particularly outside the Rhineland, liberal ideology was primarily a matter of abstract philosophy – informed by foreign historiography and political economy – not of active politics. (So, too, did Germany produce a 'socialist' philosophy in place of a workers' socialist movement.[2]) The conservative philosophical liberalism of Hegel, the moderate (seemingly 'left') philosophical liberalism of the Young Hegelians, and the petty bourgeois philosophical radicalism of the 'True Socialists' – each of which in turn Marx confronted in developing his critique of liberal ideology – were all imbued with the ideas of the French Revolution.[3]

The question for liberals had been what to make of the politics and goals of the Revolution in the context of Germany, and – for the 'left' Hegelians and 'True Socialists' who rejected Hegel's accommodation with the Prussian state – how to bring about democracy and social progress in its many backward, reactionary regimes. Hal Draper has discussed in detail the essentials of Marx's development from this left-Hegelianism, to the theory and practice of revolutionary working-class socialism, in the two volumes of *Karl Marx's Theory of Revolution*. As a young radical-democratic journalist and philosopher, deeply committed to real human emancipation – too radical for even Rhenish political respectability, but frankly ignorant of the French socialist ideas which were acquiring currency – Marx withdrew to his study in mid 1843 to undertake a systematic critical study of Hegel's *Philosophy of Right*.[4]

Through criticism of Hegel's political ideology and, subsequently, the Young Hegelian Bruno Bauer's 'radical' pronouncements on Jewish political emancipation, Marx first clearly discerned and progressively developed a conception of *social* emancipation.[5] This new goal went far beyond the merely political emancipation which the French Revolution had represented, to embody the liberation of human potentialities from the encumbrances imposed by the economic and social institutions of bourgeois society. Marx argued that the task of political emancipation was insufficient in itself – it was only a step towards *human emancipation*. This implied not only a rejection of *liberal* politics, but also of any purely democratic radicalism which did not address the inherent social limitations posed by the *particular interests* that belonged to the propertied in bourgeois society. In fact, it is already possible to see in the conception of state and civil society that Marx advanced at this early point the general outlines – still in a critical-philosophical form – of his later conception of the capitalist state and the necessity of socialist revolution.

Marx's perspective on liberal ideology was therefore *critical*, but still philosophical. In considering the means for achieving human emancipation, for example, Marx took over Hegel's concept of the 'universal class', transforming it in conjunction with the now widely held historical concept of class revolution. The result was his conception of the necessity of a *revolutionary universal class*, one whose only interests were those of humanity in itself, an idea which laid the groundwork for development of the historical materialist conception of proletarian revolution. This groundwork itself, however, remained recognizably philosophical. Taking the realization of human potentialities to be the inherent end of human existence, Marx analyzed what was *wrong* with existing society; what society must instead become to be just and emancipatory; and how the politics of the French Revolution (political emancipation) were wholly inadequate to this end because they were integral to existing society. (It must be remembered, however, that while Marx's criticisms were still couched in the terms of philosophy, he had been actively engaged as a political journalist and polemicist from the very start, and was not content with idle philosophical speculation.)

At this point – October 1843 – Marx moved to Paris, where the development of his original conceptions was greatly accelerated as a result of his work (editing the *Deutsch-Französische Jahrbücher*) and environment. Within the year he had produced the essential and recognizable foundations for historical materialist social analysis.

The first step was his argument, put forward in the 'Contribution to the Critique of Hegel's Philosophy of Right. Introduction', that all general revolutions necessarily were made by specific classes in the pursuit of their own specific interests, which equally necessarily were presented as general interests.[6] The French Revolution had brought about general political emancipation – but no more – through the pursuit of the particular interests of the bourgeoisie. Therefore, in a parallel fashion, the revolution required for true human emancipation had to be made by the class *without* particular interests: the *revolutionary universal class* which possessed nothing but its own humanity, the proletariat. Draper acknowledges the impact of Engels's 'Outlines of a Critique of Political Economy' in this development, and recognizes that Marx himself acknowledged his debt to Engels; but he still tends to understate the importance of this contribution – as have all Marxists – emphasizing the impact of Marx's exposure to the Parisian socialist workers' movements.[7] More to the point, *despite* Marx's recent exposure to political economy and the idea of proletarian revolution through Engels's critique, he was still thoroughly philosophical in his perspective, as Draper stresses, holding that 'philosophy finds its *material* weapons in the proletariat', and that 'The *head* of this emancipation is *philosophy*, its *heart* is the *proletariat*.'[8]

The Origins of Historical Materialism

According to Draper, the next step was the result of a confluence between Marx's studies and political movements and events – notably the uprising of Silesian weavers in June 1844 – which together underscored the vitality of proletarian class struggle as *self*-emancipation.[9] At the same time that Marx identified the proletariat as the universal class (the turn of 1843–4), he had undertaken his first serious encounter with political economy and began intensive study of the French Revolution. Marx attended socialist workers' meetings, and heard for himself their own consciousness of struggle with the bourgeoisie over property – a consciousness descended in part from the raising of 'the social question' during the French Revolution. He also read accounts of decades of English workers' struggles, and encountered the *assumption* by political economists that there existed an inherent opposition between wage-labor and capital. In addition, he delved into the liberal histories that emphasized the class struggle of the Revolution.

Then, in April 1844, Marx sat down to clarify for himself the lessons from his *critical* appropriation of political economy, in the notebooks that have come to us as the *Economic and Philosophic Manuscripts of 1844*.[10] In these manuscripts, he brought together the diverse strands of his study and observation, and clearly developed the central ideas of historical materialism on the specific basis of *class struggle against exploitation*.

As Draper argues, in the 'Introduction' to his critique of Hegel's political philosophy – finished in January – Marx had as yet offered no hint of the *self*-emancipation of the proletariat. By late July, however, Marx wrote an article in response to Arnold Ruge's 'The King of Prussia and Social Reform', in which the class struggle of the proletariat figures as the 'leitmotiv'.[11] Then, in *The Holy Family*, undertaken by Marx and Engels only weeks later, their central theme was the disdain of philosophers for the masses, with a clear statement that the proletariat will necessarily bring about the end of alienation and class society *themselves*, through their own socialist abolition of private property.[12] Draper is directly interested in Marx's theory of revolution, *per se*; but it is to this same rapid development of his ideas during 1844 – revealed particularly in the *Economic and Philosophic Manuscripts* – that both the origins of historical materialism, and the influence of bourgeois liberalism on some of its expressions, can be traced.

The key to the development of Marx's thought in these months is his *critical* consideration of political economy, and specifically his treatment of the issue of private property. In the 'Introduction', Marx had distinguished the proletariat as the universal class on the grounds of their propertylessness, in stark contrast to the particular interest with which property imbued the bourgeoisie. Marx then turned, logically enough, to the study of both bourgeois class interest and property; which is to say, to the study of both the history of the Revolution and political economy. As Ruge indicated in letters from that spring and summer, Marx had even planned to produce a history of the Convention.[13] Jean Bruhat closely considered Marx's intentions and ideas with regard to the Revolution, and came to the conclusion that in so far as they reveal a 'preoccupation' with the Convention, 'it was the notion of power which then interested Marx'.[14] At this point then, Marx had recognized the importance of property as a class interest, but his approach remained essentially political.

Yet, whatever the ultimate influence of his consideration of bourgeois class power and the process by which the 'political state' of bourgeois society was created – and allusions to these aspects of the Revolution are sprinkled throughout Marx's work – it is instead the idea of *private property* itself, its centrality in all aspects of human alienation, and its *developmental* character as the decisive dynamic of class history, which came alive in and almost entirely occupied Marx's manuscripts. Marx never returned to any serious investigation of the Revolution, nor produced any work upon it. Instead, his critical encounter with political economy gave a decisive new definition to his political project – the emancipation of humanity from its long history of alienated labor through proletarian class revolution. As a result, Marx's development of historical materialism would remain almost entirely restricted to his study of capitalist society, primarily through the critique of political economy.

The critical turning point is clear in the 1844 manuscripts, where Marx works through themes first encountered in Engels's critique. Although Engels's article was preliminary, superficial, and imperfect as a critique of political economy, it *first* put forward many of the ideas which Marx would correct, improve, and systematize in his life work. Among these perhaps none was so suggestive as the idea that there is a *necessary* connection between political economy and socialist revolution:

> But as long as you continue to produce in the present unconscious, thoughtless manner, at the mercy of chance – for just so long trade crises will remain; and each successive crisis is bound to become more universal and therefore worse than the preceding one; is bound to

impoverish a larger body of small capitalists, and to augment in increasing proportion the numbers of the class who live by labour alone, thus considerably enlarging the mass of labour to be employed (the major problem of our economists) and finally causing a social revolution such as has never been dreamt of in the philosophy of the economists.[15]

At the time this was written by Engels (October–November 1843) Marx himself had not yet even discovered the proletariat as the 'universal class'. While it is true that Engels still saw the Young Hegelian philosophers as constituting a real communist movement (as Draper emphasizes), Marx's *own* ideas had as yet gone no further. Though it would be Marx who would ultimately be most responsible for developing the concept of the proletariat as the exploited class of capitalism, and Marx who actually tied the critique of political economy to history, it should be recognized that Marx's agenda of study, themes of analysis, and even the specific terms in which he formulated certain problems – as revealed in the manuscripts – were taken directly from Engels.[16]

Marx read the major economists whom Engels had criticized, writing out their central ideas and his own responses to them in a series of notebooks. These 1844 manuscripts form the essential starting point for understanding the development of Marx's practice of historical materialism. The thoughts Marx works through in these pages reveal – paragraph by paragraph – the emergence of a specifically *critical* historical materialist perspective through a systematic critique of political economy.

In comparison to the later developed form of this critique, Marx's analysis here is undeniably naive, and frequently off the mark. But the continuities between these thoughts and those of the *Grundrisse* and *Capital* are striking, as Lucio Colletti has stressed, and it is in this continuity that that which is most fundamental to Marx's work is to be found.[17] Above all, the manuscripts reveal the original form of Marx's critical overview of history – that conception of a dynamically developing continuum of class society which is fundamental to historical materialism. At the core of this historical conception lies Marx's recognition that it is the 'alienation of labor' which is the basis of property – and not the reverse – and that the history of alienated labor has in fact constituted the historical course of human social development.

The concept of alienation is at the center of these manuscripts, but specifically and particularly in the form of *the alienation of labor*. Marx's usage, unfortunately, has been widely misunderstood, and the importance of its historical dimension too often ignored. These manuscripts are often read – and perhaps equally often criticized – for 'the young Marx's' philosophical insights into capitalism, seemingly stressing 'alienation' instead of class; focusing upon how capitalist production dehumanizes humanity, and why the proletariat *should* revolutionize society. Yet rather than marking some unique period in Marx's thought, for good or ill, this early analysis of alienation is fully consistent with the central thrust of his mature work, and quite valid in the terms with which it is presented.

Indeed, as will be seen, the immature philosophical leanings of the 'young' Marx are most reflected in the 'hard' determinism of his early work, rather than in its supposedly 'humanistic' focus on alienation. For in Marx's work the meaning of 'alienation' is above all *exploitation – economic estrangement –* and not some merely psychological condition. Whatever insights Marx's passages may offer into the existential condition of humanity, these manuscripts belong first and foremost to the critique of political economy. It is here, in his consideration of alienation, that Marx first undertakes to relate the situation of the proletariat within capitalism to the historical evolution of class society.

The manuscripts begin with a discussion of the ideas of political economy, 'presented', as Marx noted, 'almost in the words of the political economists'.[18] His conclusion from this is that political economy offers workers no better prospect than relative impoverishment – and for the most part only misery – and that it does so with no more consideration to the worker as a human being than it offers to 'any horse' as a factor of production.[19] Marx therefore proposes to rise above this level of political economy, and poses two momentous questions:

> (1) What in the evolution of mankind is the meaning of this reduction of the greater part of mankind to abstract labour?
> (2) What are the mistakes committed by the piecemeal reformers, who either want to *raise* wages and in this way to improve the situation of the working class, or regard *equality* of wages (as Proudhon does) as the goal of social revolution?[20]

Marx has taken a step back from the arguments and contradictions of political economy itself in order to find a critical perspective, and he has immediately identified the essential questions to be asked of capitalist class society. Indeed, the answers to these questions comprise virtually the whole of Marx's life work.

The second of these questions lays the groundwork for Marx's lifelong commitment to communist politics and the abolishment of class society, through his critique of liberal political ideology and the development of his theory of revolution. The first question, however, is more purely theoretical, and therefore was never pursued with the same practical commitment. It corresponds to Marx's critical overview of human history, and directly involves the central issue of historical materialism – the role of exploitation in the social evolution of humanity. It is upon this first question that Marx particularly focused in the Paris manuscripts. More than just a turning point in Marx's thought, this analysis represents the theoretical underpinning for his later development of the critique of political economy. Not until taking up the issue again in the rough-draft notebooks of the *Grundrisse* would he improve on this analysis, and then with a focus specifically narrowed to the distinctive relations characteristic of capitalism.

Marx's critique, and his entire analysis of the alienation of labor, turns upon the issue of property. The existence of property is taken for granted by political economy:

> Political economy starts with the fact of private property; it does not explain it to us. It expresses in general, abstract formulas the *material* process through which private property actually passes, and these formulas it then takes for *laws*. It does not *comprehend* these laws, i.e., it does not demonstrate how they arise from the very nature of private property.[21]

Explicitly rejecting a return to some 'fictitious primordial condition', of the sort that had been carried into political economy from liberal speculative history, Marx sets out instead to examine the meaning of private property and the laws of its development on the basis of *fact*.

The central point is clearly stated:

> The relationship of the worker to labour creates the relation to it of the capitalist (or whatever one chooses to call the master of labour). *Private property* is thus the product, the result, the necessary consequence, of *alienated labour*, of the external relation of the worker to nature and to himself.[22]

Thus, while it may *appear* in capitalist society that private property produces alienated labor, 'it is rather its consequence'. It is alienated labor which is the inherent problem in historical human society; even if an 'enforced *increase of wages*' were possible, it would be 'nothing but better *payment for the slave*'. It is not poverty that is the essential problem to be addressed, but relations of class exploitation, of which poverty is only an expression.

It is from this foundation that Marx continues to pursue the question of the development of property in history. In undertaking to discuss the historical antithesis between property and propertylessness, Marx in fact provides a critical overview of the whole history of class society. He argues, indeed, that the course of this history directly corresponds to the development of exploitive class relations. It is this 'movement of property' which reaches its culmination and full realization in the form of industrial capital and the factory system.

In light of the later critique of political economy represented by *Capital*, there is much in this analysis that is flawed. Nevertheless, it is this fundamental historical perspective, and particularly the recognition that property is not immutable – that it not only has origins, but *development* – which makes that later work possible. In these passages can be read Marx's first statement of the essential developmental dynamic of human history, his initial *historicization* of the critique of political economy. Nowhere else in Marx's work is it so clear that the critique of political economy is also necessarily a critique of liberal historical ideology – the speculative history of property and the 'progress of civilization' which was integral not only to the ideology of political economy, but also to the liberal materialist concept of 'bourgeois revolution'.

Through his analysis of property as alienated labor, Marx arrived at an overview of a central *developmental dynamic* to human history. It ran from the origins of the property in the alienation of labor; through that historical evolution of social institutions in general which corresponds to the development of this alienation; to the future 'transcendence of self-estrangement' – the realization of human emancipation that would follow abolition of private property and the establishment of communist society. The course of this history, as the development of '*real life* alienation', was also the history of alienated social consciousness. The transcendence of private property therefore would be not only the transcendence of *economic* estrangement, but also of alienated consciousness, and hence the real achievement of human emancipation.[23]

Unlike Hegel, Marx rooted his overview of history securely in the social *fact* of exploitation, in the fundamental reality of the alienation of labor for the great majority. It is this fact which accounts for the alienated condition of humanity, which shapes, limits, and colors all other social relations to create the general alienation of exploitive class society. From the very start, the central theme of Marx's conception was that the *dynamism* of historical development had its source in the 'movement of private property', or the historical logic of the alienation of labor. It is this conception, sharpened by his identification of the political task of the proletariat in revolutionizing society, which informs Marx's later declaration that 'the history of all hitherto existing society is the history of class struggles'.

In these crucial manuscripts, then, Marx brought together the radical ideas of his early, critical political philosophy with an understanding of working-class conditions and a criticism of political economic ideology that was first suggested by Engels. The theoretical foundations of historical materialist thought, however, are to be found in Marx's original application of a critical analysis founded on social *fact* to the key question of the origins of private property. Engels had already gone so far as to recognize that political economy took property for granted, and saw that all the 'unnatural divisions' of society – in particular that between capitalists and workers – followed from property.[24] Marx went on to ask: if private property is not to be *presumed*, what are its true origins and its role in human development?

In drawing the conclusion that it is the alienation of labor, or exploitive production, that is the basis of property – and not the reverse – Marx took the essential step by which the critique of political economy also became (if only in overview) a critique of speculative history. Here is the very core of historical materialism, its fundamental difference from liberal materialist history: where the latter takes for granted the social relations of property, which even the economists recognized as leading to great disparities in class, historical materialism instead recognizes property to be the result of specific and historical *social violence*, the exploitive alienation of productive humanity.

Neither the liberal speculative history of property nor Marx's critical overview of class history provides any real historical detail. Indeed, when it came to this detail – above all in the conception of the French Revolution as a bourgeois class revolution – Marx continued to rely upon the liberal historians. But whereas the liberal ideological perspective presumed existing class relations in order to explain property and propertylessness, Marx began with the singular historical *fact* of exploitive alienation in class society, and recognized that it was not class relations which gave rise to this fact, but the fact of exploitation which gave rise to the history of class relations. *Property*, as the organizing principle of 'the economy' (alienated social production) is not a timeless and immutable expression of human nature, nor a general necessity of social relations. Property is a historically specific expression of exploitive class relations, relations which – having gained ascendancy in a distant but real past – have since constituted, in their development, the central dynamic of class society. As will be seen, it was in pursuing this line of thought through the critique of political economy that Marx put historical materialism into practice.

Notes

1. J. Montreau [Jean Bruhat], 'La Révolution française et la Pensée de Marx', *La Pensée*, 3 (1939), 24–38, Jean Bruhat, 'La Révolution française et la formation de la pensée de Marx', *Annales historique de la Révolution française*, xxxviii (2), 1966, 125–70.
2. Marx–Engels, *The German Ideology, Parts I and III*, New York 1963, pp. 79–82.
3. See Hal Draper, *Karl Marx's Theory of Revolution,* vol. I, New York 1977, pp. 31–6.
4 Draper, *Marx's Theory*, vol I, pp. 36–76; Marx, 'Preface' to *A Contribution to the Critique of Political Economy*, Moscow 1970, pp. 19–20.
5. Marx, 'Contribution to the Critique of Hegel's Philosophy of Law', and 'On the Jewish Question', in *Collected Works* vol. III. See Draper, *Marx's Theory*, vol. I, pp. 77–125; also, Lucio Colletti, 'Introduction', to Vintage Marx Library, *Early Writings*, New York 1975.
6. Marx, 'Contribution to the Critique of Hegel's Philosophy of Law. Introduction', in *Collected Works* vol. III, pp. 184–7; Draper, *Marx's Theory*, vol. I, pp. 129–48.
7. See note 1, also below. Draper, *Marx's Theory*, vol. I, pp. 136–8, 159–62.
8. Marx, 'Critique of Hegel's Philosophy. Introduction', p. 187, quoted by Draper, *Marx's Theory*, vol. I, pp. 147–8, citing *Marx–Engels Werke* vol. I, p. 391.
9. Draper, *Marx's Theory*, vol. I, pp. 172–3, 219–21.
10. Marx, *Economic and Philosophic Manuscripts of 1844*, in *Collected Works* vol. III.
11. As Draper puts it, *Marx's Theory*, vol. I, p. 220. Marx, 'Critical Marginal Notes on the Article "The King of Prussia and Social Reform. By a Prussian" ', Marx–Engels, *Collected Works* vol. III.
12. Marx–Engels, *The Holy Family*, in *Collected Works* vol. IV, p. 37.
13. See Marx's conspectus of the *Mémoires de R. Levasseur*, in *Collected*

Works vol. III, pp. 361–74, for his summary of the struggle between the Girondins and Montagnards; footnote no. 117, p. 606, refers to Ruge's letters and explains the context.

14. Bruhat, *Annales historique de la Révolution française*, 1966, p. 141.

15. Engels, 'Outlines of a Critique of Political Economy', *Collected Works* vol. III, p. 434.

16. Compare Marx's *Manuscripts*, p. 235 and p. 266, with Engels's 'Outlines', pp. 440–41, 441–2.

17. Colletti, 'Introduction', pp. 49–56.

18. Marx, *Manuscripts*, p. 241.

19. Ibid., pp. 239–41.

20. Ibid., p. 241.

21. Ibid., pp. 270–71.

22. Ibid., p. 279.

23. Ibid., pp. 294–7.

24. Engels, 'Outlines', pp. 428–31.

7

Historical Materialism

Hobsbawm had it exactly right – it is Marx's *overview* of history, his overview of the dynamic historical development of class society, that is central to historical materialism. The 1844 manuscripts offer Marx's first statement that there is such a dynamic – and that it corresponds to the 'movement of private property', or, more precisely, to the development of the *antithesis* between lack of property and property. In so preliminary a statement, of course, the full implications could not be realized at once. Yet the germ of a conceptual framework *was* worked out within these three manuscripts, and this line of thought continues uninterruptedly through Marx's works. Since, however, Marx never pursued the historical dynamics of pre-capitalist class society in the serious and sustained manner of his critique of political economy, much of what little he did say about it is problematic. In *The German Ideology*, as will be seen, the continuity of his thought was to a certain degree deflected by a re-infusion of liberal materialist ideology, the effects of which continue to bedevil Marxist thought. Still, Marx's early insight into the historically fundamental character of class exploitation would endure, and ultimately find its mature expression in the achievement of *Capital*.

Materialism and Social Reality

This, then, is the central concept of historical materialism: that

133

the *realization* of human social existence through history has corresponded to the *development of private property* and its fundamental social antithesis of the propertied and the property-less. As Marx most notably stated the idea, 'The history of all hitherto existing society is the history of class struggles': on one hand, the history of struggle, because this has been the history of *alienated labor*, of exploitation, in its development; on the other hand, the history of hitherto existing society, for this is the history of human *social development*.

Marx as yet had very little to say about the details of this development prior to the arrival of bourgeois society; he would *never* have very much to say about these details, and much of that would be historically inaccurate. History, as such, could not match in significance the cause of revolutionary human emancipation; and it is not in previous social existence, but only in bourgeois society, that the antithesis of property is fully realized, and the 'transcendence' of estrangement – *exploitation* – becomes both possible and necessary. Marx was not an academic, and his primary commitment remained to revolutionary politics. Therefore, as a means of understanding communist society's 'process of *becoming*', and as a guide to working-class objectives in capitalist society, it would be the critique of political economy that would command Marx's attention, not history. The history of the Convention which he had planned was put aside forever.

Partly inspired by Hegelian philosophy and partly by liberal political economy, through *criticizing* both, Marx had come to recognize a line of historical development from a past that neither ideology would acknowledge, to a future that neither would accept. In making this conceptual leap, Marx did not attribute the evolution of mankind either to the development of an idea, or to a spurious unfolding of inherent human nature. Instead, he proposed for the first time a *fully materialist* conception of history, rooted in social fact rather than ideological preconception. He developed this idea in a number of pages of the 1844 manuscripts which are devoted to the specifically social character of production – particularly the social production of consciousness – arguing from a critical appropriation of social reality against speculative history.

The *social* character of Marx's materialism is central to the method of historical materialism, in that it repudiates the liberal ideology which treats history as 'natural' development. About the 'movement of property' which constituted history, Marx argued that

both the material of labour and man as the subject, are the point of
departure as well as the result of the movement (and precisely in this
fact, that they must constitute the *point of departure*, lies the historical *necessity* of private property).[1]

Which is to say that the history of social development requires
human, subjective, existence (and that, since the history of
humanity is the history of the movement of property, property is
a 'historical necessity').

Thus the *social* character is the general character of the whole movement: *just as* society itself produces *man as man*, so is society *produced* by him. Activity and enjoyment, both in their content and in
their *mode of existence*, are *social*: *social* activity and *social* enjoyment. The human aspect of nature exists only for *social* man; for only
then does nature exist for him as a *bond* with *man*. . . . Thus *society*
is the complete unity of man with nature – the true resurrection of
nature – the accomplished naturalism of man and the accomplished
humanism of nature.[2]

These passages may seem to be excessively philosophical,
the terminology obscure and marred by formalistic dualities.
Indeed, this 'philosophical', 'early' Marx is often opposed to the
hard Marxism of economic determinism, which has been presented as truly orthodox. Yet, it is in fact the social materialism
expressed here which will remain at the core of Marx's work, in
the critique of political economy; whereas the *hard* determinism
that crept into *The German Ideology* is actually a product of
liberal political economy that will fall to the wayside. In this
regard, it is notable that Marx asserts in these pages that there
can be no speculative abstraction of 'original' humanity from
humanity as it now exists; that the 'genesis' of humanity must be
sought in the *process* of human development, through social
reproduction, not with some creation of original man.[3]

The Historicization of Political Economy

A tremendously rapid intellectual transformation is crystallized
in the pages of the 1844 manuscripts. In a matter of months,
Marx had gone from his first glimpse of the proletariat as
universal class, to a materialist conception of history – and social
consciousness as its product – while carrying the critique of
political economy far beyond Engels's initial efforts. Marx still,

at this point, accepted the proposition put forward by Engels that communism would proceed from 'self-consciousness' in Germany, but from 'politics' in France, and from 'practical' need in England.[4] Yet he had already made a substantial movement away from philosophy as such:

> In order to abolish the *idea* of private property, the *idea* of communism is quite sufficient. It takes actual communist action to abolish actual private property. History will lead to it; and this movement, which *in theory* we already know to be a self-transcending movement, will constitute in actual fact a very rough and protracted process.[5]

This understanding was underscored by his reply to Ruge on the Silesian weavers' movement, emphasizing the self-directed struggle of the proletariat, which was written during the weeks he worked on these pages.[6]

Just after completing the manuscripts in August of 1844, Marx met Engels for the first time, and they outlined *The Holy Family*, in which, as Draper argues, they not only dispensed with Young Hegelian philosophy but clearly asserted that communism will be the *self*-emancipation of the proletariat through class struggle.[7]

> It is not a question of what this or that proletarian, or even the whole proletariat, at this moment *regards* as its aim. It is a question of *what the proletariat is*, and what, in accordance with this being, it will historically be compelled to do. Its aim and historical action is visibly and irrevocably foreshadowed in its own life situation as well as in the whole organization of bourgeois society today.[8]

Finally, in 1845–6, the now close friends brought together and sought to clarify what seemed to be the essential points of their critical approach, in *The German Ideology*.[9]

This first truly joint work of theirs is usually taken to be the first genuinely Marxist text. Certainly, it is the essential text for their conception of the social production of consciousness, and a primary text for many of the themes of their historical and social analysis. In relation to the whole body of their work, however, *The German Ideology* presents notable problems – most particularly with regard to its statement of materialist principles. Yet though the implications of this early confusion of historical materialism with liberal materialism have long endured within the body of Marxism, Marx's own work was thereafter specifically focused on capitalist society; and with ever-increasing acuity he criticized the quintessential liberal ideology of political economy.

This development by Marx of a consistent and thorough critique of political economy, over the whole course of his work from 1844 to the last, posthumously published volumes of *Capital*, coincides with the actual development of historical materialism, its increasing realization by Marx in practice. The essential key to this development was Marx's growing appreciation of the *historical specificity* of the categories of political economy. For, at the same time that his critique exposed the specific class character of political economic categories in capitalism, it *also* laid the basis for criticizing the ideological conceptions of *previous* class societies. It has already been noted that the very concept of 'the economy', or even 'the economic', is necessarily specific to capitalist society, with its *uniquely* economic form of exploitive surplus extraction. A major point of the present work is that Marx's study of this peculiar form of class exploitation, through his critique of political economy, provides a guide for the necessarily quite different analysis of *extra-economic* surplus extraction in pre-capitalist societies.

Perhaps the clearest discussion by Marx of the historically specific economic categories of capitalist society – such fundamental concepts as property, labor, and exchange – occurs in the section on the *method* of political economy in the *Grundrisse*.

> Although it is true, therefore, that the categories of bourgeois economics possess a truth for all forms of society, this is to be taken only with a grain of salt. They can contain them in a developed, or stunted, or caricatured form, etc., but always with an essential difference. The so-called historical presentation of development is founded, as a rule, on the fact that the latest form regards the previous ones as steps leading up to itself, and since it is only rarely . . . able to criticize itself . . . it always conceives them one-sidedly.[10]

Marx's work is full of the presentation of previous forms 'as steps leading up to' the forms of capitalism – but there is no unintentional irony in this statement. For Marx's extensive retrospective use of history in *Capital* was *conscious*, informed precisely by these insights of the *Grundrisse*, and intended to reveal the class character of these supposedly timeless forms. It is only subsequent Marxists who have taken this 'history' written from the point of view of capitalism to represent history, *per se*.

This conscious historical specificity in Marx's critique of political economy was not confined to the *Grundrisse*, but first appeared in *The Poverty of Philosophy*, in the year after *The German Ideology*. In attacking Proudhon's spurious 'synthesis' of political economy and communism, Marx observed that the economists treat the laws of capitalism as eternal, despite the fact that they also attempt to counterpose these laws to the restricted economic life of feudal society:

> Thus there has been history, but there is no longer any. There has been history, since there were the institutions of feudalism, and in these institutions of feudalism we find quite different relations of production from those of bourgeois society, which the economists try to pass off as natural and, as such, eternal.[11]

Here the link is quite apparent between Marx's critique of political economy and his *historical* conception of specific social modes of production (in which it is not the historical detail that is important, but the contrast which reveals *development*). The point is that historical development proceeds through successive epochs of *equally* specific exploitive relations of property (whatever they might be).

> In each historical epoch, property has developed differently and under a set of entirely different social relations. Thus to define bourgeois property is nothing else than to give an exposition of all the social relations of bourgeois production.
> To try to give a definition of property as of an independent relation, a category apart, an abstract and eternal idea, can be nothing but an illusion of metaphysics or jurisprudence.[12]

The continuity between the critical thought in this passage and that in the *Grundrisse* a decade later is striking. Whereas 'property' was in 1844 treated as a simple category – though one which had history – already by 1847, before the *Manifesto*, Marx conceived property relations to be historically specific expressions of the antagonistic relations of production fundamental to each particular epoch.

Marx had, then, already substantially arrived at the conceptual foundations of historical materialism. Its development followed from his perception that the central dynamic of 'historical movement' lay in the evolution of *alienated* social production – that history was the history of class exploitation and struggle. The essential accomplishment of historical materialist thought to this point had been to grasp the historical specificity of capitalist social relations, as one stage in the development of exploitive social production.

This overview of historical development did, of course, imply some actual succession of equally specific class epochs – each social mode of production being developmentally linked with those preceding and following. The essential point was that capitalism, too, was such an epoch of class society, and that it too would be superseded. It has already been suggested that the historical details which Marx attached to this overview were drawn from ideologically liberal historical conceptions of ancient slavery, feudal agriculture, and bourgeois progress. The extent to which his conception of the succession of epochs, particularly in *The German Ideology*, was influenced by the century-old theory of stages of subsistence is still to be considered. Yet with regard to the overview itself, Marx's central critical perception remains: in capitalism, the social development of relations of alienated labor and class relations have reached a logical terminus – the condition of universal commodification, encompassing even living human labor-power, as he came to express it.

The essential concepts of historical materialism – the historical overview, the fundamental role of class exploitation, the specificity of relations of production in each epoch – were, then, developed through the *critique* of political economy. The original formulation was suggested by Marx's critical treatment of 'private property', as an expression – not the cause – of alienated labor. By this, he attributed to property a process of origination and a history of development. This leap beyond the merely economic conception of property as a 'natural' category was embodied in his critical recognition of the simultaneously *exploitive* and *historical* character of property relations. Through all of Marx's work, the two essential strategies of historical materialist analysis in criticizing liberal ideology were to reveal its *class content*, and to identify the *historical specificity* of its concepts.

The only systematic application of this critical historical materialist approach was to be in Marx's lifelong study of capitalist class society. Although he never completed the major project of analyzing world capitalist society that he set for himself – which according to the *Grundrisse* was to have included 'Concentration of bourgeois society in the form of the state'[13] – the fundamental class analysis provided by *Capital* can be adequately supplemented by inferences from the major works of Marx's contemporary political analysis. Together, these form a consistent and integral picture of capitalist class society as it existed in Marx's lifetime, a genuinely historical materialist analysis, rooted in the critique of political economy.

This critique had commenced with Engels's criticism of the 'splitting apart' of capital and labor, sanctioned by political economy, but seen by Engels to be the source of working-class impoverishment.[14] Here was the initial theoretical recognition of exploitation and class struggle in capitalism. In carrying this critique further, Marx located capitalism within the whole course of the history of class exploitation – if only in overview – establishing the basis for historical materialism. Most of the real work of historicization, however, would remain no more than prospective, since the primary concern of Marx and Engels always remained capitalist class society.

Liberal ideology, on the one hand, claimed that the social relations of capitalism were natural and eternal; and, on the other hand, construed the generalized commodity market, into which human labor was dissolved, as a true and just circulation of equivalents. The critique of political economy, however, revealed the specific, historically imposed character of these relations, and so exposed a system of class exploitation in the regular exchange of labor-power for subsistence. The historical dimension is fundamental to this criticism, just as this critical conception of capitalism is essential to an understanding of the history of class society as a whole. One of the real weaknesses of Thompson's 'The Poverty of Theory' is its somewhat dismissive treatment of Marx's critique of political economy.[15] Far from having created a blind alley as Thompson has argued, Marx's '*Grundrisse* face' was the key to his achievement in developing historical materialism (although it is of course true that an enormous proportion of his energies were expended in systematic analysis of the structure of capitalist class relations, the *social* and *exploitive* character of which are realized only through the entire circuit of capital).

Problems of *The German Ideology*

After mid 1844, Marx and Engels based their thought with increasing clarity upon the central conception of history as the history of class society. The fundamental 'movement' of history was that of the social relations of production in class society: *property relations*, in the broad historical sense of 'alienated labor'; *exploitive* class relations. Engels's *The Peasants' War in Germany*, however, stands out as the only genuinely historical work written by either, and it was preoccupied with the question of revolution in Germany.[16] Overall, their account of the history of class society prior to capitalism was never more than sketchy, as in the *Manifesto*. Only in *The German Ideology* did Marx and Engels make an attempt to describe explicitly the historical operation of this dynamic of social development, and even then in broad strokes. The deeply flawed result – which, after all, they withheld from publication – must be contrasted to the general line which their thought otherwise followed.

This surely will be a contentious claim, given both the reputation and the very real attractions of this 'first' work of Marxism, and it must be emphasized that no effort will be made to repudiate *The German Ideology* as a whole. However, this early attempt at providing a 'historical' materialism for their conception of the development of exploitive alienation through the 'movement of property' resulted, unfortunately, in the wholesale incorporation of significant elements of liberal ideology.

The extraordinarily speculative account of human social development offered in *The German Ideology* immediately calls to mind the stages theory of the previous century. Nor is this a merely superficial similarity: it is the liberal four stages theory itself which provides the agenda for Marx and Engels's account. They begin with the concept of producing the *means of subsistence*:

> [Men] begin to distinguish themselves from animals as soon as they begin to *produce* their means of subsistence, a step which is conditioned by their physical organization. By producing their means of subsistence men are indirectly producing their actual material life.
>
> The way in which men produce their means of subsistence depends first of all on the nature of the actual means they find in existence and have to reproduce. This mode of production must not be considered simply as being the reproduction of the physical existence of the individuals. Rather it is a definite form of activity of these individuals, a definite form of expressing their life, a definite *mode of life* on their part. As individuals express their life, so they are. What they are, therefore, coincides with their production, both with *what* they produce and with *how* they produce.[17]

Of course Marx and Engels here have gone beyond a simple conception of 'mode of subsistence', for they offer a mode of production that is more than simply technique – it is social existence, a 'mode of life' through production. The difference is much as Meek suggested. At the same time, however, this conception of mode of production refers neither to class nor to the alienation of labor. In this, it contrasts starkly with the conception of the capitalist mode of production which emerged through the critique of political economy – and with the important passages on pre-capitalist modes of production in Volume III of *Capital*. While it is usual to read into the 'definite form' of the modes of production an understanding that they take an exploitive form in class society, *The German Ideology* remains fundamentally flawed by an uncritical focus on production as such, and an attendant precedence of productive technique over property relations. The earlier insight that it is *alienation* which is the essential moment of production in human history is undercut by the conflation of a liberal materialist approach to the origins of class.

In order to understand how and why the focus has shifted from property relations and alienation to production as such, it is essential to recall both the scope of *The German Ideology* (when the critique of political economy had not yet been carried far), and the specific purpose for which it was written. This work is an extended polemic against German idealism, in which Marx and Engels sought to counterpose to the Hegelian philosophy of history a materialist and social conception which was as broad and deep. They began, therefore, with the very origins of society, their point of departure a social conception of humanity defined by self-creation in social production. In so doing, they generalized upon Marx's earlier recognition that social institutions and modes of consciousness are founded on the social relations of production, taking this analysis back beyond the threshold of property relations, with which the original observation had started. In *The German Ideology*, the analysis begins with the fundamental role of social production in constituting society *in general*, even before the existence of exploitive class society.

With this contribution to social theory, Marx and Engels improved significantly on the long-standing liberal recognition that social forms correspond to means of subsistence. There remains, however, an essential difference between this general materialist conception of the fundamental social role of production, and Marx's recognition that history – the history of class society – begins with and is founded upon the development of specifically *exploitive* relations of production. For in this earlier insight, it is explicitly the social relationship of exploitation – the human estrangement of property – which is determinative: not production in any of its merely material aspects. This original conception, while not so *general* a contribution to social theory, specifically addressed the world-historical development of class society, culminating in industrial capitalism. It was in this specific context, indeed, that Marx first observed that 'religion, family, state, law, morality, science, art, etc.' fell under the 'general law' of the 'movement of property' – in other words, that the social forms of *class society* correspond to the development of *class exploitation*, not to production as such.

In *The German Ideology*, this focus was to a real extent displaced by an effort to contrast the real social-material foundation of all human existence with Hegelian idealism. This social-materialist conception of human society is important in its own right. Locating the issues of actual historical development within its framework, however, makes it necessary to offer some link between social production in general, and the historical emergence of specifically *exploitive* production in class society. Beginning with the distant origins of human society, as such, requires some account for the subsequent emergence of class, which is not itself an issue in considering the course of historical development *within* the continuum of class society. In *The German Ideology*, the history of 'all' hitherto existing society is *not* the history of class struggles, and the bridge to class society must somehow be made.

In order to combine the 'movement of property' in class society with a general philosophy of materialism that stood in opposition to the German idealists, Marx and Engels introduced a causal link between production in general and the exploitive production of class society – one which, unfortunately, was derived directly from liberal ideology. For, immediately following the idea of social mode of production, they assert that 'This production only makes its appearance with the increase of population.'[18] This opens their discussion of division of labor, in which the *technical* aspects of materialism seem to outweigh substantially the social aspects, and the links to the stages theory are most clearly revealed. Indeed, the most regrettable feature of *The German Ideology* from the standpoint of historical materialism is precisely the emphasis it places upon the primary social role of the division of labor, conceived in the terms of political economy and explicitly related to the observations of Adam Smith:

The relations of different nations among themselves depend upon the extent to which each has developed its productive forces, the division of labour and internal intercourse. This statement is generally recognized. But not only the relation of one nation to others, but also the whole internal structure of the nation itself depends on the stage of development reached by its production and its internal and external intercourse. How far the productive forces of a nation are developed is shown most manifestly by the degree to which the division of labour has been carried. Each new productive force, in so far as it is not merely a quantitative extension of productive forces already known . . . brings about a further development of the division of labour.

The division of labour inside a nation leads at first to the separation of industrial and commercial from agricultural labour. . . . At the same time, through the division of labour there develop further, inside these branches, various divisions among the individuals co-operating in definite kinds of labour. The relative position of these individual groups is determined by the methods employed in agriculture, industry and commerce (patriarchalism, slavery, estates, classes). . . .

The various stages of development in the division of labour are just so many different forms of ownership; i.e. the existing stage in the division of labour determines also the relations of individuals to one another with reference to the material, instrument, and product of labour.[19]

What is distinctive and new in the version of the stages theory presented by Marx and Engels is the history of the development of property. Here they transform the liberal conception, by arguing that property is simply an aspect of division of labor. Their purpose is to demystify and 'historicize' property, in contrast to the economists who regard it as 'natural'. In making property an aspect of the division of labor, they make it into a specifically social relation, derived from that division of labor by which the reproductive life of individuals is socially organized.

Their intent is clear – to bring to the materialist conception of historical development the critical insight that the basis of all social progress has at the same time been the basis for the development of exploitive human alienation. This insight is a sharp rebuke to the simple-minded liberal ideology of progress, and particularly to the German ideologists who believe they have discovered the 'resolution' to problems of modern misery, without having either experienced or understood the historical development of capitalism, of which these problems are an expression.

Yet in theorizing the social origins of property (and hence exploitation) by deriving it from the division of labor – instead of taking exploitation as the given point of departure – Marx and Engels have followed the schema of the four stages theory, and so incorporated its mechanical and 'naturalistic' conception of development. They present the history of social development in terms which are strikingly similar to the ideas of Turgot (whose work they comment on in passing), the primary difference being their focus on the process by which *inequality* develops through the joint development of property and division of labor (although Turgot, it will be recalled, also had acknowledged inequality to be the price of progressing from savage society).[20]

> The first form of ownership is tribal ownership. It corresponds to the undeveloped stage of production, at which a people lives by hunting and fishing, by the rearing of beasts or, in the highest stage, agriculture.[21]

This significantly modifies the 'modes of subsistence' model by recognizing in *all* the pre-historic stages of development, the stages which precede private property and commerce, an epoch of 'communal property'. This is an even more elegant and philosophically neat resolution of the problem presented by the stage of 'commerce' than that offered by Barnave. It is also suggestive in its potential for identifying the emergence of *private* property as the basis for real historical development. Yet telescoping the early epochs of human society into the 'undeveloped' stages of property also suggests an anachronistic conception of property as a single, timeless, and natural category of human experience, and obscures the critical point that private property is a *consequence* of exploitation, and not the reverse.

Marx and Engels follow the development of social relations from the initial elaboration of family relations in tribal society, through ancient slave society, feudal society, and, finally, modern bourgeois society and the prospect of communism. Through all this the actual historical content is limited to that provided by a general knowledge of the liberal histories of the day – a good deal of which is clearly wrong or inadequate – and their purpose and originality rest in describing the development of modes of production in conjunction with the development of property relations. It is not the faulty history which is the fundamental problem, however, but their reliance upon anachronistic conceptions of property, class, civil society, and above all the division of labor, which they have not yet begun to criticize. The endeavor to produce a unified materialist account of social development from its origins founders on their effort to establish a single dynamic of development which will lead through the long epochs of pre-history and account for both the creation of class society and its subsequent two thousand-odd years of history.

In *The German Ideology*, 'class' is something very different from the fundamentally opposed pairs of classes which Marx and Engels would offer in the *Manifesto*. 'Class' is treated as a product of the division of labor, precisely as the political economists would have it – developing within the various branches of labor 'among the individuals co-operating in definite kinds of labour', the 'relative position of these individual groups . . . determined by the methods employed in agriculture, industry and commerce (patriarchalism, slavery, estates, classes)'. Class is no more than one among many 'economic' categories of labor. T. B. Bottomore observed this difference in Marx's use of class between *The German Ideology* and the *Manifesto*, but since he himself took class to be narrowly 'economic' in character, he suggested that the earlier concept of class was the 'scientific' one while the more general concept of the *Manifesto* was problematic.[22] The truth of the matter is just the reverse. It is the use of class found in the *Manifesto* which belongs to historical materialism, which studies the supposedly economic category of class only to *criticize* it, to reveal that class is not an 'economic' category of 'income' but a politico-economic category of exploitation and conflict. The historical accuracy of the actual pairs of classes given in the *Manifesto* must be questioned, but their sense of *opposition*, of exploiters and exploited, is central to historical materialism.

The acceptance of anachronistic and liberal ideological meanings for important terms at this early point in their thought can also be seen in their use of *Bürgerliche Gesellschaft*. This term is used by both liberals and Marxists to indicate either 'civil society' or 'bourgeois society'. In *The German Ideology*, it is 'civil society' which is described as 'the true source and theatre of all history', which finally comes into its own as 'bourgeois society':

> Civil society embraces the whole material intercourse of individuals within a definite stage of the development of productive forces. It embraces the whole commercial and industrial life of this stage. . . . The word 'civil society' emerged in the eighteenth century, when property relationships had already extricated themselves from the

ancient and medieval communal society. Civil society as such only develops with the bourgeoisie; the social organization evolving directly out of production and commerce, which in all ages forms the basis of the State and of the rest of the idealistic superstructure, has, however, always been designated by the same name.[23]

This discussion of civil society, and all the discussions of property as such, still carry the same flaws as the account of the 'movement of private property' in the 1844 manuscripts: they are 'historicized' only in the abstract-formal manner of political economy. From the perspective of the *critique* of political economy, which Marx had yet to develop very far, it is not civil society which knows stages, but *class* society.

Division of Labor

Undoubtedly, however, it is the conception of the 'division of labor' – utilized to an extent unmatched in any other work by Marx – that is most problematic in *The German Ideology*. The term may be used to indicate either the *technical* division of tasks of production – as in the production of pins described by Adam Smith – or the *social* division of labor among roles and occupations (and ultimately classes). The very confusion of these quite different ideas is a consequence of the ideology of political economy, which, as Meek noted, was inclined to read back into the earliest stages of human existence the categories of political economy. This happy anachronism transformed the division of labor – which Turgot had seen to be a progressive effect of the inequalities brought about by property – into an unquestioned, natural, and apparently spontaneous impetus for increased production. For political economy even more than the stages theory, the division of labor was a virtually *natural* force, the ideological rationale by which the family, class structure, and the workshop could all be explained.

Marx and Engels to some extent exhibit a tendency to confuse the technical and social senses of division of labor, particularly in their discussion of the development of division of labor in feudal town and country.[24] Yet their focus is unmistakably upon the *social* division of labor: they emphasize the social character of production, the social character of property, and indeed the social character of all aspects of human existence, beginning with language and consciousness itself.

> The production of life, both of one's own in labour and of fresh life in procreation, now appears as a double relationship: on the one hand as a natural, on the other as a social relationship. . . . It follows from this that a certain mode of production, or industrial stage, is always combined with a certain mode of co-operation, or social stage, and this mode of co-operation is itself a 'productive force'.[25]

This observation – that social relationships may themselves be forces of production and have a *material* existence – is extremely important, yet it depends entirely upon how the social relationships are themselves conceived. If social relationships are no more than reflections of fundamentally *natural* forces, then this is simply a wrinkle upon a wholly naturalistic materialism, not an expression of a truly social materiality. If there is to be any real meaning to Marx's earlier insight that 'both the material of labour and man as the subject, are the point of departure as well as the result' of human history, then there must be a human reality which is material but more than simply 'natural'.

Not to belabor the philosophical point, it is apparent that such a reality is precisely that which is created by *consciousness* and human intention. A book is composed of natural materials, and produced through human labors that, in both muscle and machine, are material processes. Yet the material reality of the book as a human artifact must include its *meaning* as a product of consciousness, a reality which is entirely *natural* in its content, yet which cannot be comprehended in purely 'natural scientific' terms that would exclude the processes of conscious existence.

In appropriating the liberal materialism of the stages theory – notwithstanding their critical amendments and Marx's prior recognition of the social character of human material existence – Marx and Engels unfortunately succumbed to its 'technical' and 'naturalistic' conceptions, especially with regard to the social relationship of division of labor. Much as in the liberal conception, the material basis of social development is said to be *'increased productivity, the increase of needs, and, what is fundamental to both of these, the increase of population'*.[26]

> With these there develops the division of labour, which was originally nothing but the division of labour in the sexual act, then that division of labour which develops spontaneously or 'naturally' by virtue of natural disposition (e.g. physical strength), needs, accidents, etc., etc.

This process of division continues, leading to the differentiation of mental and physical labor. Here the issue of exploitation is rejoined, since 'enjoyment and labour, production and consumption . . . devolve on different individuals, and . . . the only possibility of their not coming into contradiction lies in the negation in its turn of the division of labour'.[27] Yet, though Marx and Engels label this the level of 'true' division of labor, they merely continue with the elaboration of a *single, natural* process of differentiation and development, from the act of procreation to the machine shops of Europe. Indeed, where political economy merely obscured the difference between social and technical division of labor, Marx and Engels have systematized the social division of labor *as* a technical process. While they have criticized the non-conflictual content of liberal ideology, they have not yet come to criticize its anachronisms and its technologically deterministic materialism.

The Historical Materialist and Liberal Conceptions of Class

There are many passages from *The German Ideology* – including many of those cited above – which could just as well be taken to demonstrate Marx and Engels's development of historical materialism. *The German Ideology* is, after all, a part of the continuous line of their work from 1844 until their deaths, work which as a whole embodies the development of historical materialism. For this very reason, however, it is not the presence of historical materialist concepts which must be emphasized, but the persistence of liberal concepts: liberal political economy, which would soon be criticized; liberal history, which would not; and a liberal natural-economistic materialism which was criticized, but not completely.

Ironically – although perhaps not surprisingly – the elements of liberal ideology which can be found in Marx's work have not only been generally accepted as *integral*, but even, in vulgar Marxism, as *central* to his line of thought. It is just because of this confusion – one of the clearest expressions of which has been the inability of Marxists to make an adequate response to the revisionist historians of the French Revolution – that it has been necessary to contrast clearly these two lines of thought in Marx's early work. Historical materialism, on the one hand, is based on *criticism* of political economy; it is rooted in a *social* conception of human existence, is historically *specific* in its analytical categories, and takes *exploitive* production as its starting point.

Liberal materialism, on the other hand, takes a natural-technical approach to human existence, is prone to analytical anachronisms, and begins with 'production in general'.

Before finally elaborating upon historical materialism as a *method* of analysis, it is important to demonstrate the extent to which Marx did and did not criticize the elements of liberal materialism which he had incorporated into his early work. Those elements of liberal ideology which have been magnified by subsequent Marxists as *economic determinism* must particularly be confronted and criticized, and the extent to which some of these ideas *persisted* in Marx's own thought must be accounted for. Aside from its apparent similarity to the stages theory of development, the two most significant specific instances of liberal conceptions incorporated into *The German Ideology*, and persisting with lasting effect upon Marxism, are the conflation of the liberal conception of class with Marx's own – a conflation which is at the core of the Marxist theory of bourgeois revolution – and the subordination of the history of class society to the technical development of the division of labor – which continues to underwrite the economic determinism that dogs Marxism to this day.

In his works, Marx used 'class' in quite a number of senses. It is the sense of *opposed* classes, classes which come into being through the systematic antagonisms of social relations of surplus extraction (alienated labor), that is inherent to historical materialism. The specific instance of opposed classes which is peculiar to capitalism is the opposition of the capitalist and working classes. These take the *appearance* of merely economic categories in political economy, because of the uniquely economic character of exploitation through the commodification of labor-power. Hence, Marx's 'economic' use of the term, indicating the modern economic classes, is really a specific and critical instance of the general *exploitive* sense. Marx also used 'class' in a variety of other instances to describe social groups demarcated by particular social interests within the dynamic workings of capitalist society – these included the classical political economic 'class' of the landlords (which he recognized to be a part of the capitalist class, in capitalism), the peasantry, the petty bourgeoisie, etc. In the earlier works in particular, however, one can detect not only uncriticized political economic uses of the term, but also the use of 'class' to mean social *rank*: precisely as in liberal history, the history of the 'lower', 'middle', and aristocratic 'upper' classes.

Marx took over whole the liberal history of the progress of the bourgeois 'golden mean'. He criticized it only partially, by insisting that bourgeois society was itself a class society. Even his conception of the proletariat as the universal class carried the sense of the *last* rank in a series. It would rise up *in its turn*, bringing an end to class society for the reason that it alone, possessing nothing but its humanity, would pursue no particular interest:

> For each new class which puts itself in the place of one ruling before it, is compelled, merely in order to carry through its aim, to represent its interest as the common interest of all the members of society. . . . The class making a revolution appears from the very start, merely because it is opposed to a *class*, not as a class but as the representative of the whole of society; it appears as the whole mass of society confronting the one ruling class. It can do this because, to start with, its interest really is more connected with the common interest of all other non-ruling classes. . . . Every new class, therefore, achieves its hegemony only on a broader basis than that of the class ruling previously, in return for which the opposition of the non-ruling class against the new ruling class later develops all the more sharply and profoundly.[28]

That there is important insight in this well-known passage will not be denied. Yet it is perplexing that its sequential *ranking* of classes – in so general form as to suggest many classes, though the usual stack is only of three – should go unremarked. It is clearly at odds with the conception of two fundamental classes locked in struggle over exploitation; classes here come into opposition not through exploitive relations, but because a 'rising' class confronts the class at the top.

Indeed, it is hard to see how any sense can be made of bourgeois revolution, in its usual form, from the perspective of class exploitation. For the peasantry, who might be expected to be opposed to the feudal aristocracy, are not usually included at all – even in Lefebvre's history, the episode of 'peasant revolution' is little more than the work of few weeks in the summer of 1789. The enduring struggle is that of the bourgeoisie and the urban people against the aristocracy. Where do relations of *exploitation* figure among these classes – particularly since it is always emphasized that the sans-culottes were not proletarians? And if the bourgeoisie *were* to be taken as capitalists, *whom* do they exploit? If no one (or so few as not to count), on what grounds do they become a ruling class? What internal dynamic of class society can have led to this peculiar constellation of classes, and to a class struggle with no apparent basis in exploitation? It is little wonder that the French Marxists have had such difficulty in finding a satisfactory response to the revisionists, once Cobban showed the right questions to ask.

The inherent problem is that the liberal conception of class which originally gave rise to the theory of bourgeois revolution cannot be reconciled to the historical materialist conception of exploitive class society. The impact of this contradiction can be seen not only in Marxist confusion over the French Revolution, but also in the Sweezy–Dobb transition debate.[29] Sweezy's position can be seen as a reluctance to allow a bourgeois class to emerge *between* feudal lords and serfs, preferring to accept its emergence only through a process *external* to feudalism altogether – the growth of trade. Dobb instead insisted upon identifying an inherent connection between the aristocracy and the bourgeoisie, whatever the problems, in order to retain the sense of an *internal dynamic* in class history. Sweezy, however, did approve of Dobb's assertion that feudalism, *per se*, was dead long before genuine capitalism emerged, and he argued for an intervening period of 'pre-capitalist commodity production' under the mediation of the Absolutist state.[30] Though there are problems with this aspect of Sweezy's analysis – particularly with his separation of the question of the ruling *classes* (he sees *at least* two) from the question of specific relations of class exploitation – the idea is not dependent upon his very problematic reliance on the external growth of trade. There is indeed a great deal to be said for an intervening period between feudalism and capitalism, as will ultimately be seen.

What is perhaps most striking about the transition debate is that all of the contributors offered significant insights, without any being able to make complete sense out of Marx's analysis. Their positions must be recognized as competing attempts at resolving a very *real* contradiction, one that is inherent in Marx's conflation of the liberal and the historical materialist meanings of class in describing the origins of bourgeois society. Since the contradiction is really in Marx's work, each attempt at resolution can offer a measure of plausibility, but in its turn will reveal an aspect of fundamental incoherence. The partial insights can only be brought together and made sense of by abandoning the orthodoxy of 'what Marx said' about pre-capitalist society, and striking out anew solely on the basis of the historical materialist method.

In making this criticism of Marx's conceptions of pre-capitalist society – and particularly his account of bourgeois revolution – it is perhaps necessary to emphasize again how much Marx got *right*, given his purposes. Aside from his uniquely perceptive and fundamental critique of political economy – in which most, if not quite all, of the purposes of historical materialism were achieved with regard to capitalist society – and his overall conception of dynamic human social development through the history of class society, there remains the fact that Marx's interpretation of the French Revolution was essentially *correct* with respect to the purpose it was meant to serve. For the essential point of Marx's interpretation was the critique of liberal and purely radical-democratic politics. That is to say, the politics of the French Revolution ultimately offered the proletariat nothing more than the possibility of liberal democracy in class society. Therefore, proletarian revolution was necessary.

Since Marx's conception of the dynamics of proletarian revolution was so intimately connected to his understanding of bourgeois revolution, much of his analysis of the *coming* of proletarian revolution must also be critically reconsidered. Yet most of Marx's thought on revolution had to do with what it must *be*, what socialist revolution must accomplish, not when or how it will arrive. And this thought, derived from his understanding of the structure of capitalist society achieved by the critique of political economy, is *not* called into question by these criticisms.

Historical Materialism vs. Economic Determinism

The purpose behind Marx's historical materialism, including both the critique of political economy and his political works, was exposure of the specific class character of capitalist society, against liberal ideological claims to the contrary. His works were to serve as a guide and a complement to the development of socialist revolutionary class struggle. Except for *The German Ideology*, Marx's work is entirely preoccupied with capitalist society, and only glances *retrospectively* at pre-capitalist social relations. His comments on pre-capitalist social forms belong, for the most part, to the critique of political economy, and their point was to describe the specific form such relations take under capitalism. Such comments were intended to distinguish what the relations had become from what they had been, always from the point of view of the evolution of capitalism and without serious regard for their actual roles in pre-capitalist class societies.

This was a conscious approach. It was for Marx's purposes sufficient to assert that the history of human social development has been the dynamic history of exploitive class society. The historical details might be interesting, they might in some ways be suggestive, but they were not *essential* in the way that the detailed critique of political economy and close political analysis of contemporary class society were; a rough overview of history was adequate, the rest could be presumed. For this reason, the one aspect of liberal ideology which remained largely uncriticized by Marx was history. The consequent failure of Marx's 'historical' formulations to describe the conditions and processes of pre-capitalist class societies really has no bearing on his life work. It is the misguided efforts by Marxists to construct a history of pre-capitalist modes of production from his paltry sketches and retrospective analyses that is problematic; the errors in his published works do not significantly affect the purposes for which they were intended.

If Marx's failure to criticize liberal historical conceptions can be attributed to the fact that history lay outside his focus of study, the same cannot fairly be said of those suggestions of economic or technological determinism which can be found in his work. Correcting the impression that historical materialism is economic determinism has been a major theme of Marxist thought in recent years.[31] Yet while it has been argued that economic determinism contradicts Marx's historical material-ism, and runs directly counter to the critique of political economy, it must be admitted that support for such determinism can genuinely be found in a number of the brief statements of their work that were made by Marx and Engels, qualifications notwithstanding.

An inclination towards economic determinism – and at times the straightforward embrace of it – has therefore persisted within Marxism. The economic determinist argument – which may imply or even be frankly stated in terms of a *technological* deter-minism, as in G. A. Cohen's *Karl Marx's Theory of History: A Defense* – is rooted in the metaphor of 'base and superstructure', as undeniably utilized by Marx and Engels, most notably in the Preface to *A Contribution to the Critique of Political Economy*.[32] An exhaustive treatment of the subject of base and superstruc-ture is not possible here, but from the foregoing discussion of the origins and character of historical materialism, it should be clear that the point of departure and continual focus of Marx's central work was not 'the economic base' but *class exploitation*.

It was with relations of exploitive production – alienated labor – that Marx began, not the idea of the determination of social behavior by the structured activities of production. Indeed, it was only in *The German Ideology* that Marx came to state his basic historical conception of social development in terms of determination by stages in the process of production – terms which are strongly redolent of the liberal mode of subsistence theory. All subsequent Marxist formulations of economic/technical determinism clearly are derived from that account. Yet, by attributing the development of both class and property forms – and so, by his analysis, the whole line of human social development – to the effects of the 'division of labor', in a conception rooted in natural/technical processes, Marx was engaging in the sort of abstract-formal and anachronistic analysis which he soon came to criticize.

Marx and the Division of Labor

Marx would never again attribute so central a role to the concept of the division of labor. Indeed, in the course of his critique of political economy – in which one might expect the category to loom large, judging from Adam Smith's heavy emphasis upon it – the role of the division of labor is remarkably limited. In his important introductory essay in the *Grundrisse*, in which he clarifies his analysis of 'production in general', the 'general relation between production, distribution, exchange and consumption', and 'the method of political economy', he barely mentions the division of labor. The entire point of his analysis is to situate the subject of political economy in the context of global and historical human production. Yet, precisely because Marx *rejects* the idea of 'production in general', which the bourgeois economists present

> as encased in eternal natural laws independent of history, at which opportunity *bourgeois* relations are then quietly smuggled in as the inviolable laws on which society in the abstract is founded, [33]

he has no room for an abstracted conception of the division of labor as some universal driving force of production. Instead, he indicates only that *exchange*, a category in which he is very much interested as an aspect of the production of commodities, requires the division of labor, and that division of labor is numbered among the 'determinant, abstract, general relations' which the political economists first analyze, in order to reconstruct the operation of the economic system as a whole.[34] This penetration of the abstract operation of 'the economy', however, is predicated upon first recognizing the specificity of its subject: *capitalist* production. In *A Contribution to the Critique of Political Economy*, a redraft of one of the chapters of the *Grundrisse*, Marx again makes limited reference to the division of labor: he observes that the social division of labor might be developed *without* commercial exchange, but since he is concerned with political economy and capitalism, he simply notes its necessary underpinning of the production of commodities.[35]

Finally, in *Capital*, Marx devotes one chapter to the division of labor, out of the thirty-three contained in Volume I. Here, he not only settles accounts with the difference between social and technical division of labor, but he makes the point that the role of the division of labor with which the political economists were preoccupied is *unique* to capitalism. In the first place,

> in spite of the numerous analogies and links connecting them, division of labour in the interior of society, and that in the interior of a workshop, differ not only in degree, but also in kind.[36]

The social division of labor is found in *all* societies, 'whether such division be brought about or not by exchange of commodities'.[37] The production of commodities – which is the essential focus of *Capital* – is, of course, predicated upon the social division of labor. This, however, does not mean that the production of commodities is itself in any way a 'natural' necessity: on the contrary, the organization of social production based on quite elaborate division of labor, *without* internal commodity exchange, has existed in a number of societies, such as ancient Egypt.

Moreover, not only is there a basic difference between the production of commodities, as such, and social division of labor in the production of articles for use, but there is an even more profound difference between the social production of commodities and the *technical* division of labor in the workshop. The latter 'is a special creation of the capitalist mode of production alone'.[38] Whereas the social division of labor is a means of organizing social production as a whole, the division of labor in the workshop is a specific means of maximizing the production of surplus-value for the capitalist. The 'natural' drive to increase productivity, the very association with the progress of *technique*, is specifically historical in character:

> By decomposition of handicrafts, by specialisation of the instruments of labour, by the formation of detail labourers, and by grouping and combining the latter into a single mechanism, division of labour in manufacture creates a qualitative gradation, and a quantitative proportion in the social process of production; it consequently creates a definite organisation of the labour of society, and thereby develops at the same time new productive forces in the society. In its specific capitalist form . . . manufacture is but a particular method of begetting relative surplus-value, or of augmenting at the expense of the labourer the self-expansion of capital. . . . It creates new conditions for the lordship of capital over labour. If, therefore, on the one hand, it presents itself historically as a progress and as a necessary phase in the economic development of society, on the other hand, it is a refined and civilised method of exploitation.[39]

To underscore the distinctive quality of *this* division of labor, Marx points to the fact that political economy conceives of the division of labor exclusively in terms of 'the means of producing more commodities with a given quantity of labour', whereas the authors of classical antiquity entirely ignored any quantitative implications of division of labor, and instead saw in it the means to improve the *quality* of the product, and the talent of the producer.[40]

From the perspective of his fully mature work, then, it is clear that the conception presented in *The German Ideology* of a natural and strongly technical impetus behind the division of labor as the fundamental source of social development could no longer be sustained. For that conception attributes the specific and peculiarly *economic* character of the division of labor found in the capitalist workshop to the social division of labor in the abstract. Such an application of economic concepts to societies *in general* is an anachronism of the first order:

> Labour seems a quite simple category. The conception of labour in this general form – as labour as such – is also immeasurably old. Nevertheless, when it is economically conceived in this simplicity, 'labour' is as modern a category as are the relations which create this simple abstraction.[41]

It is this line of critical thought, the *critique* of political economy, which was central to Marx's work, emphasizing the *social* determination of relations of production in contrast to their supposedly 'natural' character, revealing the class exploitation disguised by this ideology.

The relatively uncritical use of political economic ideas in *The German Ideology*, in conjunction with the general schema of the stages theory of development, permitted the excessively philosophical and abstract-formal conception of point-by-point correlation between technological development, division of labor, forms of property, and class structure. Marx and Engels had arrived at the view that production is 'social'; but both production and society were still conceived by them in the terms of political economy, and were not yet *historicized* by any criticism of abstract-formal materialism.

Yet no more than a year passed before, in his next important work, *The Poverty of Philosophy*, Marx explicitly criticized Proudhon precisely for his anachronistic and technical conception of division of labor:

> The division of labour is, according to M. Proudhon, an eternal law, a simple, abstract category. Therefore the abstraction, the idea, the word must suffice for him to explain the division of labour at different historical epochs. Castes, corporations, manufacture, large-scale industry must be explained by the single word *divide*. First study carefully the meaning of 'divide', and you will have no need to study the numerous influences which give the division of labour a definite character in each epoch.[42]

Marx argued that it was not the natural unfolding of the division of labor that gave rise to Adam Smith's workshop; but the imposition of new social relations by the exercise of capital, which made possible the workshop and made *necessary* the further increase in division of labor.[43] This analysis clearly belongs to the line of the critique of political economy. Marx had already abandoned the problematic terminology of *The German Ideology*, and its tendency towards a natural-deterministic conception of social development, and once again emphasized the role of class relations instead.

The Confusion of Liberal and Historical Materialism

Still, some Marxists have persevered in treating the base and superstructure metaphor, which Marx occasionally used, as the essence of his historical materialist method. Against this form of economic or technological determinism – specifically G. A. Cohen's conception of the 'social' as determined by the 'material' – Ellen Meiksins Wood has argued that it ignores or misinterprets the whole thrust of the *Grundrisse* and *Capital*:

> Marx's object is to criticize the mystifications of political economy which are achieved precisely by beginning with 'material production in general' and then proceeding to treat the process of producing *capital* abstractly as if it were the process of production *as such*.[44]

Any conception of historical development which is rooted in 'nature' or 'material existence' reveals an underlying liberal ideological orientation which displaces class exploitation as the central fact of history.

Materialism in the abstract is not enough, and it is not Marxist. Wood states the matter clearly: the essence of *historical* materialism 'in contrast, say to the materialism of the political economists – is precisely that it *socializes* and *historicizes* the material base'.[45] Any conception of the 'social' or 'social production' which does not *begin* its analysis of a historical (Western) society with the fact of its *class character* ultimately must reproduce liberal ideology by deriving 'class' from some presumed 'natural' social relations of humanity, in just the manner that political economy itself derives 'classes' and 'property' from relations of 'exchange' and the division of labor, taken in the abstract. Classes do not *emerge* in a given society, through the operation of pre-existing social processes. Instead, class is the *initial* and *fundamental* determinant of social relations in exploitive class societies – a defining characteristic of those societies. This is the cardinal point of historical materialism, the point Marx recognized in 1844, and which forms the historicizing context for his critique of political economy.

It may be objected that this conception of historical materialism is not *generally* applicable to all human societies, in the way that determination by relations of production, as such, claims to be – that it could not, for example, be meaningfully applied to Trobriand Islanders in the social formation which preceded their engagement with the commercial circuits of the modern capitalist world. Indeed, the point is well taken. A major contribution of Marx's thought is the general principle that *every* society can be fruitfully examined in terms of its relations of production, and particularly the production and appropriation of *surplus*, known to every human society. The structure of these relations may be egalitarian in some non-class societies, and hierarchical in others.

Marx, however, was *specifically* concerned with those societies in which production and surplus appropriation are organized in *class* ways; and the historical dynamism he describes is specifically that of class society. This is not to suggest that there is a mystical separation of Western class society from other types of society; nor that the *origins* of class society cannot be considered by historical materialism. On the contrary. There is, however, an all-important qualitative difference between recognizing that class relations of production have been the specific basis of Western social reproduction, on the one hand; and on the other, merely recognizing in production a general social character, without acknowledging the fundamental impact of *exploitive* social relations. The latter has been the tendency in both liberal political economy (and economic history) and liberal materialist history (including demographic 'social' history). Unfortunately, as Robert Brenner in particular has argued, this is also characteristic of a tendency towards 'neo-Smithian' Marxism, which approaches the origins of capitalist development from the perspective of 'economic growth', or the rise of trade, in order to account for underdevelopment as an aspect of world capitalism.[46] Brenner's series of articles ranks among the most important efforts to apply historical materialism to precapitalist societies, and at their core is a return to the history of class exploitation and struggle which is exemplary.

While it is clear that staunch economic determinists have failed entirely to recognize the meaning of the *critique* of political economy, it must again be admitted that the ambiguity and contradictions in Marx and Engels's work are real. The *persistence* of certain liberal concepts and perspectives in their thought is a matter that must be accounted for. After Marx's initial criticism of Hegel and liberal politics, his development of historical materialism remained for a time associated with both philosophy and political economy. Only after the development of a more complete critique of political economy did Marx produce an analysis, specifically limited to capitalist society, which was inherently free of liberal ideology. There still remained, however, three main contradictory areas of Marx's thought, in which – for a variety of reasons – liberal conceptions were taken to be *consistent* with historical materialism, and therefore were never properly criticized as ideological.

In the first place, liberal materialist history had already recognized classes, seen struggle between them as central to political history, and asserted that economic progress was the key to bourgeois class strength – so much is clear from Hume, Mignet, Guizot. It was not Marx who claimed that the bourgeoisie was triumphant, but the bourgeois themselves. The French Revolution was their own – within limits, and save for the subversive, radical democracy of the popular movement, whose raising of the 'social question' called for stern measures. Since Marx's essential political point was precisely that the politics of the French Revolution served only the bourgeois class, and his primary concern thereafter was with bourgeois class rule in capitalist society, he simply had no cause to doubt the bourgeoisie's own claim to a class revolution.

Marx also had no reason to call into question the pervasively held general historical interpretations of progress, which recast in class terms seemed only to support his overall conception of history. He could not have had reason to question them, unless he were to investigate pre-capitalist society seriously, on its own terms. Not only was the theory of bourgeois revolution standard history, dramatically turned to serve Marx's purposes, but it recommended a historical precedent for *proletarian* class revolution, and evoked the memories of earlier popular action. Remembering that Marx's thought *began* with the class politics of the French Revolution, it is not surprising that he never criticized liberal history as a whole.

In the second place, while a criticism of liberal materialism was implicit in the developed critique of political economy, the liberal materialist presumption that social development followed from economic development did appear to provide an adequate account for the dynamic of liberal class history. The contradiction was not immediately apparent, and without creating an entire alternative history it would have been difficult to specify any different dynamic. After *The German Ideology*, of course, Marx did not attempt actually and specifically to describe the dynamic of class history (and he never published that work). Instead, a simple correlation of the stages of social relations of production with stages of the forces of production continued to offer a convenient framework for history, and an apparent explanation for the emergence of classes. The ambiguity created by endowing the 'forces of production' with a broadly social definition *appeared* to raise the argument above the level of determination by the division of labor, *per se* – without actually contradicting it. This ambiguity can only be resolved in favor of either the economic determinism of base/superstructure, *or* the dynamism of class exploitation in the social relations of production. Historical materialism clearly, if implicitly, requires the latter.

A similar approach to explaining this ambiguity in Marx's overall conception of historical development is offered by Melvin Rader in his somewhat problematic *Marx's Interpretation of History*. Rader asserts that Marx's mature insights are most faithfully expressed in the metaphor of *organic structure* – which implies that the political and the economic are inseparable, and that 'production in its organic totality is internally related to "moments" that are not usually thought of as economic'; in short, that society as an organic *whole* is characterized by class.[47] Yet, he argues, there remained a need for the base/superstructure metaphor also, in order to emphasize the priority of *production* within this structure, as opposed to the role of consciousness.

There were in fact two different senses of 'priority of production' for Marx to convey. With regard to development within *class* societies, on the one hand, the fundamental priority of 'production' can be taken to mean the priority of 'alienated labor' – the extraction of social surplus – in class relations. Class is not a function of ideology, status, etc. – though it takes those forms as well – but a manifestation of the exploitation of producers of social surplus that is inherent to certain, historically specific social relations of production. The organic totality of class society is a function of these class relations of production; and however imperfectly, the metaphor of base and superstructure helped to convey that 'at bottom' real issues of the creation, possession and enjoyment of surplus product were at stake in such relations.

With regard to social existence generally, on the other hand, it is the materiality of social reproduction, the fundamental reality of human self-creation, which must be stressed – a reaffirmation of the broad materialist perspective argued in *The German Ideology*. In so far as the base/superstructure metaphor underscores the priority of material reproduction in social existence, it serves this purpose. To the degree, however, that the metaphor implies the determination of social development uniquely, or even predominantly, at the level of productive *technique*, it comes into contradiction with historical materialism. Because the only developmental link which Marx ever offered between the generally fundamental character of social production and the specific dynamic of exploitive class relations was that of progress in the division of labor, and because he never entirely repudiated the association of level of technique with stage of society, Marx's use of the metaphor must be recognized to involve real contradictions.

Finally, the liberal conception of the French Revolution had a lasting impact on Marx's political thought and his expectations for proletarian revolution. Marx began as a radical-democratic critic of both absolutism and liberalism, in the wake of the French Revolution. He had decided on the 'necessity' of revolution by a universal class, and had seen this class in the proletariat, *before* he developed historical materialism through the critique of political economy. His further studies – and exposure to proletarian movements – confirmed his belief that such revolution was needed, and led him to announce its inevitability. Together with Engels, Marx became an active communist – in the main, a journalist and propagandist for proletarian and democratic revolution, against utopian, 'feudal', and petty bourgeois socialism. Then, with the passing of 1848, and a return to capitalist prosperity for another cycle, Marx accepted that the immediate prospect of revolution was gone, but *not* its inevitability.[48]

Marx's Conflation of Historical Necessities

The issue of 'necessity' in Marx's writings is problematic, and is essential to a full understanding of the persistence of liberal materialism in Marxist thought. Marx's critique of political economy, as historical materialism, is *not* being challenged here. The many arguments which have been raised over *Capital*, and the supposed necessity for revising its analysis, as claimed by some Marxists, relate to the prognosis for capitalism and its ability to sustain growth – in other words, these arguments ultimately concern the *prospect* of proletarian revolution. In hindsight, it can be seen that Marx and Engels leapt forward a whole era in their understanding of capitalism's class dynamics, mistaking the struggles of *early* capitalist society for its death-throes. To what extent this misperception, the erroneous con-

ception of bourgeois class revolution, and the various philosophical tinges of determinism which were never fully repudiated, may have combined to produce misleading conclusions
about the specific processes to be expected in proletarian revolution is an issue which must still be taken up by historical
materialists. What becomes apparent from a consideration of the
history of Marxism is not that the belief in the 'necessity' of
proletarian revolution is wrong, but that the various meanings of
this necessity have been confused.

Historical materialism, recognizing exploitation in the very
fabric of history, is inherently *value-laden* as well as 'scientific' –
and this is no less true of the critique of political economy, as
Lucio Colletti, in particular, has often argued.[49] Colletti's perspective is a corrective to E. P. Thompson's evaluation of the
critique of political economy. Thompson goes too far in criticizing Marx's '*Grundrisse* face' precisely because he recognizes the
tendency among many Marxists to 'disinfect' *Capital* of its essential value-judgements.

> Marx does not only lay bare the economic processes of exploitation,
> but he also expresses (or presents his material so as to evoke) indig-
> nation at suffering, poverty, child labour, waste of human poten-
> tialities, and contempt for intellectual mystifications and apolo-
> getics.[50]

This 'moral' attitude is not, however, simply an addition to
Marx's argument, as Thompson seems to suggest. It is rather the
impetus for the critique of political economy, on the one hand,
and the very substance of that critique, on the other: capitalism is
revealed to be only one system of exploitation among many,
while also the most dehumanizing.

Thompson criticizes *Capital* on the grounds that if the
'moralistic' elements are removed,

> a very considerable part of that work – the major part – could be taken
> *just as* 'what the English call "the principles of Political Economy" ':
> an analytic critique of the existing 'science', and an exposition of an
> alternative 'science', of economic functions, relations, and laws. That
> is, if we did not (for exterior 'reasons' of value) disapprove of exploi-
> tation, waste and suffering, then we would find ourselves presented
> with an alternative lawed structure of economic relations.[51]

Certainly many Marxists do attempt to disinfect *Capital*. Yet
Marx did not intend it to be disinfected; it was consciously

written as *both* critical exposition of the Law of Value, *and* the critical analysis of capitalism as class society.

In revealing capitalism to be an exploitive class society, in challenging bourgeois ideological conceptions of human existence, in exposing the full measure of dehumanization and its sources, and in pointing up the just, heroic, and purposeful character of class struggle, writ large and small – in all this, *Capital* accomplishes no less than that which the best historical studies of class society hope to do. It is *not* a history, and at this late date a history of capitalist society is indeed overdue. Still, capitalism cannot be understood as class society unless the hidden operation of the extraction and distribution of surplus-value – and the attendant contradictions of development – are revealed. This, in both abstract-analytical and concrete terms, is what *Capital* does.

The *dialectical* character of Marxism, as science *and* ideology, has been a special concern of Colletti's. He has considered the impact of this quality – particularly the extent to which Marxism has been falsified by refusals to accept this union – and the implications it ought to have. Of particular importance is his argument that there is a real dialectic in the combination of science and ideology, grounded in a real opposition. Many Marxists have mistakenly attempted to 'resolve' this through the *theory of the crash*: the theory that capitalism must crash because it cannot grow infinitely, and that the crash necessitates revolution.

As Colletti argues, there are grounds in the critique of political economy for recognizing the impossibility of infinite capitalist expansion, but this *cannot* be stated in the purely formal and structural terms of a capitalist 'law', whatever else the implications of the 'laws' of capitalism. Instead, 'necessity' must be based on the historical prospect of *class struggle*:

> The system is not destined to an inevitable 'crash' through a mechanical impasse. The only factor that *can* destroy it is the clash of classes, a clash in which, besides objective material conditions, all the subjective factors like 'class consciousness', the degree of class unity and organization, and the efficacy of each class 'political instrument' participate.[52]

This once again emphasizes the dynamic centrality of class exploitation and class struggle in historical materialism: the reproduction of society and the creation of history, by human subjects, bound by class relations. No mechanical, structural determinism can replace the *process* of history. The necessity of communism can only be the historical necessity of real human action; a revolutionary necessity – comprising moral, scientific, philosophical, political necessities, etc. – not an 'objective', 'natural', unilinear necessity.

Yet it is true that Marx and Engels did reveal a tendency to *conflate* these necessities, to confound the logically distinct forms of 'necessity' in their revolutionary perspective. All of these necessities are implied by historical materialism and the critique of political economy, but they have varying senses, and rest on different grounds. Marx argued the *necessity* of humans realizing their emancipation and full potential in classless society; the *necessity* of capitalist economic relations being limited by the contradictions of their growth; the *necessity* of working-class struggle in its own interests; the *necessity* of replacing irrational and atomized production for profit with conscious production for social needs. These are all 'necessities' for socialist revolution, but they are so in logically quite distinct ways. In their *different* senses they each make a contribution towards the determination of socialist revolution.

One of the most regrettable consequences of the persistence of liberal materialism, and the inclination towards a natural-scientific determinism of the 'base', is that all of these differences become dissolved together in a single overriding *economic necessity*. Clearly, in expressing their belief in a revolutionary future, Marx and Engels were sometimes tempted by the certainty suggested by this sort of materialism; most of their followers have *insisted* upon it. Yet historical materialism cannot impose a false logical identity on such differing 'necessities'; it cannot make socialism *more* necessary than it really is by confounding different logics. The task of historical materialism remains to bring together science and ideology, to integrate these differing necessities in a concrete analysis of the ongoing dynamic of class history.

The Method of Historical Materialism

The central idea of historical materialism is that antagonistic class relations have provided the central dynamic of human historical development – specifically of the development of

Western society in its rise to world ascendancy. These antagonistic class relations center, of course, upon the direct confrontation between producing class and exploiters: both as it is
routinized in regular contention over the production and distribution of surplus in the 'normal' relations of class society, and as
it occasionally erupts in conflict over the very existence of the
exploitive relations. Yet it is perhaps important to emphasize
that the antagonistic relations of social development are not
restricted to direct class struggle between the ruling class and the
exploited. For, in the class relations of Western societies, surplus
is appropriated by the *individual* members of a *class* of exploiters. Each individual ruling-class member enjoys formal
equality with regard to the essential relations of surplus extraction (proportional to the possession of property), and *competes*
with other members of the ruling class in the class careers of
acquiring power and surplus (in the forms specific to each
society).

It is this *competition* of the ruling class, within itself, which is
the primary form of conventional political history, with the
material interests of individuals, families, or factions usually
figuring centrally. This competition also is, of course, essentially
an expression of the class exploitation/struggle which under-
writes it. That is, in pre-capitalist class societies, where class
exploitation takes directly extra-economic and political forms,
politics and/or conquest are the definitive ruling-class careers, in
which differential access to surplus through the state or plunder
can be gained, maintained, or even squandered by individuals
and families of the ruling class. Intra-ruling-class conflicts may
also very well become directly associated with, or emerge as a
response to, the conflict between the fundamental classes over
exploitation: all of the French revolutions between 1789 and
1871 can be offered as examples of ruling-class struggles associated with popular movements that were at least in some sense
rooted in exploitation and its social effects. Yet, though the
potential for intra-ruling-class conflict is created in the first place
by exploitation/fundamental class struggle, it has an identity of
its own – witness feudal warfare – and it may sometimes have a
contradictory bearing upon the struggle of exploiter and exploited – as when capitalists facing a shortage of workers bid up
wages, or East Prussian lords lured peasants with advantageous
terms.

With regard to capitalism, of course, Marx himself explicitly
recognized this general character of ruling-class competition:

> On the other hand, if all the members of the modern bourgeoisie have the same interests inasmuch as they form a class as against another class, they have opposite, antagonistic interests inasmuch as they stand face to face with one another.[53]

Competition is certainly recognized as integral to capitalism, yet it is rarely treated as *real* competition among members of the ruling class. It is even more rarely, if ever, acknowledged that competition is a general feature of class society, in a form specific to each society. Yet simply considering its role in feudal and capitalist societies reveals the extent to which competition within the ruling class has been an important aspect of historical dynamism, and a key to the peculiar nature of the state in class society.

It should by now be clear that the basic question to be asked of any class society is: what are the specific antagonistic relations which define opposing classes in fundamental exploitive production, and generate the dynamics of politico-economic development? It is precisely in the very important and oft-cited discussion of ground-rent in Volume III of *Capital* that Marx emphasized the importance of this question.

> The specific economic form, in which unpaid surplus-labour is pumped out of direct producers, determines the relationship of rulers and ruled, as it grows directly out of production itself and, in turn, reacts upon it as a determining element. Upon this, however, is founded the entire formation of the economic community which grows up out of the production relations themselves, thereby simultaneously its specific political form. It is always the direct relationship of the owners of production to the direct producers – a relation always naturally corresponding to a definite stage in the development of the methods of labour and thereby its social productivity – which reveals the innermost secret, the hidden basis of the entire social structure, and with it the political form of the relation of sovereignty and dependence, in short, the corresponding specific form of the state.[54]

No single passage of Marx's work can be said to give the 'key' to the whole. Yet, once the general line of historical materialism is recognized, the idea of developmental determination by 'production in general' is set aside, and liberal historical judgements are dispensed with – above all, once the strictures imposed by a 'theory' based on an *a priori* set of modes of production are removed – then this passage can be seen to offer a striking condensation of the central themes of historical materialism.

For the 'base' on which 'the entire social structure' is founded is not said to be production in any general sense, but 'the specific economic form in which unpaid surplus-labour is pumped out of direct producers'. Even 'the entire formation of the economic community' *grows up out of* these class relations of production – not the reverse. Here is the organic unity of the political and the economic in class exploitation, clearly asserted. The entire social structure, including both economic relations and the specific form of the state, is based upon the fundamental opposition of classes in exploitation. Admittedly, the exploitive relations are once again problematically said to be 'always naturally corresponding to a definite stage in the development of the methods of labour and thereby its social productivity' – which, if we recognize technology to be a *product* of class society, seems once again to leave the horse behind the cart. Yet this assertion is something of an aside, and if allowance is made for Marx's inclination to associate historical materialism with liberal-scientific materialism – a tendency even more notable in Engels, and enthusiastically embraced by their followers – the statement poses no real problem. Indeed, the 'direction' of this correspondence can be reversed from what is usually understood, and priority can instead be given to the *exploitive relationship*, as it relates to 'the development of the methods of labour'.

More to the point, the *determination* which Marx has in mind here is of the historical and limit-setting variety – not that of strict causation – as he specifies in the passage immediately following:

> This does not prevent the same economic basis – the same from the standpoint of its main conditions – due to innumerable different empirical circumstances, natural environment, racial relations, external historical influences, etc., from showing infinite variations and gradations in appearance, which can be ascertained only by analysis of the empirically given circumstances.[55]

This perhaps could be read as just a gloss on an underlying economic determinism; but if so, it is at most a hollow principle, wholly undermined by the effects of the historical situation. In the context of Marx's development of historical materialism, however – taking the emphasis upon *production* to mean alienated labor and exploitation – this statement expresses the real importance of historical specificity in the determination of class society.

This social determination is not only historical, but also dialectical – for the relationship between rulers and ruled which is determined by class exploitation 'in turn reacts upon it as a determining element'. It is no less true that the *economic relations*, which *also* grow out of the nexus of exploitation, also in their turn react back upon it. The central relationship of exploitation thus provides the 'class logic' for an entire class-based system of relations of social reproduction. These relations, in turn, constitute the essential fabric of social life, and as such, the field of struggle between the classes; hence, they continue to interact with the opposition of exploiters and exploited as it develops. If history is the development of class relations of exploitation and struggle, here, then, is an abstract sketch of its dynamic operation.

The analysis is suggestive, if only a sketch. It is also, however, an interpolation of the method Marx brought to bear on capitalism, through the critique of political economy. Within Marx's work, the critique of ideological conceptions is the first, essential step in an analysis of class society – the specification of the class relations of exploitation, identification of the actual relations of surplus extraction. Understanding the whole body of Marx's analysis of capitalist society to be founded on the critique of political economy, the outlines of a method can be inferred which 'operationalizes' the central idea of historical materialism, and makes it applicable to any class society.

Outline of the Method of Historical Materialism

1. *Identification of Class Exploitation*

In any class society, the key to social analysis is the specific relationship by which surplus extraction is effected. Knowledge of this relationship cannot be presumed in advance, but must emerge from a critical historical investigation. Liberal historical accounts are unlikely to reveal surplus-extractive relations directly, as such; but they may be traced through the circuit of social surplus which is so often revealed in such accounts. The production of surplus-value in capitalism – the analysis of which was the enormous task undertaken by Marx in his '*Grundrisse* face' – is by far the most complex case, because exploitation is inherent in the moment of production, and operates on a macro-social scale, through the Law of Value. In pre-capitalist societies, the overwhelmingly agrarian production was for the most part *openly* subjected to surplus appropriation through extra-economic relations, which included (but were not restricted to) the exaction of rents from tenants.

Recognition of the fundamental exploitive relationship is necessarily also recognition of class struggle, and the specific character of the classes arising through exploitation and struggle. The specific form of exploitation will create specific conflicts of social interest: the concrete basis for class struggle, and the concrete basis for ruling-class competition. In capitalism, these can be recognized in the struggle over wages, over the right to organize unions, over the welfare functions of the state, etc., on the one hand; and in capitalist competition, monopolization, state regulatory policies, imperialism, etc., on the other.

There is, finally, the question of the developmental *logic* that is dynamically generated by class struggle and competition. This logic is not simply abstract-formal, but historical. It includes not only the implications for development deducible from the *form* of exploitation, but the implications of specific historical and cultural forms of class behavior as well, as they enter into and are created during the historical epoch. Thus, in capitalist society the logic of the historical dynamic is *not* reducible to the 'logic of capital' in the abstract – although its implications are central – but must include the heritage of political activism (or apathy), the form and extent of democracy, the legacy of trade unionism, the national 'logic' of state intervention, the history of international relations, the potential for implementing welfare reforms, etc.

2. *Characterization of the State*

Class exploitation is intrinsically *political* as well as *economic*, and a permanent system of surplus extraction presupposes a permanent system of political power. Vitally important to the specific form of the Western class state is the *class* structure of social exploitation: personal ownership of exploitive property by a class of individuals. This necessarily implies a very different and far more dynamic structure than that characterized by the coincidence of surplus extraction with the state itself, as in the great temple civilizations. As Marx indicated, the specific form of the basic exploitive relationship is a determinant of the specific form of the state. In this discussion, Marx noted that for both Western feudalism and the 'Asiatic' state, the fundamental relation of exploitation can be identified as the necessarily *extra-economic* extraction of ground-rent. Yet in the Asiatic case there is no 'ownership' of land, except on the part of the central bureaucratic state. In feudalism, however, property is *personal*, and the personal possession of state power by each lord is integrated in the political system of the feudal class 'state' – descended from the post-Roman successor kingdoms, and providing the *form* for development of the later Absolutist state.

One consequence of the real inseparability of the political and the economic, however – which holds even for the unique case of capitalism, in which the politico-economic character of exploitation is obscured by the *formal* separation of apparently exclusive systems of 'politics' and 'the economy' – is that despite the *class* structure of exploitation, the state itself will have a role directly in exploitive relations. Even in capitalism, the state does not simply provide an 'external' shield for 'economic' exploitation: it is intimately involved in the relations of surplus extraction, through the law, property relations, regulation, mediation, etc. In turn, there must necessarily be some relationship between the state and the dynamic created by the contradictions of class relations. As a result, not only will the state be the 'arbiter' of normal class struggle, and the primary opponent of class insurrection, but it may itself become directly implicated as the *object* of struggle between the classes.

Consequent developments in state relations will, of course, in their turn become determinants of the social relations of exploitation. Ruling-class competition plays an important role: the Roman Imperial state was very much a product of the civil wars within the Roman ruling class during the final century of the Republic; yet, in turn, the existence of the Imperial state-form gave a new structure to ruling-class action, and as such had a major determining effect upon exploitive relations over the succeeding centuries. Marx's own political analyses, plus the role the state has obviously played in imperialism, fascism, welfare reformism, Keynesianism, austerity programs, etc., leave little doubt that the state is intimately involved in the dynamic of capitalist development. Also, the autonomy of the capitalist state relative to the capitalist class (whether or not this constitutes 'relative autonomy') has generally been recognized. The relationship between state apparatus and ruling class has, in fact, been problematic *throughout* Western class history – an expression of dynamic development in exploitive relations, the individual possession of class power, and the contradictory conflicts that are typical of ruling classes.

3. *Recognition of Historical Continuities*

Each era of class society is marked off by a *specific*, but *dynamic*, continuity of exploitation within the larger continuum of class history. Class relations are, as a whole, constantly changing – even the central nexus of exploitive relations develops over time – at the same time that, within any society, they retain their essential, abstract identity. This is, of course, inherent in the character of real historical development *as* the development of class relations. It is not that the fundamental relations of exploitation remain unaltered, while creating historical change in the surrounding society – only somehow to be transformed in the twinkling of an eye at the moment of 'transition'. Throughout a historical epoch marked by essentially continuous relations of surplus extraction, *development* nevertheless will occur.

In capitalism, for example, there has been an essential continuity in the fundamental form of exploitation: the creation of surplus-value through the commodification of labor-power. Yet there have been enormous changes in capitalist productive relations, and these have not been restricted to the substitution of new techniques for old. Structural developments have included: the creation of joint-stock companies, then monopolistic giants, then multinational conglomerates; the winning of effective collective bargaining and trade union representation; the introduction of the 'social wage' through state services, and state regulation of myriad sorts; the structural incorporation of inflation through monopoly pricing; the dramatic expansion of white-collar employment. None of these changes, not even those so frequently denounced as 'socialism', has in any fundamental way altered the *capitalist* character of class relations; yet, alone and together, they make for significant *development* of these relations.

The impetus for this development comes both from logical determinations of structure and from historical determinations, in a structured historical *process*. The constraints upon this process are themselves also both structural – created by the form of exploitation – and historical. Yet, notwithstanding the strictures and continuity of relations of exploitation over long periods, from epoch to epoch the essential class forms *have* been transformed. Without change in the underlying fact of class exploitation, and with substantial continuity in the relations of property, the developmental contradictions of one exploitive form must eventually be resolved by the creation of a new (also dynamic) form. Through the particular and concrete processes of class struggle which have developed in a given society, new relationships of exploitive class production are introduced in specific, historical forms, bringing 'transition' from one era to another.

'Mode of production' must be taken to refer to the essential, abstract identity of the fundamental exploitive relationship which is continuous over an epoch. Yet this is neither a category of 'the economy', nor an abstract-formal relationship. Because of the *unique* character of the formal separation of politics and the economy in capitalism, the formal economic category of surplus-value may be sufficient to define the capitalist mode of production. *All* pre-capitalist modes of production, however, (including those of ancient Greece and Rome) involved the exploitation of peasants, and the category of 'ground-rent' is not adequate to specify any one of them; the specific relations of extra-economic surplus extraction are essential to any definition of a pre-capitalist mode of production.

Each such 'mode of production' – implicit in the term is *exploitive* production, and one might better say 'mode of exploitation' – possesses a *history* of class struggle against exploitation and the exercise of state power, within each of its societies. As E. P. Thompson has emphasized, it is in these class struggles that exploited classes have *made themselves* as historical subjects: out of the situations defined by exploitation; through the creation of social relations – and consciousness – of common interest, solidarity, and active resistance.[56] No class society can be conceived as a static thing, moving and 'changing' only within a mechanical fixity. The history of class relations – the actual course and balance of class struggle against relations of exploitation and state power; the actual development of contradictions between ruling-class roles and those same relations – is essential to understanding the structure and dynamic of class society at any given point. From an understanding of the specific historical dynamism of a mode of production over time, finally, it is possible to recognize the conflicts and contradictions which lead to transition: the specific *logic* and *balance* of class forces which lead class exploitation to new forms and relations – and new struggles.

The Practice of Historical Materialism

Such an abstract exposition of the analytic method of historical materialism cannot really be satisfactory. Its high level of abstraction is almost a denial of real historical class analysis; it is at most an indication of what must be accomplished through historical practice. In fact, the foregoing exposition is not truly a *methodology*, but an anticipation of what is to be learned – a partial systematization of what historical materialist analysis can yield. The methodological injunction of historical materialism is to locate in actual history the dynamism of class exploitation and struggle, and to reveal the source of historical social change and human self-development in the dialectical determination of social structure by relations of class. It is Thompson, again, who has put it best:

> We have often been told that Marx had a 'method', that this method lies somewhere in the region of dialectical reason, and that this constitutes the *essence* of Marxism. It is therefore strange that, despite many allusions, and several expressions of intent, Marx never wrote this essence down. . . . If he had found the clue to the universe, he would have set a day or two aside to put it down. We may conclude from this that it was not written because *it could not be written*, any more than Shakespeare or Stendhal could have reduced their art to a clue. For it was not a method but a practice, and a practice learned through practising.[58]

The history of class society *itself* provides the structure of knowledge, not any methodology of analysis. *Of course* the initial decision must be made to structure historical knowledge in terms of class; nothing can be understood without conceptual structures. This is exactly the point of Marx's critique of liberal ideology, to provide a critical basis of knowledge against the contrary assertion that class is an accidental byproduct of human nature and natural development. This, however, provides only the point of entry, without guarantees, into historical knowledge.

With his somewhat too critical evaluation of Marx's '*Grundrisse* face', Thompson unfortunately sees in *Capital* a work entrapped by the system of political economy, and not a work of historical materialism: 'Marx's hope of himself developing historical materialism in practice remains, very largely, unfulfilled.'[59] Thompson does not sufficiently credit the necessity of practicing the critique of political economy in capitalist society – a society in which the *effects* of class exploitation may be apparent in the lives of workers, but not the *form* of exploitation, nor its pervasive penetration of the whole fabric of society. Yet it remains true that even Marx's historical materialist analysis of

capitalism was never completed, or even advanced in properly
historical terms. The analysis of pre-capitalist societies – including the *history* of the transition to capitalism – was never even
attempted. The task of historical materialism still lies ahead: to
improve and extend the analysis of capitalist society, and to
make a comparable analysis for the rest of class history.

On the whole, this history will have little to do with Marx's
retrospective glances at the antecedents to the political economic
categories with which he was primarily concerned. In general,
Marx's specific suppositions can be expected to be proved
wrong. Yet it is not hard to perceive that his overall conception of
history will be vindicated. There is much that can be recovered
from the histories that have already been written. And already in
Thompson's and Brenner's works can be found that focus on the
concrete history of class relations and the balance of class
struggle which is essential to historical materialism. Particularly
in the contributions they have made to the *history* of the transition to capitalism, the leading edge of historical materialism
can be seen emerging from the heavy fog of 'Marxist theory'.

While a historical materialist interpretation of the French
Revolution can only truly follow from a great deal more work
upon the society that lay behind it – and not the society that lay
ahead – the present work would not be complete without some
effort to anticipate how the method outlined here might reveal a
structure of exploitive class relations in the ancien régime and
relate it to the political conflict of 'bourgeois' and 'aristocrats'.
The conclusion which follows will therefore offer a preliminary
historical synthesis, incorporating most of the data the revisionists have used to criticize the social interpretation. The
evidence clearly suggests that the Revolution was indeed the
direct result of the conflicts and contradictions generated by class
relations of exploitation in the ancien régime, though in a fundamentally different way than is usually associated with 'bourgeois
revolution'.

Notes

1. Karl Marx, *Economic and Philosophic Manuscripts of 1844, Collected
Works* vol. III, p. 298.
2. Ibid.
3. Ibid., pp. 304–6.
4. Ibid., p. 313.
5. Ibid.

6. Marx, 'Critical Marginal Notes on the Article "The King of Prussia and Social Reform. By a Prussian" ', *Collected Works* vol. III.

7. Hal Draper, *Karl Marx's Theory of Revolution*, vol. I, New York 1977, pp. 221–6.

8. Karl Marx and Frederick Engels, *The Holy Family, Collected Works* vol. IV, p. 37.

9. Marx and Engels, *The German Ideology, Parts I and III*, New York 1963.

10. Marx, *Grundrisse*, New York 1973, p. 106.

11. Marx, *The Poverty of Philosophy, Collected Works* vol. VI, p. 174.

12. Ibid., p. 197.

13. Marx, *Grundrisse*, p. 108.

14. Engels, 'Outlines of a Critique of Political Economy', *Collected Works* vol. III, pp. 430–31.

15. Thompson, 'The Poverty of Theory', in *The Poverty of Theory and Other Essays*, London 1978, pp. 249–62.

16. Engels, *The Peasants' War in Germany*, London 1956.

17. Marx–Engels, *German Ideology*, p. 7.

18. Ibid., p. 8.

19. Ibid., pp. 8–9.

20. Ronald Meek, *Social Science and the Ignoble Savage*, Cambridge 1976, pp. 70–71, quoting from Turgot's well-known letter to Madame de Graffigny, as cited in Chapter 3 above.

21. Marx–Engels, *The German Ideology*, p. 9.

22. T. B. Bottomore, *Classes in Modern Society*, New York 1966, pp. 21–2.

23. Marx–Engels, *The German Ideology*, pp. 26–7.

24. Ibid., p. 13.

25. Ibid., p. 18.

26. Ibid., p. 20, emphasis added.

27. Ibid., p. 21.

28. Ibid., p. 41.

29, Maurice Dobb, *Studies in the Development of Capitalism*, New York 1963; R. Hilton, P. Sweezy, M. Dobb, *et al.*, *The Transition from Feudalism to Capitalism*, London 1976.

30. Hilton, Dobb, Sweezy, *et al.*, *Transition*, pp. 49–50, 107–8.

31. The work of Lucio Colletti can be cited, particularly his essays 'Marxism as Sociology' and 'Bernstein and the Marxism of the Second International', both in Colletti, *From Rousseau to Lenin*, London 1972, and 'The Theory of the Crash', *Telos*, 13 (1972), reprinted in Bart Grahl and Paul Piccone, *Towards a New Marxism*, St Louis 1973. Raymond Williams's critical discussion of the major categories of Marxist analysis in *Marxism and Literature*, Oxford 1977, is particularly good. For an excellent discussion from a perspective that is more philosophical than Marxist, see Melvin Rader's *Marx's Interpretation of History*, New York 1979. For a direct confrontation of contemporary economic determinism, see Ellen Meiksins Wood, 'The Separation of the Economic and the Political in Capitalism', *New Left Review*, 127 (May 1981), 66–95.

32. G. A. Cohen, *Karl Marx's Theory of History: A Defense*, Oxford 1978; Marx, op. cit.

33. Marx, *Grundrisse*, p. 87.

34. Ibid., pp. 99–100.

35. Marx, *Contribution to the Critique of Political Economy*, Moscow 1970, pp. 60, 208; 51, 92.

36. Marx, *Capital* vol. I, Moscow 1954, p. 334.

37. Ibid., p. 339.
38. Ibid.
39. Ibid., p. 344.
40. Ibid.
41. Marx, *Grundrisse*, p. 103.
42. Marx, *Poverty of Philosophy*, p. 179.
43. Ibid., p. 186.
44. Wood, 'Separation', p. 71.
45. Ibid., p. 74.
46. Robert Brenner, 'On the Origins of Capitalist Development: A Critique of Neo-Smithian Marxism', *New Left Review*, 104 (1977).
47. Rader, *Marx's Interpretation*, p. 59.
48. Draper, *Marx's Theory*, II, p. 250.
49. See the works cited in note 31 above.
50. Thompson, 'Poverty of Theory', p. 250.
51. Ibid.
52. Colletti, 'Theory of the Crash', p. 187.
53. Marx, *Poverty of Philosophy*, p. 176.
54. Marx, *Capital* vol. III, p. 791.
55. Ibid., pp. 791–2.
56. For a discussion of Thompson's important but widely misunderstood ideas, see Ellen Wood's 'The Politics of Theory and the Concept of Class: E. P. Thompson and His Critics', *Studies in Political Economy*, 9 (1982), 45–75.
57. Thompson, 'Poverty of Theory', p. 306.
58. Ibid., p. 258.

Conclusion:
Towards a Marxist
Interpretation of the
French Revolution

Historical materialist analysis of the French Revolution must begin with an investigation of the fundamental structure of exploitive class relations in the ancien régime. It is the fundamental social relations which define the classes that must first be identified. Then, both the immediate social interests of these classes and the whole dynamic structure of exploitive relations must be related to the political conflicts that brought down the absolutist state and gave rise to the Revolution. This virtually necessitates an original analysis of the whole social order of the ancien régime, as well as confronting the lingering misconceptions of 'bourgeois revolution'. It will also mean dealing with the temptation to invest a few of the same old categories with new meaning.

The analysis which is called for must be so far-ranging, and synthesize such a wealth of historical evidence on the complex society of the ancien régime, that it cannot reasonably be undertaken here in any adequate detail. Yet it seems necessary to indicate at least the outlines of an analysis which would replace the social interpretation as an account of the Revolution in terms of *class*. What follows will therefore primarily be interpretive, based on a preliminary synthesis of much of the work which has contributed to or been inspired by the revisionist challenge, coupled with a comparison of development in English and French agrarian history. This conclusion is really no more than an anticipation of future work, offered here to demonstrate how the Revolution may be conceived to be a product of the exploitive relations of class society *without* being a bourgeois capitalist class revolution.

'Bourgeois Revolution' and the Ancien Régime

Class analyses of the French Revolution have always begun with the 'classes' – bourgeoisie and aristocracy – not with class *relations*. Then, once these classes have been identified as the principal historical actors in the Revolution, it is assumed that nascent capitalism, early capitalism, a period of the transition, or whatever can be read back into the ancien régime – and perhaps a few obvious social relations may be identified as 'corresponding' to the classes. Because these classes have for so long been accepted as *given*, without first considering their actual basis in the class relations of the ancien régime, it may be valuable once again to underscore the arguments presented in previous chapters *against* describing the nobility and the bourgeoisie as the fundamentally opposed social classes of the Revolution.

The bourgeoisie certainly was not a capitalist class. Lawyers and owners of non-noble state offices – notaries, bailiffs, lower-ranking magistrates, etc. – along with the far less numerous private professionals, together formed the largest group within the bourgeoisie.[1] They may have been as much as 60 percent of the whole; they certainly were not much less than a majority. The next largest group, at about one-third of the total, were the rentiers, who lived off the income from their property. Of the remainder who were engaged in commerce or industry at all, the overwhelming majority were merchants, eager to acquire enough wealth to buy land and a dignified, and preferably ennobling, office.

The most important forms of property for the bourgeoisie were land (small- to medium-sized plots let to peasants for rent and provisions, for the most part), state offices (for sale on an open market at prices that fluctuated over time), and *rentes* (virtually permanent loans or private debentures that returned fixed and low rates of interest).[2] The bourgeoisie were understood to be those persons not having noble status who owned sufficient property – or in rare and usually marginal cases, had sufficient 'talent' – not to be obliged to engage in demeaning manual labor (which included retail trade). There simply were no capitalist relations – no appropriation of *surplus-value*, as opposed to mere commercial profit making – that can be attributed to the bourgeoisie, not even that supposed 'agrarian capitalism' which has been claimed for the relations between seigneurs and their tenant farmers.

Property relations were, in the usual Marxist sense, 'bourgeois', in that property was absolute and fully alienable (with insignificant exceptions in a few areas), and contractual relations were the norm, fully codified and protected in law. Yet all this was no less true for the property of the nobility. Indeed there was no differentiation in the forms of property of nobles and bourgeois at all. Nobles lost their status if they engaged in trade, but their investment in trade or industry on a large enough scale (or well enough disguised) was acceptable and widespread (in fact heavy industry was virtually a preserve of the nobility). All land and forms of property – seigneuries and other 'fiefs' or *roturier* parcels, feudal dues or *rentes*, noble or *roturier* offices – were first and foremost *property* and subject to ownership by persons of *either* noble or *roturier* status. A bourgeois might own a seigneurie, whose feudal dues he chose to lease to a noble, who in turn owned an allodial 'peasant' property. If few seigneuries were actually owned by bourgeois, it was because few of those able to afford a great estate retained bourgeois status.

In fact no social boundary at all existed between the bourgeoisie and the nobility except for noble status itself, and that was readily acquired through purchase of a noble office. Some offices conferred immediate and fully inheritable nobility; others conferred qualified degrees of nobility that matured with time (or death in office). All were sources of income as well as status, and many were actually legitimate careers. The great majority of nobles could trace their nobility no farther than to their grandfathers, and there were many *anobli* whose statuses were unsecured or still 'raw'.[3]

These were not the transient features of a society on the brink of collapse, but the enduring and characteristic social relations of the absolutist regime. As for the need to break 'feudal fetters', it should be noted that 'bourgeois' patterns of efficient estate management had become widespread in the nobility, even among the great houses of 'ancient' nobility. French state administration had already been 'rationalized' in significant ways, and it worked tolerably well in everything except the public fisc. Indeed, state finances were handled well, given their decentralized basis and the policy of pursuing bankrupting wars.[4] With regard to further state reforms, the monarchy was itself the chief proponent.

Many of the Enlightenment's basic ideals were widely

accepted by the nobility, and the most prominent advocates of political and economic liberalism were high-ranking nobles. Opposition to the absolutist monarchy actually originated among the great nobility, while the leaders of the Revolution were quite typical of the bourgeoisie in that they were lawyers, officials, and professionals, rather than men of commerce and industry. On the whole, then, there is no evidence to support any aspect of the 'theory' of bourgeois revolution except that, in some sense, the leadership of the Revolution came to rest with the bourgeoisie, and that they identified their opponents as the aristocracy.

Yet between an understandable reluctance simply to break with bourgeois revolution, and the inclination of those consider-ing the rise of capitalism in France to follow Marx, and find parallels with Britain, it is difficult to leave the matter at that. It has been asked if, in so far as the typical members of the bour-geoisie were not capitalist, some other group might not be identi-fied that was? Or whether there might not in fact be some sense in which capitalism was at least 'emerging' in the ancien régime?

Capitalism and the Ancien Régime

When people speak of emerging capitalism – as has been seen in earlier discussion of 'the transition' – they often seem to mean that capitalism was somehow already present in the interstices of its predecessor, without reference to a dynamic of *class relations* leading to the emergence of a new, capitalist organization of production. Capitalism does not seem to emerge out of class relations at all. Instead, capitalist class relations appear to emerge out of some disembodied pre-existing capitalism – some-times neatly described as 'commercial capitalism' – perhaps as a result of the 'natural' law of progress and technological improve-ment. In this sense, the notion of emerging capitalism is opposed to historical materialism and its essential conception of history as the *development of class relations*.

If the fundamental exploitive class relations of capitalism can simply be said to 'emerge', then the claims of bourgeois-liberal ideology have been conceded from the start: economic relations naturally develop out of production in general, private property is to be presumed, and 'social problems' are only an unfortunate byproduct of progress. If capitalism can simply be 'emerging', without reference to a dynamic of class relations giving rise to it, then the historical materialist overview of developing class society goes out the door. Capitalism can, of course, be said to be emerging from *something*; but in the absence of any prior historical materialist analysis that actually leads to this conclusion, this is simply to re-import the teleological perspective of 'the transition'. From the point of view of historical interpretation, it is a matter of the utmost importance whether or not some set of social relations in the ancien régime were, or verged on being, *capitalist*. It is not a matter to be settled superficially.

In recent years, Marxists have taken to heart the idea that industrial enterprise cannot simply be equated with capitalism, and even more significantly, that capitalism does not only mean industry. It has become widely accepted that agrarian capitalism preceded industrial capitalism – and specifically that British industrial capitalism developed upon the social framework created by the agrarian capitalism of the English gentry and tenant-farmers. This idea has followed from Dobb's position in the original transition debate that capitalism must have developed through an *internal* dynamic of class society. It has since found its way into most discussion of the origins of capitalism, including both the structuralist conception of the articulation of modes of production, and Soboul's suggestion that French 'kulak'-type capitalism lay behind the Revolution. In fact, recent discussion of the emergence of capitalism in France has almost entirely focused on agriculture: either on the process of transforming feudal ground-rents into capitalist rent, or on the kulak-type *laboureur* tenant-farmers. From either point of view, the heartland of this supposed agrarian capitalism has been located in the Paris basin. If, therefore, capitalism can be said to have existed, or to have been emerging, anywhere in the ancien régime at all, the test must be the tenant-farming of the Paris basin.

The leasing of farms at money rents was far from peculiar to this region – it was in fact found nearly everywhere in the ancien régime, with a wide range of variance in local frequency. Near Paris, however, not only were farms rented on short-term (but not annual) money rents, but the farms were large and relatively consolidated; they were worked by wealthy tenant-farmers with hired labor; production was specialized in grain for the Paris market; the majority of rural inhabitants were very nearly landless; and the common wastes of the region had virtually disappeared through the efforts of the seigneurs. In short, in innumerable superficial ways, agrarian production in the Paris basin *appears* to have been capitalist.[5]

This brings us back to the work of Gilles Postel-Vinay. For whereas Pierre-Philippe Rey's work was no more than a theoretical reconstruction of the transition, based entirely on Marx's *Capital*, Postel-Vinay's work is based on original historical research, and appears to reveal the actual transition from feudal to capitalist social relations of production in agriculture during the ancien régime. Since his theoretical perspective has been taken directly from Rey, it is only because of the seeming plausibility and detail of the historical analysis he offers that it must be given further consideration – on the chance that *despite* its theoretical premises it might in fact have uncovered capitalist agriculture in eighteenth-century France.[6]

Postel-Vinay's stated purpose is to establish that the development of capitalism in agriculture is a historically specific process, and he challenges the concept of a 'classic' path of agricultural development based on the inexorable and uniquely successful growth of large-scale capitalist farming. The survival of a large *peasant* sphere of production in France has often been recognized in its relation to the development of capitalism. Postel-Vinay's intention is to examine the actual historical development of large-scale agriculture in the Paris basin, hoping to show that it too has followed a specifically determined path, based on a specific form of articulation of the capitalist mode of production in a specific developed context of the feudal mode of production.

Rey's work had been intended to establish that the articulation of the capitalist mode of production always preserves essential aspects of the pre-existing mode during the process of transition. There is no mistaking that Rey is concerned with *the* transition – he is not absolutely clear about the role of the non-agrarian capitalists to which he alludes, but it is certain that agrarian capitalists and landlords figure centrally in the transition to a genuinely capitalist society. Postel-Vinay, however, is not concerned with the transition as such, but with the development of agricultural capitalism. In referring so definitively to Rey concerning the articulation of modes of production, he seemingly commits himself to situating his work in the general transition to capitalism. In fact, however, he is inclined not merely to focus on agriculture, but even to separate it from the general development of capitalism. This introduces an underlying theoretical incoherence to his account, which is not, however, immediately apparent from its historical presentation.

Postel-Vinay focuses on the patterns of rent relations around Soissons between the sixteenth and twentieth centuries, and particularly differentiates between the levels of rent paid by poor peasants, middling peasants, and the tenants of the large farms. Briefly, as far as concerns the question of capitalism in the ancien régime, he argues that there was a change in rent relations in the eighteenth century that corresponds to a dramatic reversal in dominance and the ascendancy of capitalism over the feudal mode of production. He finds that up to the end of the seventeenth century, a general pattern of heavy rent increases fell proportionally on all sectors of the peasantry, large tenant-farmers included.[7] Indeed, towards the end of the century, the burden on tenant-farmers became such that they found it difficult to sustain their positions, and many faced ruin; the seigneurs frequently forgave rent arrears in order to retain their farmers, and sometimes resorted to direct management of their estates due to the difficulty of finding viable farmers.

In the eighteenth century, however, the tenant-farmers were able to prevent the rate of their rents from being increased so rapidly as the rents on all the rest of the peasantry.[8] Postel-Vinay argues that they accomplished this in part through intimidation and violent resistance, though he claims that the *fermiers* as a result found that their contradictions with the landowners – with whom their rent relations now represented a sharing of surplus-value, instead of direct exploitation – were reduced to a merely secondary level (just as Rey had suggested). The ever-increasing burden of rents on the poor peasantry, meanwhile, increasingly forced them to sell their labor to the tenant-farmers – without, however, entirely dispossessing them. (Typically, they owned a scrap of land, and rented a bit more.) The middle peasants were progressively reduced to the status of the poor peasants.

According to Postel-Vinay, this process corresponds to the conjunction of the feudal and capitalist modes of production in a specific form of articulation – one which leads to capitalist relations of the sharing of surplus-value produced on large farms, but which also leads to a *dependent* labor force, and which blocks the operation of fully commodified labor-power. In this regard, Postel-Vinay not merely recognizes that this form of agricultural capitalism is specifically quite different from that which arose in England, but also argues that it does not correspond to the full realization of the capitalist mode of production in agriculture (which would require the commodification of labor-power).[9] Moreover, precisely because the labor force is kept dependent on its own subsistence production instead of being fully proletarianized, the actual material processes of production are blocked from technological progress, and virtually the whole body of traditional peasant community practices, rights, and obligations remain in force.[10]

The remainder of the book follows the development of this specific agricultural formation, particularly in the limitations it continues to reveal. Much of what Postel-Vinay has to say throughout the book adds to an appreciation of the specific historical development of this agrarian capitalist sector. The essential question remains, however: has he actually revealed the specific form of the existence of *capitalism* in the ancien régime?

The difference between Postel-Vinay's argument and Rey's is striking, although ironically neither of them recognizes it. Yet there is no question that what Postel-Vinay has described is fundamentally different from the model of transition which Rey originally proposed for England. There, the transformation of the agricultural sector through articulation of the capitalist mode of production in conjunction with the internal logic of rent was argued to be *central* to the indigenous transition to capitalism. What Postel-Vinay has described seems instead to correspond to an articulation of capitalism from *outside*, since the development of capitalism in agriculture remains partial and blocked. The only sense which can be made of this as the transition to capitalism in France is if in fact the real achievement of the capitalist mode of production were occurring in non-agricultural sectors. Postel-Vinay does not explicitly argue for this, but he does refer to the existence of *urban capitalism* in even the seventeenth century, when capitalism was supposed to be completely blocked in the countryside.[11] He offers, however, neither evidence nor rationale for the existence of this highly problematic 'urban capitalism'.

Postel-Vinay clearly must be arguing for a real transition to capitalism, since despite the historically specific and limited character of the agrarian capitalism he describes, he explicitly attributes the production and distribution of *surplus-value* to the capitalist farms. Also, like Rey, he attributes the Revolution to the uniting of *all* capitalists to force a resolution of their 'secondary' contradiction with the landowners. Because, unlike England, this transition cannot be springing primarily from the logic of the agricultural sector – or there would be no basis for a real transition – we are implicitly asked to accept that it is occurring elsewhere. It is, of course, precisely because no other capitalist sector has been found that attention has been focused on agriculture in the first place, so this whole analysis simply gives another spin to the circular logic of 'the transition'.

Using Rey as a theoretical guide, Postel-Vinay has looked for a convergence in interest between capitalist farmers and seigneurial landowners. Apparently finding one in the relatively lower rents paid by tenant-farmers over most of the eighteenth century, he simply attributes this to the transition to capitalism. (The two subsequent periods when these 'capitalist' rents rise *faster* than peasant rents, he attributes to the development of 'internal contradictions'.) Yet, even if the completely circular logic of this analysis and the absence of the necessary capitalist sectors could be ignored, what does this 'transition' in agriculture really turn out to be?

In the first place, substantial commercial production on the large farms was in existence long before the eighteenth century, and according to Postel-Vinay it was essentially capitalist in form, but blocked from realization. In fact, however, all that was blocking it appears to have been the high rents charged the farmers. Once the tenant-farmers applied sufficient pressure to hold their rents down, feudalism became capitalism (and those same rents ceased to be exploitive and became instead distributional). Clearly, in this view, capitalist agricultural relations were already fully developed in the ancien régime in the form of commercial tenant-farming based on hired peasant labor – which had in fact existed since before the fourteenth century! It needed only for its fetters to be burst, and in the event the 'capitalist' farmers did not even need a revolution to accomplish that.

In the second place, nowhere in his analysis does Postel-Vinay actually examine the social relations of production of the hired farm workers to show that they are capitalist. He simply assumes that they are producers of surplus-value because they are paid. There is no change in social relations between the poor peasants and the *fermiers* they work for at the moment of 'transition' – all that happens is that, as rents continue to rise, more peasants are forced into paid labor in addition to their subsistence farming. Postel-Vinay is quite explicit that the organization of production itself was essentially unaffected. This contrasts dramatically with the systematic imposition of new forms of work-discipline that E. P. Thompson shows emerged in English agrarian capitalism as early as the mid seventeenth century, as part of the continuous development of capitalist social relations that laid the groundwork for capitalist industrial revolution.[12] According to Postel-Vinay, however, poor peasants who remained in precisely the same relationship to the tenant-farmers that their ancestors had for centuries suddenly became producers of surplus-value without *any* basic change in their class relations of production.

In short, what Postel-Vinay has done is simply to identify the specific form of development for agrarian capitalism in the Paris basin as its peasant-based commercial grain production – which had grown, but was little changed, since its origins in the medieval period. He attributes the historic limitations of large-scale farming in France to this specific form, so he can hardly argue that it is the driving force of capitalist transition. Any fundamental changes in the actual relations of production on the farms must be dated to before the fourteenth century, yet it is argued that agrarian capitalism definitely did *not* exist as late as the end of the seventeenth century. The only evidence put forward to support a subsequent transition in the eighteenth century is the relative success of tenant-farmers, at the center of regional commercial production, in limiting their rent increases to a level that gave them a share in the general prosperity enjoyed by merchants and landowners during a long period of commercial growth.

What Postel-Vinay has in fact produced is a history of *commercial grain production* in the Paris basin that reveals a truly remarkable continuity between the sixteenth and twentieth centuries. Clearly, at some point in this history, it must in some sense have become a sector of capitalist agriculture, since France has certainly become a capitalist society. Yet it is equally clear that this transformation did not spring from any internal dynamic, and that it presumably follows instead from the development of capitalist industry – quite unlike the sequence of development in Britain. If this is the case, what possible grounds can there be for identifying this transition at any time before the Revolution? There is nothing in Postel-Vinay's account which requires recognition of anything beyond commercial production, and every indication that this commercial production continued to be markedly different from capitalism long after the Revolution had passed.

In purely superficial terms, it might appear that the social forms of capitalism existed in the tenant-farming of the Paris basin: the landlord/tenant-farmer/wage-labor structure seems comparable to that of agrarian capitalism in England. Yet the differences are fundamental when viewed in a fully historical perspective. The fact that French commercial agriculture was notoriously non-dynamic is merely indicative of a far more important absence of fundamental transformation in the basic relations and organization of production. As Postel-Vinay himself argues, French agriculture was to an astonishing extent untouched by the revolutionary techniques of improved farming which had swept England over the previous century or century and a half. Indeed, ignoring the new implements and crops of the agricultural revolution, not even the most important techniques that dated back centuries in English practice – particularly convertible, or up-and-down husbandry – were employed in France, except as the special projects of Anglophile agronomists.[13]

It is not, of course, that techniques themselves in any sense create or embody capitalism. Nor that the French farmers lacked entrepreneurial spirit: for aggressive commercial profit making, shrewd bargaining over rents, careful accounts, and specialized production of wheat have all made it easy for non-Marxists to refer to this agriculture as 'capitalist'. The significant point is that nowhere in the ancien régime was agricultural production caught up in the specific logic of capitalist accumulation. Nowhere was there the necessary capitalist drive to increase productivity through control over the labor process and constant technological improvement – which is the specific characteristic of capitalist appropriation through the extraction of relative surplus-value. This lack of dynamic growth reflects the restriction of agrarian production and surplus extraction to a sphere of traditional peasant production which *included* commercial farming, but which stood in opposition to the transformation of productive practices by the complete mastery of capital over producers selling their commodified labor-power. For a host of specific historical reasons that are mostly beyond the scope of the present work (having to do with basic differences in class relations between England and France in the *medieval* period) agrarian production in France remained bound by the considerations and social relations of peasant community reproduction – even in production under tenant farmers on consolidated seigneurial farms.

Again, it is not that French capitalism was emerging, but was as yet weak or inexperienced, or that it was faced with the fetters of aristocratic class society. Commercial tenant-farming had quite as long a history in France as in England, but the histories diverged dramatically. In England, tenant-farming of all forms occurred on land which the landlord could by right enclose. Enclosures, whether of domainal lands, the manorial wastes, or open-field strips by common assent – and whether originally to create manorial farms, or later to create sheep runs, or finally to establish convertible husbandry – always involved the complete subtraction of that land from the peasant sphere of production. This implied the freedom to introduce and organize whatever production the farmer saw fit. English tenant-farmers were absolute masters over the production process (subject to the good repair clauses and occasional convenants in their leases) in a way that they never were in France. This is a basic manifestation of the fundamentally different histories of agrarian class relations in the two countries.

As farmers prospered, rents were increased and more land was enclosed. English customary tenants never acquired the title to their lands that French peasants had, nor did their rights to the practices of the 'commons' (gleanage, etc.) extend to the farms. English peasants were not kept in place to be 'squeezed' by rents; if more was to be had through enclosure, then they were evicted, or forced to compete in the ever more competitive marketplace. As the middling sort of peasants and yeomen increasingly failed, except for those who themselves became successful farmers, the country population was increasingly divided into the characteristic wealthy landowners, capitalist tenant-farmers, and rural working class of agrarian capitalism.

It was not French property law that hindered such a pattern of development, but the continued focus of surplus extraction in the *ancien régime* on the exploitation of the peasant *community*, of which the *laboureur* was in a sense a specialized member. The *laboureur* functioned as a leader of the local peasant community; often at odds with it, he was ever a part of the whole. The *laboureurs* organized production on the seigneurial farms for the landowners, but this production always remained bound by the collective existence and social reproduction of the entire peasant community. The farm workers themselves remained peasants, producing their own subsistence on land for which they also had to pay landowners exploitive rents. As Postel-Vinay argues, this underlying structure of exploitation and subsistence production required maintenance of the traditional structure of peasant rights, obligations, and practices.

Why is it that French surplus extraction remained bound to such an undynamic system of production? All across the open-field grain region of France, the common wastes had been under attack from encroaching landowners for generations, and in the Paris basin they had all but disappeared. The fields were 'open', but the farms were consolidated; there was no *compulsory* rotation of specific fields at given times, and farmers were in many respects formally free to make decisions regarding production. Thus, despite the open-field absence of permanent hedges and fences, many of the advantages of 'enclosure' would seem to have pertained. Yet written into every farm lease, over the whole history of the ancien régime, with no apparent opposition or non-compliance, was the guarantee that three-field rotation, with its regular one winter in three of fallow, would be scrupulously observed.

Agronomists such as Arthur Young were wholly taken aback by this apparent backwardness. Replacing three-field rotation with convertible husbandry was recognized as the crucial first step of improved farming, leading to *enormously* increased yields. Convertible husbandry allowed the all-important increase in livestock that produced the quantities of manure required for greater yields. French livestock was recognized to be notoriously inadequate for modern farming requirements. Yet instead of treating manure as a private resource, the practice of *vaine pâture* – pasturing village livestock in common herds on each property owner's fallow land in succession – was universal. Also universal were the 'commons' rights of gleanage, and gathering straw off the seigneurial farm. These practices were essential to the peasant community because of the shortage of wastes. By universal convention, throughout all the open-field regions where commercial tenant-farming was predominant, convertible husbandry was a social and contractual (but not *legal*) impossibility. On the one hand, peasants had won, and fought to preserve, certain rights important to their collective existence; on the other hand, the system of surplus extraction conformed to and reinforced the specific characteristics of this social reproduction.

Increased surplus extraction was achieved in England by adoption of social relations predicated upon a higher achievement of the social mastery of property – expressed in the ultimate mastery of the lord, and the immediate mastery of the tenant-farmer over the means of production. Development took the specific form of ever-intensifying production, through the coupling of capitalist farmers who exercised absolute control over the means and processes of production with property owners who exacted reasonable, but growing levels of rent – rents which presumed the increasing levels of productivity. Peasant small producers became *irrelevant* to the extraction of surplus, and they were either expropriated outright, or abandoned to the inevitably destructive forces of market competition. In France, however, the extraction of rent did not encourage, or even allow, innovation. It simply *squeezed* the peasant community when population increased and rents and prices were bid up. Agrarian relations as a whole – especially as they affected the state, the significance of which will be seen shortly – simply reinforced the fundamental structure of peasant demography.

A really adequate discussion of the comparative development of commercial agriculture in England and France would require close historical analysis of their respective structures of social relations from the thirteenth to the eighteenth centuries, and this analysis can be carried no further at this point. Very much the same argument as to these contrasts, however, has been made by Robert Brenner, with more stress on the *scale* of farms than on specific 'improved' farming practices, as a manifestation of the use of class power in England to transform the peasant structure of production.[14] The essential point remains that precisely in what has been supposed to be the heartland of French capitalism, the social relations reveal a profound departure from that line of development which produced capitalism in England. French commercial agriculture was highly developed, but nothing in its structure showed any of the characteristic internal dynamism and that dissolution of traditional relations of production which is fundamental to capitalism. The ancien régime, then, shows no sign of either developed capitalism or its emergence. Tenant-farming and wage-labor had changed little since the crisis of the fourteenth century, despite all the demographic cycles of expansion and contraction; whereas capitalism had totally transformed the agriculture of England. Agriculture would *remain* largely unchanged long after the Revolution, until after the substantial development of capitalist industry.

This historical view of the dynamic of capitalist development underscores the mistake of identifying a simple social relationship of production, even one so specific as wage-labor, with the specific exploitive relationship of capitalism. Wage-labor in agriculture has been common throughout Western history. Usually it has been an adjunct to peasant production: often a great many peasants would have been unable to survive without this employment, and some have had little else. In itself, increasing the degree of dependence on wage-labor, or even the numbers dependent upon it, is not enough to change the basic character of peasant production, or introduce the dynamic logic of the capital accumulation and its expanded reproduction through intensified production. What is required for capitalism is not merely wage-labor, but a system entirely structured about commodity production as the self-expansion of capital through the reduction of labor to *labor-power* – a commodity wholly abstracted from the community of human experience, and subjected absolutely to the dictates of capital, as another factor of production. French farm hands were peasants, employed in peasant production. English farm hands were increasingly subjected to a radically different system of production – intrinsically structured as a process of capital accumulation – as if they were living machines.

Class Relations in the Ancien Régime

If even the production of grain for Paris was not capitalist, then the whole structure of surplus production and extraction throughout the ancien régime certainly was not. The specific forms of agrarian class relations varied widely over France. Aside from the small and recently acquired French Flanders, whose agriculture had little to do with the ancien régime as such, France was composed of three major agrarian zones, with innumerable further variations.[15] Across the north was the belt of open-field grain production; the west and center were characterized by the *bocage* country of hedged tracts of fields and far more extensive wastes; the Midi saw varieties of light and extensive farming well adapted to the arid climate. If the peasant community was intact even in the open-field regions, the peasant household was everywhere else the preponderant basis of production.

The great majority of peasants were landowners, yet there was only a minority who had near enough land to subsist from it – and they for the most part lacked sufficient livestock. Only a very small minority of well-to-do peasants – the *laboureurs* – had sufficient land and livestock to be truly independent. As a result, peasants everywhere engaged in leasing land: tiny parcels; small plots to combine with an inadequate patrimony; whole units of production to provide for family subsistence; additional fields to increase the yields of a well-to-do household; or large tenant-farms to operate commercially. The money-lease – a standard 'bourgeois' private contract, essentially the same as found in England – was virtually universal in the open-field regions and was increasingly widespread elsewhere. There was also a wide range of contractual sharecropping agreements, particularly typical of the west and center. A variety of relatively rare 'feudal' tenures were found throughout the country, in some cases corresponding to the abject misery of the otherwise propertyless, and in other cases to fairly prosperous tenancies of substantial units of production. In certain areas it was also common for peasants to lease livestock, usually through a sharecropping agreement with bourgeois owners.

The essential form of surplus was, then, *rent* – extracted from peasant producers in a variety of ways which reflected the divergences of climate and social history. These divergences were not 'natural' developments, however, but the product of class struggle in all its forms – the ravages of war, defense of the peasant community, competition resulting from population growth, the concentration of class power near the capital, etc. The basic structure of rent was based on what Marxists have called 'bourgeois' property rights: rents associated with the economically *contractual* tenancy of property – for in even the rare cases of onerously 'feudal' properties, the peasants were *personally* quite free.

To this basic structure must be added the surviving structure of 'feudal' rents and dues. These had become merely different forms of property – additional sources of income with no intrinsic connection to noble status, that were alienable from possession of the land to which they nominally were attached. These ranged in total impact from a fairly light surcharge on the basic contractual rents, to a major component of the income of landed property in some of the more 'backward' areas. The overall structure of rents was therefore extraordinarily varied and complex. What all these rents had in common was that they were fundamentally different from the specific structure of true feudal *manorialism*, which had passed from the scene before the fourteenth century, yet were entirely unrelated to the distribution of *surplus-value* through capitalist rent that characterized contemporary English agriculture.

This extraction of rent through the various forms of private property was the most widespread and fundamental form of surplus appropriation in the ancien régime. Agriculture was the overwhelmingly predominant sector of social production. Most of the surplus distributed through commercial profits was directly agricultural in origin – not only the grain trade, but also the island trade and the wine trade; and that surplus which was produced and extracted through manufacturers essentially conformed to this general commercial agrarian structure. It certainly was no more capitalist in character than the surplus produced in Roman manufactures.

This fundamental basis of social surplus in agrarian production – drawn off in the form of rent and in turn supporting trade and manufactures – is perfectly reflected in the Physiocratic conception that agriculture was the *unique* source of wealth. The concept was also accepted by Turgot, who recognized the differentiation of 'capitalist Entrepreneurs and ordinary Workmen' in industry, but described them as *together* constituting a 'stipendiary Class' who were ultimately dependent upon the truly *productive* 'Cultivators', and the 'Proprietors' (who took the whole social surplus in the form of rent).[16] (At very nearly the same time, of course, Adam Smith conceived that labor produced value in every field of production, and though writing of an overwhelmingly *agrarian* capitalist society, he described the all-important division of labor in terms of the increased productivity and improved technique of the workshop.)

Private rent, however, was not the only form of agrarian surplus extraction in the ancien régime. An enormous edifice of state offices and jurisprudence, a huge military, and the powerful Gallic Church, all rested upon the further extraction of surplus from peasants through taxes, fees, and tithes. Of course the fact that these many official positions were themselves *property*, bought and sold on the open market (or virtually property in the cases of the Church and private lawyers) simply underscores the extent to which this surplus extraction was another, historically specific, sort of 'rent'. Purchase of an office was an *investment* in a career – or in some cases simply in noble status – for which it was not difficult to secure loans, and by which an 'honorable' income was obtained. Just as the bourgeoisie and the nobility *both* owned the properties rented by peasants, so offices belonged to both bourgeois and nobles. Perhaps a majority of the bourgeoisie either owned state offices – from local notaries and bailiffs, to subaltern military officers, to senior provincial magistrates – or were similarly associated with the processes and revenues of the state through one of the many grades of the legal profession.

Noble offices were at once the means by which large numbers of the wealthiest, most successful, and/or best-connected bourgeois attained noble status for themselves and their families, and also the field of competition for ambitious nobles – eager to increase their social standing and with it the prospects of auspicious marriages, advantageous social connections, or royal favor. Through the extension of administration, the munificence of the royal court, and the proliferation of sinecures, the state had become a central nexus of surplus extraction on a grand scale. Commerce was the primary route by which sufficient wealth could be acquired for a bourgeois to enter the nobility, but aside from land itself, the state was the real locus of bourgeois social interest. Among nobles and the *anobli*, at the same time, differential access to surplus extraction through the careers and favors of the state was the principal means, directly or indirectly, of increasing wealth and achieving social advancement.

Both bourgeois and nobles, then, shared in the essential social relations of property ownership and state office which were the fundamental forms of surplus extraction in the ancien régime. The very acquisition of noble status was itself a function of these relations, and commercial enterprise was primarily a means of acquiring the wealth for landed property and office – only the very few 'international' merchant families of the ports remained bourgeois or stayed in commerce after becoming rich. It is clear, then, that if landed property and state office were the joint basis of class relations of exploitation in the ancien régime, the bourgeoisie and the nobility *together* made up its ruling class.

Too often it is forgotten that within a ruling class the range of wealth and social power is typically very great: even today, one does not have to be a Rockefeller to be a capitalist. Equally often are forgotten the real tensions, divisions, and conflicts with which a ruling class may be marked. Much as poor knights and great kings who were frequently at war were all together the members of a feudal ruling class, so both the great nobles of the realm and petty legal officials were comprised by the ruling class of the ancien régime.

Class Interest in the French Revolution

What, then, was the social basis for the French Revolution? If it was not a conflict between a declining feudal class and a rising capitalist class, if there was no fundamental social division between the forms of property and economic interests of the bourgeoisie and nobility, was the Revolution simply a political contest between rival factions of a single 'elite'? Are 'bourgeois' and 'aristocrat' – and even 'sans-culotte' – in fact no more than *political categories*, as Cobban argued? Of course not. The

French Revolution was a specific product of the class relations of the ancien régime, *directly* related to fundamental issues of surplus extraction.

There has always been an important element of truth in the 'social interpretation' of the French Revolution; otherwise it could hardly have persuaded such a wide range of historians for so long. The conflict between 'bourgeoisie' and 'aristocracy' was the essential core of that interpretation, a confrontation which was first defined by the revolutionaries themselves, and which even Cobban saw no grounds for challenging. The great weakness of the revisionist analyses has been precisely that they have been unable to account for this real and virulent conflict.[17]

The general character of the bourgeoisie has been broadly sketched above, and it corresponds both to a real social category of the ancien régime (but not a separate class!) and to the 'political' category of the revolution. The bourgeois revolutionaries, in both the great national assemblies and the municipal governments across France, in the Jacobin clubs and the National Guard, were property owners, office holders, and lawyers. Not all the 'bourgeoisie' in the period of the Revolution had been bourgeois *roturiers* in the ancien régime, however; for with the Revolution had come a polarization between 'bourgeois' and 'aristocratic' ideologies which forced a choosing of sides, or a careful low profile. This was particularly true for the *anobli*, of course. Even members of the oldest and wealthiest noble families chose to stand with the bourgeoisie and the prospect of liberalism; shorn of their privileged status, they differed from other bourgeois only in the magnitude of their possessions. The bourgeoisie was precisely the ruling class of property and state office *without* the special privileges of noble status.

What was the aristocracy then? In the context of the Revolution, of course, it was the section of the ruling class *standing for* the privileges of nobility, a political position to which even *roturiers* could adhere. Yet 'aristocracy' had a real meaning which pre-dated the Revolution, a meaning which did not simply coincide with noble status. It referred, of course, to the highest and most exclusive inner circles of the nobility.

Among the aristocracy must first be included the immediate royal family, the Princes of the Blood, the Peers of France, the highest ranks within the Church, and the Court nobility. Then there were perhaps a few hundred houses of 'ancient' nobility, who by preserving and renewing inherited wealth, and carefully cultivating connections, had managed to maintain or restore their reputation – and the prospect of royal favor. The magistrates of the Paris *parlement* also ranked high among the aristocracy: if most enjoyed noble status of comparatively recent vintage, they all boasted the enormous wealth and good reputation necessary to purchase the supreme venal offices in the land.[18]

Enjoying somewhat lesser status, but generally recognized to be arriving as aristocrats, were the great noble financiers: the nobility of the tax farm and the other royal fiscal offices. Nomination to the ranks of the *Fermiers-Généraux*, in fact, was generally a form of co-optation – it was a royal favor that bestowed very great wealth, noble status, and entry to the aristocracy. Sons of the *fermiers* usually purchased magistracies or other positions more appropriate to the new family status. The entire financial administration, in fact, served as a means of pumping surplus directly into the aristocracy – to the profit not only of the financiers, but also of the many other artistocrats who lent at interest the money needed to advance the state funds.

Besides this great national aristocracy, there were of course the provincial aristocracies. These nobles were also truly rich, if not so rich, and they tended to enjoy multiple claims to aristocratic status. Provincial *parlementaires*, for example, usually belonged to the richest houses of the province, and enjoyed nobility of much greater lineage than the recently ennobled, but in turn richer, families of the *parlement* of Paris. Provincial aristocrats rarely advanced to national rank, though Turgot came from an old and respected Norman family, and Montesquieu was a president of the *parlement* of Bordeaux.

The ranks of the great nobility, then, formed an informal and co-optative but nonetheless real *aristocracy* of the best-connected and wealthiest members of the ruling class. Even including the whole of provincial aristocracies, however, this aristocracy constituted only a small minority among the hundreds of thousands of nobles. What particularly distinguished them was precisely what Sieyès pointed to in criticizing the aristocracy: they monopolized 'all the best posts'. The aristocracy enjoyed privileged access to royal favor and the chief offices of Church and state. They were at once the greatest property owners and the pre-eminent beneficiaries of the surplus extractive powers of the state. To be close to the aristocracy, and eventually to be co-opted into it, was the essential goal of the ambitious. Aristocrats embodied the whole of the political life of the ancien régime – both administering the royal state, and contending with it for power.

As previously noted, in the political ideology of the ancien régime there were two basic positions: that of aristocrats opposed to royal power, and that of the aristocratic supporters of absolutism.[19] Just as the former position became codified in the terms of the Enlightenment as an aristocratic *constitutionalism* that sought to offset royal power (as most notably expressed in *The Spirit of the Laws*), so the latter became associated with 'enlightened' progressive state policies, and eventually with liberal constitutionalism. So it happened that, in 1787, the chief ministers of France attempted to put through a far-ranging program of political and fiscal reforms, only to be opposed and eventually defeated by a coalition of aristocratic constitutionalists and liberal aristocrats.

For the liberals, the intention was to replace absolutism with a British-style constitutional monarchy. For the remainder of the aristocracy, however, the purpose was to 'repossess' the powers of the state. In limiting the absolute monarchy, the conservative aristocrats sought to arrogate to themselves – through traditional political forms which acknowledged their status – additional privileged access to state power. This naturally had important implications with regard to the major surplus extractive functions of state: high civil and military offices, the administration of taxes, and the network of co-optative patronage and favor.

These two great aristocratic positions were of course mutually exclusive, despite having in common a desire to end absolutism. And so, in September 1788, the aristocratic coalition which had brought about the surrender of the monarchy – a coalition in which the bourgeoisie had played virtually no role, aside from the legal professionals in the cities of the *parlements* – suddenly split apart over whether or not the Estates General were to be called following the procedures of 1614.[20] If so, then the privileged Estates of the Church and nobility would be both twice as numerous and, in voting by order rather than by head, possessed of formal state dominance.

The minority of liberal aristocrats who looked to emulate Britain were determined not to let the Paris *parlement* have the last say on the calling of the Estates. Sponsoring 'patriot' pamphleteers, groups such as the Committee of Thirty publicized the fact that the bourgeoisie would be denied effective political voice in the new constitution if the aristocrats had their way. Though the bourgeoisie had shown little evidence of involvement or interest to this point, there was an immediate and unprecedented flowering of bourgeois liberal political activism. It is particularly the suddenness of bourgeois politicization – from general inactivity to a mobilization that included hundreds of resolutions, petitions, and illegal assemblies in the space of a few weeks – which calls for a social explanation. No significant bourgeois political movement had previously existed, though it is true that the Masonic lodges brought together a good deal of generally liberal opinion. The only credible explanation for the sudden and general mobilization of bourgeois opinion against the aristocratic proposal for calling the Estates is the central role of the state in the surplus extractive relations of the ruling class, and its direct importance to so much of the bourgeoisie. The social interests which underlay the political emergence of the bourgeoisie were thus themselves *directly* political. The central struggle of the French Revolution was *about* the state precisely because the state itself was so central to the interests of the antagonists.

The French Revolution was essentially an *intra-class* conflict over basic political relations that at the same time directly touched on relations of surplus extraction. It was a civil war within the ruling class over the essential issues of power and surplus extraction. The focus of the struggle was the nature of the state, giving the conflict its specifically *political* form, because the fundamental social interests at stake were directly tied to state relations. While private rent relations constituted the preponderant basis of class exploitation, the offices of the state played a key role: they were of extraordinary importance to the maintenance of the wealth of the aristocracy, essential to any hope for advancement by the lesser nobility, and at the same time the basis of the major part of bourgeois careers.

The French state was peculiarly involved in the class relations of surplus extraction, and so was more directly the subject of immediate class interests than would be the case in capitalist society. This class interest in the state itself also explains the impossibility of an across-the-board compromise on some neutral state power – virtually no one wanted what Robespierre called the 'virtuous' state. The lesser legal and official bourgeoisie were most interested in a state administration open to talent and a more democratic system of representation. The great aristocrats (and many of their poorer noble supporters) had vested interests in a state with virtually no democracy, and a premium on personal status. Innumerable gradations of interest, roughly corresponding to greater or less liberalism, could be carved out in between. The bringing down of the absolutist monarchy threw open the whole question of formal state power at the same time that it eliminated effective mediation between the privileged and unprivileged sectors of the ruling class.

Victory by the aristocracy would not necessarily have made them into a new, more exclusive ruling class – but the potential for damage to bourgeois interests was very great. Issues of state power are always of the greatest significance to possessors of exploitive property; but when political power is itself directly linked to access to surplus extraction, the stakes are very high indeed. It was not the form of property and exploitation which was at issue in the Revolution, not the predominance of one *kind* of appropriating class over another – the bourgeoisie and aristocracy both took for granted the importance of private property and state careers. Instead, the issue was the continued security of a substantial portion of the ruling class, which was both directly and indirectly threatened by the aristocracy's effort to translate their privileged status – and hence also their privileged access to state resources – into a formal constitutional monopoly as well. It is clear, therefore, that the opposition of bourgeoisie and aristocracy – of liberalism and reactionary privilege – was not a 'merely political' conflict, but a product of the fundamental class dynamics of exploitive relations in the ancien régime.

From this conflict of bourgeois liberalism and political 'aristocracy' emerged much of the particular ideological content of European liberalism, including the idea of bourgeois class revolution. The terms of the conflict, and its ideological expression, were, however, escalated in scope and intensity by the unforeseen involvement of the people on behalf of the Third Estate. In this respect, the conflict of social interests between owners of exploitive property and non-exploitive direct producers entered into the Revolution, prolonging the upheaval and affecting its outcome as previously discussed.

The popular movement played a specific and integral role in the political development of the Revolution: without the politicization of the Paris crowds the Third Estate would undoubtedly have been defeated in 1789, and the willingness of successively more radical groups to carry further the conflict with aristocracy would not have been translated into the policies of successive revolutionary governments. Inherent to the overall politics of the Revolution, therefore, is not merely the opposition of aristocracy and liberalism, but also the radical promise of democracy and social justice. The Revolution did not actually produce a political perspective that wholly transcended liberal ideology, but it put such a politics on the agenda.

Yet while the French Revolution did so much to define the politics of the nineteenth century, it did very little in the way of transforming the essential social relations of production. The Revolution was not fought by capitalists, and it did not produce capitalist society. Instead, the Revolution further entrenched small-scale peasant production, and with it the extraction of agrarian surplus through rent, mortages, etc., by redistributing church lands among the bourgeoisie and peasantry. At the same time, if the *venality* of offices was ended, and state positions more opened to 'talent', the importance of state careers was if anything *increased*: in 1863, the salaries of the Ministry of Finance alone consumed *one-quarter* of the taxes it levied.[21] The lure of a state career did not disappear with the end of the ancien régime.

There is in fact no better testimony to the fundamentally unchanged role of the French state in surplus extraction than that offered by Marx himself in *The Eighteenth Brumaire*. Marx wrote, in *1852*:

> In France the executive has at its disposal an army of more than half a million individual officials and it therefore constantly maintains an immense mass of interests and livelihoods in a state of the most unconditional dependence; the state enmeshes, controls, regulates, supervises and regiments civil society from the most all-embracing expressions of its life down to its most insignificant motions. . . . [T]he *material interest* of the French bourgeoisie is most intimately imbricated precisely with the maintenance of that extensive and highly ramified state machine. It is that machine which provides its surplus population with jobs, and makes up through state salaries for what it cannot pocket in the form of profits, interest, rents and fees.[22]

Again:

> The executive power possesses an immense bureaucratic and military organization, an ingenious and broadly based state machinery, and an army of half a million officials alongside the actual army which numbers a further half million. This frightful parasitic body, which surrounds the body of French society like a caul and stops all its pores, arose in the time of the absolute monarchy, with the decay of the feudal system, which it helped to accelerate. The seignorial privileges of the landowners and towns were transformed into attributes of the state power, the feudal dignitaries became paid officials, and the variegated medieval pattern of conflicting plenary authorities became

the regulated plan of a state authority characterized by a centralization and division of labour reminiscent of a factory. The task of the
first French revolution was to destroy all separate local, territorial,
urban and provincial pøwers in order to create the civil unity of the
nation. It had to carry further the centralization that the absolute
monarchy had begun, but at the same time it had to develop the
extent, the attributes and the number of underlings of the govern-
mental power. Napoleon perfected this state machinery. The Legiti-
mist and July monarchies only added a greater division of
labour. . . . [23]

Marx's approach to the Revolution is here, too, determined by
his interest in contemporary society, but it is far from absolutely
clear that the 'bourgeois society' of which he is writing is *capitalist*. Indeed, the state-centered surplus extraction which he
describes, the centralized rent extracted directly from the
peasantry, seems to be a clear example of the 'extra-economic'
modes of surplus extraction that Marx associated with *non*-
capitalist societies in Volume III of *Capital*. Marx was simply too
good an observer of class society to write an analysis of
nineteenth-century French society which neatly conformed to his
account of bourgeois revolution. The extent to which *The
Eighteenth Brumaire* and Marx's other writings on France need
either to be corrected, or merely reinterpreted, in light of a new
understanding of the society of which he was writing, is yet
another question which must be addressed in future work. In any
case, it is clear that the peculiarly important role of the state
administration in France, and the pre-eminence of the *Ecole
Nationale de l'Administration*, belong to a historically specific
pattern of development of long standing.

It finally remains to be asked whether there is any sense in which
the concept of 'bourgeois revolution' can still figure meaningfully in historical analysis. It can no longer be supposed that
'bourgeois' society – contractual property relations, the rule of
law, a centralized state, etc. – is co-extensive with *capitalist*
society. Social relations which may be necessary for the existence
of capitalism are by no means sufficient to create it. Therefore, if
there is any sense in which it may be useful to consider the French
Revolution a 'bourgeois revolution', it cannot imply a connection to the emergence of capitalism, smuggling in through the
back door a meaning which is plainly unsupported by the
evidence.

Nevertheless, Robert Brenner has recently put forward an

interpretation of the English Civil War which may again suggest structural similarities with France; but if so, with fundamental differences as well.[24] According to Brenner, the revolution behind the Civil War was simply the ruling class repossessing its state power as a class, dispossessing the monarchy of its surviving 'private' feudal character. He sees this initially as the act of a virtually united class, creating a distinctly *public* state through Parliament's constitutional limitation of the monarchy. The Civil War, Brenner suggests, resulted from the growth of substantial conservative opposition to the involvement of popular elements in the affairs of state – encouraged by Parliamentary Independents – and the attendant danger that the revolution would get out of hand to threaten the ruling class itself.

It is clear that the English ruling class, having developed an increasingly important 'economic' mode of surplus appropriation through agrarian capitalism, had no significant need for state-centralized surplus extraction, and was in a unique position to create a fundamentally new relationship between class and state. Indeed, although 'Old Corruption' sat in power for some time after the Glorious Revolution, its use of state power for surplus extraction – insignificant in comparison to that of the French state – was opposed by much of the ruling class *as* corruption. Hence, the Civil War might be said to mark a significant separation of the state and civil society, which has often been regarded to be a central characteristic of 'bourgeois revolution'.

It may possibly be useful to consider the French Revolution in terms which are to some extent similar: the act of a united ruling class, dispensing with the 'feudal' prerogatives of royal absolutism to create a *constitutional class state*. In the case of France, however, it is not possible to link this to the separation of the state from civil society – since the role of the state in extra-economic surplus extraction was neither challenged nor ended by the Revolution. The separation of the public political sphere of the state from the economic sphere of civil society never really occurred in France before the establishment of the Third Republic, by which time capitalism can at last also be said to have existed.

If there is any value at all in pursuing the concept of 'bourgeois revolution' in these terms, it is not immediately apparent whether it would better refer to the ruling-class revolution against absolutism, on the one hand – which would apply to 1787–8, and once again create a parallel between the English Civil War and the French Revolution (on political, if not social grounds), or to the revolutionary separation of state and civil society, on the other hand – which might better refer to 1871, or perhaps to the whole history of French revolutions from 1787 to 1871. It must be asked, however, to what extent this would really serve to shed light on the essential relations of state and society, and to what extent it would merely serve to salvage for Marxism some conception of 'bourgeois revolution'. Considering its ideological origins, it may be better simply to drop the idea of bourgeois revolution once and for all, in favor of systematic historical materialist studies of the developing structural relationships between class and state in each social context.

If our purpose is to understand the world, the better to change it, we must begin with analyses which are rooted in the historical processes of class exploitation and class struggle. Assumptions which have long been dear will have to be discarded in order to engage in real historical investigation. The ideas sketched above are in many ways no more than preliminary anticipations of the real work of historical materialism which remains to be done. Marx drew attention to two thousand years of class struggles. Their history is still to be written.

Notes

1. It is extremely difficult to provide figures for the various groups within the bourgeoisie; the figures suggested here are derived from Soboul's estimates in *The French Revolution, 1787–1789*, vol, I, pp. 44–6, *after discounting* the petty artisans and shopkeepers, which make up two-thirds of what he defines there to be the 'bourgeoisie'. This hardly makes for an adequate statistical measure, but it does correspond to the sense of proportions which is conveyed in many other works: Pierre Goubert cites Beauvais as an average town, but one in which the textile trade was extremely important; there were 99 'merchants', but 136 rentiers and 159 lawyers and officers, plus 22 medical professionals (*The Ancien Régime*, New York 1974, pp. 225–6). Claude Journès found that in Bourg, rentiers made up 42 percent of the bourgeoisie, and 30 percent were officers and professionals; but of the 25 percent who were 'merchants', the great majority were shopkeepers and retailers who were not truly bourgeois, making the other groups larger ('Les classes sociales à Bourg pendant la Révolution (1785–1799)', *Bulletin d'histoire économique et sociale de la Révolution française–Année 1977*, Paris 1978, pp. 95–116). Considering the numbers of modest rentiers and petty officials to be found in the larger villages across France, the proportions offered here seem to be roughly correct. If there is an error, it likely is an underestimate of the rentiers.

On the forms of property, see George V. Taylor, 'Non-capitalist Wealth and the Origins of the French Revolution', *American Historical Review*, lxxii (1967), 469–96, Colin Lucas, 'Nobles, bourgeois and the French Revolution', *Past and Present*, 60 (1973), 84–126, and William Doyle, *Origins of the French Revolution*, Oxford 1980, pp. 128–35.

3. Virtually all of this basic objection to the social interpretation is ably reprised by Doyle, with ample references to the most relevant texts.

4. See particularly J. F. Bosher, *French Finances 1770–1795: From Business to Bureaucracy*, Cambridge 1970.

5. See Marc Venard, *Bourgeois et Paysans au vxiie siècle*, Paris 1957, and Jean Jacquart, *La Crise rurale en Ile-de-France 1550–1670*, Paris 1974, as well as the relevant sections of the economic and rural history texts cited in note 13, below.

6. Gilles Postel-Vinay, *La Rente foncière dans le capitalisme agricole*, Paris 1974, pp. 10, 15.

7. Ibid., pp. 19–30.

8. Ibid., pp. 31–75.

9. Ibid., pp. 16, 80.

10. Ibid., pp. 107–8.

11. Ibid., pp. 30, 63.

12. E. P. Thompson, 'Time, Work-Discipline, and Industrial Capitalism', *Past and Present*, 38 (December 1967), p. 43.

13. On the early development of commercial agriculture in England and France: Georges Duby, *Rural Economy and Country Life in the Medieval West*, Columbia, SC 1968; Hugues Neveux, 'Déclin et reprise: la fluctuation biséculaire 1330–1560', in G. Duby and A. Wallon, eds, *Histoire de la France rurale*, 4 vols, Paris 1975–6, vol. 2; Marc Bloch, *Les caractères originaux de L'Histoire Rurale Française*, 2 vols, Paris 1952, 1961; J.Z. Titow, *English Rural Society, 1200–1350* London 1969; Lord Ernle, *English Farming, Past and Present*, 6th edn, London 1961 (and particularly the Introduction by G. E. Fussell); F. R. H. Du Boulay, 'Who Were Farming the English Desmesnes at the End of the Middle Ages?', *Economic History Review*, 17 (1965), 443–55. On English agrarian capitalism: Ernle, *English Farming*; Eric Kerridge, *The Farmers of Old England*, London 1973; G. E. Mingay, 'The Agricultural Revolution in English History: A Reconsideration', in W. E. Minchinton, ed., *Essays in Agrarian History*, 2 vols, Newton Abbot 1968. On the structurally very different French agriculture: Robert Forster, 'Obstacles to Agricultural Growth in 18th Century France', *American Historical Review*, 75 (1970) 1600–12; E. Labrousse, P. Léon, P. Goubert, *et al.*, *Histoire économique et sociale de la France moderne*, vol. II, Paris 1970; J.-P. Houssel, J.-C. Bonnet, S. Dontenwill, R. Estier, and P. Goujon, *Histoire des paysans français du xviiie siècle à nos jours*, Roanne 1976; Emmanuel Le Roy Ladurie, 'De la crise ultime à la vraie croissance, 1660–1789', in Duby and Wallon, eds, *France rurale*, vol. 2; Arthur Young, *Travels [in France] During the Years 1787, 1788 & 1789*, 2 vols, 2nd edn, London 1794 (facsimile, 1970).

14. Robert Brenner, 'The Agrarian Roots of European Capitalism', *Past and Present*, 97 (1982), 16–113.

15. Excellent overviews of production in each zone are offered in Duby and Wallon, *France rurale*, Labrousse, Léon, Goubert, *et al.*, *Histoire économique*, and Houssel *et al.*, *Histoire des paysans*.

16. A. R. J. Turgot, *Reflections on the Formation and the Distribution of Wealth*, in Ronald L. Meek, ed., *Turgot on Progress, Sociology and Economics*, Cambridge 1973, pp. 123, 126, 153; Meek considers these ideas in his Introduction, pp. 21–6 and 31–3.

17. As Colin Lucas argues, 'Notable against Notable', *Times Literary Supplement*, May 8, 1981, p. 525.

18. On the aristocracy: Guy Chaussinand-Nogaret, *La Noblesse au xviiie siècle. De la féodalité aux lumières,* Paris 1976; Robert Forster, *The House of Saulx-Tavanes*, Baltimore 1971, and *The Nobility of Toulouse in the 18th Century*, Baltimore 1960; François Bluche, *Les Magistrates du Parlement de Paris au xviiie siècle (1715–1771)*, Paris 1960; Yves Durand, *Les Fermiers-Généraux au*

xviiie siècle, Paris 1971; Jonathan Dewald, *The Formation of a Provincial Nobility*, Princeton, NJ 1980, Jean Egret; 'L'aristocratie parlementaire français à la fin de l'Ancien Régime', *Revue historique*, ccviii (1952), 1–14.

19. Nannerl Keohane, *Philosophy and the State in France*, Princeton, NJ 1980.

20. See particularly Jean Egret, *La Pré-Révolution française, 1787–1788*, Paris 1962; also, Elizabeth L. Eisenstein, 'Who Intervened in 1788? A Commentary on *The Coming of the French Revolution*', American Historical Review, lxxi (1965), 77–103.

21. Georges Dupeaux, *French Society, 1789–1970*, London 1976, p. 28. On the general absence of economic transformation as a result of the Revolution, and the lingering 'stagnation' which was only dissipated after the building of railroads for largely *political* purposes, see Roger Price, *An Economic History of Modern France, 1730–1914*, London 1981.

22. Marx, *The Eighteenth Brumaire of Louis Bonaparte*, in Vintage Marx Library, *Surveys From Exile*, New York 1974, p. 186.

23. Ibid., p. 237.

24. Robert Brenner, Colloquium at Vanier College, York University, March 10, 1982.

Select Bibliography

Works on France and the Revolution

Books

Aulard, Alphonse. *The French Revolution: A Political History 1789–1804*. 4 vols. New York, 1910.

Barber, Elinor G. *The Bourgeoisie in 18th Century France*. Princeton, 1955.

Bergeron, Louis. *Banquiers, négociants et manufacturiers parisiens du Directoire à l'Empire*. Paris, 1978.

Bloch, Marc. *Les caractères originaux de L'Histoire Rurale Française*. 2 t. Paris, 1952, 1961.

Bluche, François. *Les Magistrates du Parlement de Paris au xviiie siècle (1715–1771)*. Paris, 1960.

Bois, Guy. *Crise du féodalisme*. Paris, 1976.

Bois, Paul. *Paysans de l'Ouest*. Paris, 1971.

Bosher, J. F. *French Finances 1770–1795: From Business to Bureaucracy*. Cambridge, 1970.

Brinton, Crane. *The Anatomy of Revolution*. Vintage, New York, rev. edn, 1965.

— *A Decade of Revolution: 1789–1799*. New York, 1963.

Butel, Paul. *Les négociants Bordelais, l'Europe et les Iles au xviiie siècle*. Paris, 1974.

Chaussinand-Nogaret, Guy. *La Noblesse au xviiie siècle. De la féodalité au lumières*. Paris, 1976.

Chill, Emanuel, ed. *Power, Property, and History* (Barnave's *Introduction à la Révolution française*). New York, 1971.

Cobb, Richard C. *The Police and the People: French Popular Protest*

1789–1820. Oxford, 1973.

Cobban, Alfred. *Aspects of the French Revolution*. Paladin, London, 1971.

— *A History of Modern France*. 3 vols. Penguin, 1963.

— *The Social Interpretation of the French Revolution*. London, 1968.

Cochin, Augustin. *Les Sociétés de Pensée et la Révolution en Bretagne*. 2 t. Paris, 1925.

Corvisier, André. *L'armée française de la fin du xviie siècle au ministère de Choiseul*. 2 t. Paris, 1964.

Dawson, Philip. *Provincial Magistrates and Revolutionary Politics in France, 1789–1795*. Cambridge, 1972.

Dewald, Jonathan. *The Formation of a Provincial Nobility*. Princeton, 1980.

Doyle, William. *Origins of the French Revolution*. Oxford, 1980.

Duby, Georges, and Wallon, Armand, eds. *Histoire de la France rurale*. 4 t. Paris, 1975.

Dupeaux, Georges. *French Society, 1789–1970*. London, 1976.

Durand, Yves. *Les Fermiers-Généraux au xviiie siècle*. Paris, 1971.

Egret, Jean. *La Pré-Révolution française, 1787–1788*. Paris, 1962.

Farmer, Paul. *France Reviews its Revolutionary Origins*. New York, 1963.

Forrest, Alan. *Society and Politics in Revolutionary Bordeaux*. London, 1975.

Forster, Robert. *The House of Saulx-Tavanes*. Baltimore, 1971.

— *The Nobility of Toulouse in the 18th Century*. Baltimore, 1960.

Furet, François. *Penser la Révolution française*. Paris, 1978.

— , and Richet, Denis. *La Révolution française*. 2e edn. Paris, 1973.

Garden, Maurice. *Lyon et les Lyonnais au xviiie siècle*. Paris, 1970.

Gerard, Alice. *La Révolution Française: Mythes et Interprétations*. Paris, 1970.

Goubert, Pierre. *The Ancien Regime: French Society, 1600–1750*. New York, 1974.

— *Beauvais et le beauvaisis de 1600 à 1730*. Paris, 1960.

Guizot, François. *L'Histoire de France, racontée à mes petits-enfants*. 5 t. Paris, 1877.

— *Historical Essays and Lectures*. Edited by Stanley Mellon. Chicago, 1972.

Hampson, Norman. *A Social History of the French Revolution*. Toronto, 1966.

Higonnet, Patrice. *Class, Ideology, and the Rights of Nobles During the French Revolution*. Oxford, 1981.

Hinrichs, E., Schmitt, E., Vierhaus, R., eds. *Vom Ancien Régime zur Französischen Revolution*. Gottingen, 1978.

Hobsbawm, Eric J. *The Age of Revolution, 1789–1848*. New York, 1962.

Houssell, J-P. (ed.), Bonnet, J-C., Dontenwill, S., Estier, R., and Goujon, P. *Histoire des paysans français du xviiie siècle à nos jours*. Roanne, 1976.

Hufton, Olwen H. *The Poor of Eighteenth Century France, 1750–1789.* Oxford, 1974.

Jacquart, Jean. *La crise rurale en Ile-de-France, 1550–1670.* Paris, 1974.

Jaurès, Jean. *Histoire Socialiste de la Révolution française.* Edited by A. Soboul. 4 t. Paris, 1969.

Kafker, Frank A., and Laux, James M. eds. *The French Revolution: Conflicting Interpretations.* 2nd edn. New York, 1976.

Kaplow, Jeffry, ed. *New Perspectives on the French Revolution.* New York, 1965.

Kennedy, M. *The Jacobin Club of Marseilles, 1790–1794,* Ithaca, NY, 1973.

Keohane, Nannerl O. *Philosophy and the State in France.* Princeton, 1980.

Labrousse, C. E. *La crise de l'économie française à la fin de l'Ancien Régime et au début de la Révolution.* Paris, 1944.

—, Braudel, F., Léon, P., Goubert, P., *et al. Histoire économique et sociale de la France moderne, II, (1660–1789).* Paris, 1970.

Lebrun, François. *Les Hommes et la Mort en Anjou.* Paris, 1971.

Lefebvre, Georges. *The Coming of the French Revolution.* Princeton, 1947 (Vintage, New York, n.d.).

— *Etudes orléanaises.* 2 t. Paris, 1963.

— *Etudes sur la Révolution française.* Paris, 1954.

— *The Great Fear of 1789: Rural Panic in Revolutionary France.* New York, 1973.

— *Les Paysans du Nord pendant la Révolution française* 2ᵉ edn. Paris, 1972.

Le Goff, T. J. A. *Vannes and its Region.* London, 1981.

Le Roy Ladurie, Emmanuel. *Les Paysans de Languedoc.* 2 t. Paris, 1966.

Lüthy Herbert. *La Banque protestante en France, de la révocation de l'édit de Nantes à la Révolution.* 2 t. SEVPEN, 1959, 1961.

Mathiez, Albert. *The French Revolution.* New York, 1928.

Mazauric, Claude. *Sur la Révolution française. Contributions à l'histoire de la révolution bourgeoise.* Paris, 1970.

Mellon, Stanley. *The Political Uses of History.* Stanford, 1958.

Michelet, Jules. *Histoire de la Révolution française.* 2 t. Angers, 1952.

Mignet, François. *History of the French Revolution. From 1789 to 1814.* London, 1913.

Moore, Barrington, Jr. *Social Origins of Dictatorship and Democracy.* Boston, 1967.

Mousnier, Roland. *The Institutions of France under the Absolute Monarchy 1598–1789.* Chicago, 1979.

Palmer, R. R. *The Age of Democratic Revolution.* 2 vols. Princeton, 1959, 1964.

Patrick, Alison. *The Men of the First French Republic.* Baltimore, 1972.

Postel-Vinay, Gilles. *La Rente foncière dans le capitalisme agricole.* Paris, 1974.

Price, Roger. *An Economic History of Modern France, 1730–1914*. London, 1981.

Rey, Pierre-Philippe. *Les alliances de classes*. Paris, 1978.

Richard, Guy. *Noblesse d'affaires au xviiie siècle*. Paris, 1974.

Robin, Régine. *La société française en 1789: Semur-en-Auxois*. Paris, 1970.

Rudé, George. *The Crowd in the French Revolution*. London, 1967.

— *Ideology and Popular Protest*. New York, 1980.

— *Interpretations of the French Revolution. Historical Association Pamphlets, General Series*, 47, Rev. edn. London, 1972.

— *Robespierre, Portrait of a Revolutionary Democrat*. London, 1975.

Sée, Henri. *Economic and Social Conditions in France During the Eighteenth Century*. New York, 1968.

Shaffer, John W. *Family and Farm: Agrarian Change and Household Organization in the Loire Valley 1500–1900*. Albany, NY, 1982.

Sheppard, Thomas F. *Lourmarin in the Eighteenth Century*. Baltimore, 1971.

Sieyès, E. M. *What is the Third Estate?* London, 1963.

Soboul, Albert. *The French Revolution 1787–1799*. 2 vols. London, 1974.

— *The Parisian Sansculottes and the French Revolution, 1793–4*. Oxford, 1964.

— *Les sans-culottes parisiens en l'an II: mouvement populaire et gouvernement révolutionnaire, 2 juin–9 thermidor an II*. Paris, 1958.

— *A Short History of the French Revolution 1789–1799*. Berkeley, 1965.

Solnon, Jean-Francois. *215 Bourgeois gentilshommes au xviiie siècle*. Paris, 1980.

Thierry, Augustin. *Oeuvres Complètes*. Paris, 1851.

Tocqueville, Alexis de. *The Old Régime and the French Revolution*. Garden City, NY, 1955.

Venard, Marc. *Bourgeois et Paysans au xviie siècle*. Paris 1957.

Vovelle, Michel. *La Chute de la monarchie, 1787–1792. Nouvelle histoire de la France contemporaine*, t. 1. Paris, 1972.

— *Ville et compagne au 18e siècle (Chartres et la Beauce)*. Paris, 1980.

Young, Arthur. *Travels During the Years 1787, 1788, & 1789*. 2nd edn. 2 vols. London, 1794 (facsimile 1970).

Articles

Behrens, Betty. 'Nobles, Privileges and Taxes in France at the end of the Ancien Regime.' *Economic History Review*, xv (1962–3) 451–75.

Bien, D. D. 'La Réaction aristocratique avant 1789: l'exemple de l'armée.' *Annales: économies, sociétés, civilisations*, xxix (1974).

Bruhat, Jean. 'La Révolution française et la formation de la pensée de Marx.' *Annales historique de la Révolution française*, xxxviii 2 (1966) 125–170.

Cavanaugh, G. J. 'Nobles, Privileges and Taxes in France. A Revision Reviewed.' *French Historical Studies*, viii (1974) 681–92.

Chaussinand-Nogaret, Guy. 'Aux origines de la Révolution: noblesse et bourgeoisie.' *Annales: ESC*, xxx (1975).

Corvisier, André. 'La Noblesse militaire. Aspects militaires de la noblesse française du xve et xviiie siècles.' *Histoire Sociale*, xi (Nov. 1978) 336–55.

Doyle, William. 'The Parlements of France and the Breakdown of the Old Regime, 1771–1788.' *French Historical Studies*, vi (1970) 415–58.

— 'Was There an Aristocratic Reaction in Pre-Revolutionary France?' *Past & Present*, 57 (1972).

Egret, Jean. 'L'aristocratie parlementaire française à la fin d l'Ancien Régime.' *Revue historique*, ccviii (1952) 7–14.

— 'The Origins of the Revolution in Brittany (1788–1789).' Jeffry Kaplow, *New Perspectives on the French Revolution*, New York, 1965, 136–152 (trans. from *Revue historique*, ccxiii (1955) 189–215).

— 'The Pre-Revolution in Provence (1787–1788).' Ibid., 153–170, (trans. from *A.h.R.f.*, (1954) 97–126.

Eisenstein, Elizabeth L. 'Who Intervened in 1788? A Commentary on *The Coming of the French Revolution*.' *American Historical Review*, lxxi (1965) 77–103.

Ellis, Geoffrey. 'The "Marxist Interpretation" of the French Revolution.' *English Historical Review*, xciii (1978) 353–76.

Forster, Robert. 'The Noble Wine Producers of the Bordelais in the Eighteenth Century.' *Economic History Review*, xiv (1961) 18–33.

— 'Obstacles to Agricultural Growth in 18th Century France.' *American Historical Review*, 75 (1970).

— 'The Provincial Noble: A Reappraisal.' *American Historical Review*, lxviii (1962–3) 681–91.

— 'Seigneurs and their Agents.' E. Hinrichs, *et al. Vom Ancien Régime zur Französischen Revolution*, 169–187.

— 'The Survival of the Nobility during the French Revolution.' *Past & Present*, 37 (1967) 71–86.

— 'The "World" between Seigneur and Peasant.' *Studies in Eighteenth-Century Culture, Vol. 5*, 1976, R. C. Rosbottom, ed., Univ. Wisconsin, 401–21.

Furet, F., Mazauric, C. and Bergeron, L. 'The Sans Culottes and the French Revolution'. Kaplow, *New Perspectives*, 226–53.

Gauthier, Florence. 'Théorie de la voie unique de la révolution bourgeoise ou négation de la Révolution française.' *La Pensée*, 187 (1976) 38–48.

Gindin, Claude. 'Autour de la Révolution française: à propos de la théorie marxiste de la rente foncière.' *La Pensée*, 203 (1979) 123–40.

— 'La rente foncière en France de l'ancien régime à l'Empire.' *A.h.R.f.*, 247 (1982) 1–34.

Goubert, Pierre. 'The French Peasantry of the Seventeenth Century: A Regional Example.' *Past & Present*, 10 (1956) 55–77.

Grenon, Michel, and Robin, Régine. 'A propos de la polémique sur l'ancien régime et la Révolution: pour une problématique de la transition'. *La Pensée*, 187 (1976) 5–30.

Gruner, Shirley. 'Le concept de classe dans la révolution française: une mise à jour.' *Histoire Sociale-Social History*, ix (1976) 406–23.

Guibert-Sledziewski, Elizabeth. 'Du féodalisme au capitalisme: transition révolutionnaire ou système transitoire?' *La Pensée*, 173 (1974) 22–36.

Gullickson, Gay L. 'The Sexual Division of Labour in Cottage Industry and Agriculture in the Pays de Caux: Auffay, 1750–1850.' *French Historical Studies*, 12 (1981) 177–99.

Jacquart, Jean. 'Immobilisme et catastrophes.' G. Duby and A. Wallon, eds, *Histoire de la France rurale,* II, Paris, 1975, 175–353.

— 'La rente foncière, indice conjonctural?' *Revue historique*, 253 (1975) 355–76.

Jones, P. M. 'The rural bourgeoisie of the southern Massif-Central: a contribution to the study of the social structure of *ancien régime* France.' *Social History,* 4 (1979) 65–83.

Journès, Claude. 'Les Classes sociales à Bourg pendant la Révolution (1785–1799).' *Bulletin d'histoire économique et sociale de la Révolution française, Année 1977*, Paris, 1978, pp. 95–116.

Kennedy, M. 'Foundation of the Jacobin Clubs and the Development of the Jacobin Club Network.' *Journal of Modern History*, 51 (1979) 701–33.

Lefebvre, Georges. Review of *The Myth of the French Revolution.* *A.h.R.f.,* xxviii (1956) 337–45.

Le Goff, T. J. A., and Sutherland, D. M. G. 'The Social Origins of Counter-Revolution in Western France.' *Past & Present*, 99 (1983) 65–87.

Lemarchand, Guy. 'Idéologie et société dans la France de 1789.' *La Pensée*, 161 (1972) 97–108.

Le Roy Ladurie, Emmanuel. 'De la crise ultime à la vraie croissance, 1660–1789.' G. Duby and A. Wallon, *Histoire de la France rurale*, II, 355–599.

— 'Pour un modèle de l'économie rurale.' *Cahiers d'Histoire*, 1974, 5–26.

Lucas, Colin. 'Nobles, Bourgeois and the Origins of the French Revolution.' *Past & Present*, 60 (1973) 84–126.

— 'Notable against Notable.' *Times Literary Supplement*, May 8, 1981, p. 525.

Lyons, Martin. 'The Jacobin Elite of Toulouse.' *European Studies Review*, 7 (1977) 259–84.

Montreau, J. (Jean Bruhat). 'La Révolution française et la Pensée de Marx.' *La Pensée*, 3 (1939) 24–38.

Neveux, Hugues. 'Déclin et reprise: la fluctuation biséculaire (1330–1560).' G. Duby and A. Wallon, *Histoire de la France rurale*, II, 11–173.

Richet, Denis. 'Autours des origines idéologiques lointaines de la Révo-

214

lution francaise: Elites et despotisme.' *Annales: ESC*, xxiv (1969) 1–23.

Robin, Régine. 'La nature de l'état à la fin de l'ancien régime: Formation sociale, Etat et Transition.' *Dialectiques*, 1–2 (1973) 31–54.

Salmon, J. H. M. 'Venality of Office and Popular Sedition in Seventeenth-Century France.' *Past & Present*, 37 (1967) 21–43.

Soboul, Albert. 'Du féodalisme au capitalisme: la Révolution française et la problématique des voies de passage.' *La Pensée*, 196 (1977) 61–78.

— 'L'Historiographie classique de la Révolution française.' *Historical Reflections/Réflexions historiques*, i (1974) 141–167, (also *La Pensée*, 177 (1974) 40–58).

— 'Qu'est-ce que la Révolution?' *La Pensée*, 217/218 (1981) 33–45.

Taylor, George V. 'Noncapitalist Wealth and the Origins of the French Revolution'. *American Historical Review*, lxxii (1967) 469–96.

— 'Revolutionary and Nonrevolutionary Content in the *Cahiers* of 1789: An Interim Report.' *French Historical Studies*, vii (1972) 479–502.

— 'Types of Capitalism in Eighteenth Century France.' *English Historical Review*, lxxix (1964).

Stone, Bailey. 'Robe against Sword: The Parlement of Paris and the French Aristocracy, 1774–1789.' *French Historical Studies*, ix (1975) 278–303.

Vovelle, M. and Roche, D. 'Bourgeois, Rentiers and Property Owners: Elements for Defining a Social Category at the End of the Eighteenth Century.' Kaplow, *New Perspectives*, 25–46.

Works of Marxist Theory and Debate

Books

Anderson, Perry. *Arguments Within English Marxism*. London, 1980.
— *Lineages of the Absolutist State*. London, 1974.
Bottomore, T. B. *Classes in Modern Society*. Vintage, New York, 1966.
Dobb, Maurice. *Studies in the Development of Capitalism*. New York, 1963.
Draper, Hal. *Karl Marx's Theory of Revolution*. 2 vols. New York, 1977, 1979.
Hilton, R., Sweezy, P., Dobb, M., *et al*. *The Transition from Feudalism to Capitalism*. London, 1976.
Holloway, J., and Picciotto, S., eds. *State and Capital, A Marxist Debate*. London, 1978.
Marx, Karl. *Capital*. 3 vols. Moscow, 1954, 1956, 1959.
— *The Civil War in France. The First International and After, Marx Library, Political Writings, Vol, III*. New York, 1974, 187–235.

— *The Class Struggles in France: 1848 to 1850. Surveys From Exile, Marx Library, Political Writings, Vol. II.* New York, 1974, 35–142.
— *Contribution to the Critique of Hegel's Philosophy of Law.* Marx–Engels *Collected Works*, III, 3–129.
— *A Contribution to the Critique of Political Economy.* Moscow, 1970.
— *Economic and Philosophic Manuscripts of 1844.* Marx–Engels *Collected Works*, III, 229–346.
— *The Eighteenth Brumaire of Louis Bonaparte. Surveys From Exile, Marx Library, Political Writings, Vol. II.* New York, 1974, 143–249.
— *Grundrisse. Marx Library.* New York, 1973.
— *The Poverty of Philosophy.* Marx–Engels *Collected Works*, VI, 105–212.
Marx, Karl and Engels, Frederick. *Collected Works.* 50 vols. Volumes III, IV, and VI. New York, 1975, 1976.
— *Correspondence, 1846–1895.* Translated by Dona Torr. London, 1934.
— *The German Ideology, Parts I & III.* New York, 1963.
— *The Holy Family.* Marx–Engels *Collected Works*, IV, 5–211.
— *Manifesto of the Communist Party.* Marx–Engels *Collected Works*, VI, 477–519.
Poulantzas, Nicos. *Classes in Contemporary Capitalism.* London, 1974.
— *Political Power and Social Classes.* London, 1968.
Rader, Melvin. *Marx's Interpretation of History.* New York, 1979.
Thompson, Edward P. *The Making of the English Working Class.* Penguin, 1968.
— *The Poverty of Theory & Other Essays.* London, 1978.
Williams, Raymond. *Marxism and Literature.* Oxford, 1977.

Articles

Bois, Guy. 'Against the Neo-Malthusian Orthodoxy.' *Past & Present*, 79 (1978) 60–69.
Brenner, Robert. 'Agrarian Class Structure and Economic Development in Pre-Industrial Europe.' *Past & Present*, 70 (1976) 30–75.
— 'The Agrarian Roots of European Capitalism'. *Past & Present*, 97 (1982) 16–113.
— 'On the Origins of Capitalist Development: a Critique of Neo-Smithian Marxism.' *New Left Review*, 104 (1977).
Colletti, Lucio. 'Introduction'. Karl Marx, *Early Writings, Marx Library*, New York, 1975, 7–56.
Cooper, J. P. 'In Search of Agrarian Capitalism.' *Past & Present*, 80 (1978) 20–65.
Croot P., and Parker, D. 'Agrarian Class Structure and Economic Development.' *Past & Present*, 78 (1978) 37–47.
Engels, Frederick. 'Outlines of a Critique of Political Economy.' Marx–Engels *Collected Works*, III, 418–43.

216

Hill, Christopher. 'A Bourgeois Revolution?' J. G. A. Pocock, *Three British Revolutions: 1641, 1688, 1776*, Princeton, 1980, 109–139.
— 'The English Civil War as Interpreted by Marx and Engels.' *Science and Society*, xii 1 (1948) 130–156.
Historians' Group of the Communist Party (UK). 'State and Revolution in Tudor and Stuart England.' *Communist Review* (July 1948) 207–14.
Hobsbawm, Eric J. 'Introduction'. Karl Marx, *Pre-Capitalist Economic Formations*, New York, 1965, 9–65.
— 'Karl Marx's Contribution to Historiography.' Robin Blackburn (ed.), *Ideology in Social Science*, Collins, 1972, 265–83.
Laclau, Ernesto. 'The Specificity of the Political.' *Economy and Society*, 1 (1975).
Lefebvre, J.-P. 'Marx: deux classes ou trois?' *La Pensée*, 225 (1982).
Le Roy Ladurie, Emmanuel. 'A Reply to Professor Brenner.' *Past & Present*, 79 (1978) 55–9.
Marx, Karl. 'Contribution to the Critique of Hegel's Philosophy of Law. Introduction'. Marx–Engels *Collected Works*, III, 174–87.
— 'Critical Marginal Notes on the Article "The King of Prussia and Social Reform. By a Prussian." ' Marx–Engels *Collected Works*, III, 189–208.
— 'From the *Mémoires de R. Levasseur (De La Sarthe). Paris, 1829.*' Marx–Engels *Collected Works*, III, 361–74.
— 'Moralising Criticism and Critical Morality.' Marx–Engels *Collected Works*, VI, 312–40.
— 'On the Jewish Question'. Marx–Engels *Collected Works*, III, 146–74.
— 'Review of Guizot's "Pourquoi la Révolution d'Angleterre a-t-elle réussi?" ' Marx–Engels *Collected Works*, X, New York, 1978, 251–56.
— 'Summary of Frederick Engels' Article "Outlines of a Critique of Political Economy." ' Marx-Engels *Collected Works*, III, 375–6.
Miliband, Ralph. 'Poulantzas and the Capitalist State.' *New Left Review*, 82 (1973).
— 'Reply to Nicos Poulantzas.' *New Left Review*, 59 (1970), reprinted in Blackburn, *Ideology*, 253–62.
Poulantzas, Nicos. 'The Capitalist State: A Reply to Miliband and Laclau.' *New Left Review*, 95 (1976).
— 'The Problem of the Capitalist State.' *New Left Review*, 58 (1969), reprinted in Blackburn, *Ideology*, 238–53.
Samuel, Raphael. 'British Marxist Historians, 1880–1980: Part One.' *New Left Review*, 120 (1980).
Thompson, Edward P. 'The Peculiarities of the English.' *Socialist Register*, 2 (1965), reprinted in *The Poverty of Theory & Other Essays*.

Wood, Ellen Meiksins. 'Marxism and Ancient Greece.' *History Work-shop Journal*, 11 (1981) 3–22.
— 'The Politics of Theory and the Concept of Class: E. P. Thompson and His Critics.' *Studies in Political Economy*, 9 (1982) 45–75.
— 'The Separation of the Economic and the Political in Capitalism.' *New Left Review*, 127 (1981) 66–95.

Works on England and Other Works

Books

Butterfield, Herbert. *The Whig Interpretation of History*. London, 1931.
Duby, Georges. *Rural Economy and Country Life in the Medieval West*. Columbia, SC, 1968.
Lord Ernle. *English Farming, Past and Present*. 6th edn. London, 1961.
Hill, Christopher. *The Century of Revolution, 1603–1714*. London, 1966.
— *Reformation to Industrial Revolution*. Penguin, 1967.
Hume, David. *The History of England*. London, 1840.
Kerridge, Eric. *Agrarian Problems in the Sixteenth Century and After*. London, 1969.
— *The Farmers of Old England*. London, 1973.
Meek, Ronald. *Social Science and the Ignoble Savage*. Cambridge, 1976.
Mingay, G. E. *English Landed Society in the Eighteenth Century*. London, 1963.
— *The Gentry*. London, 1976.
Tawney, R. H. *The Agrarian Problem In The Sixteenth Century*. New York, 1967.
Thirsk, Joan. *Tudor Enclosures. Historical Association Pamphlets*, G41. London, 1959.
Titow, J. Z. *English Rural Society, 1200–1350*. London, 1969.

Articles

Du Boulay, F. R. H. 'Who Were Farming the English Desmesnes at the End of the Middle Ages?' *Economic History Review*, 17 (1965) 443–55.
Habakuk, H. J. 'Economic Function of English Landowners in the Seventeenth and Eighteenth Centuries.' W. E. Minchinton, ed., *Essays in Agrarian History*, I, Newton Abbot, 1968, 187–201.
Jones, E. L. 'Agriculture and Economic Growth in England, 1660–1750: Agricultural Change.' Minchinton, *Essays in Agrarian History*, I, 203–19.

Kerridge, Eric. 'The Movement of Rent, 1540–1640.' *Economic History Review*, vi (1953) 16–34.

Mingay, G. E. 'The Agricultural Revolution in English History: A Reconsideration.' Minchinton, *Essays in Agrarian History*, II, 9–27.

— 'The Size of Farms in the Eighteenth Century.' *Economic History Review*, 14 (1962) 469–88.

Thirsk, Joan. 'The Peasant Economy of England in the Seventeenth Century.' *Studia historiae oeconomicae,* x (1975) 5–16.

Index

224